Praise for
Self-Regulation in the Classroom

"This action-ready, comprehensive, beautifully organized resource full of power tools for student self-regulation is all a teacher needs to bring daily success to students."
—LeAnn Nickelsen, M.Ed., coauthor of *Deeper Learning* and *Bringing the Common Core to Life*

"Richard Cash brings his high energy, positive approach to education, providing a road map of how to develop 21st century learners through an empathic understanding of the role of affect, behavior, and cognition. Excellent resource for teachers, psychologists, parents, and administrators."
—Teresa Argo Boatman, Ph.D., psychologist and gifted specialist

"As a teacher for nearly thirty years, it is exciting to find a strategy that energizes me as an educator. *Self-Regulation in the Classroom* is grounded in research, user friendly, and chock full of strategies and activities to guide all students toward finding their own 'sweet spot' for learning. Dr. Cash has a superb understanding of how the mind works and how to tap into its fullest potential."
—Monica Fitzgerald, teacher, grade 3

"Dr. Cash's in-depth, well-researched, and insightful book addresses both the socio-economic and the academic-intellectual needs of all students. It is filled with sound theory, interesting concepts, and practical strategies. Throughout the book, he emphasizes the world of 21st century students with its information overload and constant distractions. He offers ways for kids to learn how to focus, build self-confidence, set goals, think deeply, manage their time and their stressors, and study effectively. I highly recommend this book not only for those new to the profession but also for veteran teachers who sometimes bemoan, 'The kids today just aren't like the ones I used to teach years ago.'"
—Carolyn Coil, Ed.D., educational consultant and author

"*Self-Regulation in the Classroom* is a comprehensive and practical guide for the classroom teacher, school administrator, and school support staff. Cash addresses the need for innovative educational strategies when teaching our 21st century, technology-driven students. Grounded in theory and up-to-date research, this book serves to educate the reader and provide tools that will promote student engagement and autonomy in learning. *Self-Regulation in the Classroom* has my highest recommendation and will become an essential text to be used when developing career and college readiness skills in my students."
—Sandra Mortensen, licensed school counselor, Bloomington Public Schools, Minnesota

"Rich in research and theory but practical enough for Monday morning classroom activities, this book is for anyone looking to increase student engagement and help students regulate their thinking and behavior. Dr. Cash draws from his expertise to provide research-based strategies and ideas to help the highest achieving student or most reluctant learner. Whether you are a classroom teacher addressing diverse learning needs, a principal wanting to provide some key strategies for your teachers, or a district administrator searching for a professional development resource, *Self-Regulation in the Classroom* will be an invaluable resource you can return to again and again."

—Nathan Warner, M.Ed., assistant principal

"Dr. Cash provides frustrated teachers and parents with research-based strategies and answers to their questions. We know that students have a lot of information coming at them. They need our help and support to sort it, make sense of it, and use it to love learning. This book is exactly what we need."

—Patricia F. Willems, reading specialist, Bloomington Public Schools, Minnesota

"Dr. Cash has an uncanny ability to get right to the heart of the matter on how to become a self-regulated learner in any environment. He gives user-friendly strategies on how to create a personal desire within an individual to persevere in becoming a lifelong learner in our ever-changing society. *Self-Regulation in the Classroom* is a must read for any person who wants to assist others in becoming the best they can be."

—Barbara Morrison, M.Ed., multi-categorical instructor,
Wittenberg-Birnamwood High School, Wisconsin

"*Self-Regulation in the Classroom* is full of practical, specific ideas backed by current research for supporting all learners in today's classroom. Teachers now have *the* preeminent tool at their disposal for supporting self-regulation for learning."

—Tim Robinson, elementary GATE program coordinator, Washoe County School District, Nevada

"A gem for all 21st century teachers, this book will help educators guide their students toward self-discovery, effective production, and improved self-esteem. Used frequently as a guide to classroom environment, the end result of *Self-Regulation in the Classroom* should be a student-centered classroom culture, enhanced self-esteem, and improved outcomes for ALL!"

—Joy Lawson Davis, Ed.D., associate professor and chair, Department of
Teacher Education, Virginia Union University

Self-Regulation in the Classroom

Helping Students Learn How to Learn

RICHARD M. CASH, Ed.D.

Library of Congress Cataloging-in-Publication Data
Names: Cash, Richard M.
Title: Self-regulation in the classroom : helping students learn how to learn / Richard M. Cash.
Description: Minneapolis, MN : Free Spirit Publishing, 2016. | Includes bibliographical references and index.
Identifiers: LCCN 2015043605 | ISBN 9781631980329 (paperback) | ISBN 1631980327 (soft cover) | ISBN 978-1-63198-083-1 (Web PDF) | ISBN 978-1-63198-084-8 (epub)
Subjects: LCSH: Learning. | Self-culture. | Classroom environment. | BISAC: EDUCATION / Teaching Methods & Materials / General. | EDUCATION / Elementary. | EDUCATION / Secondary.
Classification: LCC LB1060 .C375 2016 | DDC 371.5—dc23
LC record available at http://lccn.loc.gov/2015043605

Image credits: page 27 © Get4net | Dreamstime.com, page 57 © Gabe9000c | Dreamstime.com, page 60 © Lukas Blazek | Dreamstime.com, page 62 © Copacool | Dreamstime.com, page 62 © Wavebreakmedia Ltd | Dreamstime.com, page 62 © Praneat | Dreamstime.com, page 83 © Connie Larsen | Dreamstime.com, page 91 © Davooda | Dreamstime.com, page 104 © Igor Zakowski | Dreamstime.com, page 125 © Mikateke | Dreamstime.com, page 125 © Chi Chiu Tse | Dreamstime.com, page 125 © Olena Skokan | Dreamstime.com, page 132 © Martina Vaculikova | Dreamstime.com, page 132 © Dimas1980 | Dreamstime.com, page 133 © Milo827 | Dreamstime.com, page 144 © Blumer | Dreamstime.com, page 144 © Vladimir Yudin | Dreamstime.com, page 144 © Andrei Tarchyshnik | Dreamstime.com, page 144 © Hemul | Dreamstime.com

Cover and interior design by Colleen Rollins
Edited by Meg Bratsch and Carla Weiland

10 9 8 7 6 5 4 3
Printed in the United States of America

Free Spirit Publishing Inc.
6325 Sandburg Road, Suite 100
Minneapolis, MN 55427-3674
(612) 338-2068
help4kids@freespirit.com
www.freespirit.com

Dedication

To Craig Feltmann, for all your love and support in the development of this book.

Acknowledgments

Much appreciation goes out to Margie Lisovskis and Judy Galbraith for making sure this book got from my head onto paper.

To my editors, Meg Bratsch and Carla Weiland, thanks for your diligence in helping me finesse my thinking and fine-tune my writing.

To Susan Swinick and John Cash, thanks for your contributions and continued support of what I love doing.

Thank you to my friend, colleague, and collaborator, Dr. Katie McKnight, for fanning the flame of self-regulation and assisting me in putting it into practice in the many places we go.

Contents

List of Figures

Figures with asterisks are available as reproducible downloads in the digital content. They can be downloaded at **freespirit.com/SRC-forms.** Use password **2learn.**

List of Reproducible Forms

Customizable digital versions of all the reproducible forms can be downloaded at **freespirit.com/SRC-forms**. Use password **2learn.**

Foreword

by Jonathan Plucker, Ph.D., Julian C. Stanley Professor of Talent Development, Johns Hopkins University

Countries around the world are starting to refocus their education systems on the skills and attitudes that will contribute to success in our rapidly changing world. I rarely visit a country where people aren't talking about "21st century skills" and attempting to find ways to help students prosper in a world that's constantly changing. Our current situation would have been inconceivable to our great-grandparents.

For example, who could have imagined even a decade ago that we would have handheld devices that let us access the vast majority of the world's information, cars that can brake for us or run on alternative energy sources, or machines that allow doctors and researchers to scan our brains to see how we think? We take such developments for granted now, yet these advances were hardly obvious before they happened. We are living in an era of unprecedented development and progress, and it's easy to be optimistic about where we will go next.

However, preparing students for a world 20 years into the future leads to one big obstacle: It is almost impossible to predict what the world will look like in 10 years, let alone 20 or more. We can't predict the jobs of tomorrow (for example, not even a decade ago, working in the smartphone industry would have been nonsensical), we can't predict the technology of the future, we can't predict much of anything.

To complicate things further, today's students are expected to be less industry-driven and more flexible about the types of jobs they seek. Some estimates suggest they will switch jobs—and often careers—every few years throughout their lifetimes. How do we ready them for life and workplace success in a world where the only constant is change?

Regardless of the field in which today's students will one day work, research suggests that cognitive skills and creativity will be increasingly necessary for workplace and life success. A crucial piece of these skills is the ability to regulate one's own thinking and behaviors. Students who take responsibility for their own learning, who use study strategies based on how they learn best, who challenge themselves and seek out problems to solve, are not only likely to be lifelong learners, they are likely to be productive, happy adults—regardless of when, where, or in what field they choose to work.

In this way, self-regulation is a foundational 21st century skill—if not *the* foundational skill for future success and well-being.

This book is an excellent introduction to helping students improve their self-regulation skills. The overarching model is straightforward but comprehensive (as opposed to simplistic) and provides a helpful affective-behavioral-cognitive framework for thinking about self-regulation and how to help students develop it. But the extensive strategies for teachers to use with their students are the strength of the book. While reading, I found myself taking notes on strategies that I could adapt for use with my college students, with the children that I coach on the weekends, and even with my own children. I can't remember the last time I came away from a book with both a better conceptual understanding of a topic *and* pages of notes on practical strategies that I could use immediately.

Best of all, Richard is never pedantic. He knows firsthand the challenges teachers face, and his vast experience, both in the classroom and as a teacher educator, comes through in every chapter as he provides advice on how educators can help their students learn self-regulation skills. He is a serious scholar and among the world's most effective teacher educators. Richard's work is thoughtful and insightful, and I often find myself asking him for advice on a wide range of educational topics. Do yourself (and your students) a favor and read his book.

Jonathan Plucker, Ph.D.

Introduction

It's fine to celebrate success, but it's more important to heed the lessons of failure.

—Bill Gates

Over the nearly three decades I've been a teacher, district administrator, and consultant, I've witnessed a steady change in how children prefer to learn. In my early years as a teacher, I could entice my students through stories, novelty, and interesting demonstrations. In those days, we competed with television and the first video games. Today, through my work with hundreds of teachers and thousands of students, I find the challenges of engaging children in learning have risen exponentially.

Not only are our students contending with hundreds of broadcast television channels, continuous on-demand media, hyper-sophisticated computer games, and "get-it-quick" information, but also they are in constant contact through social media and texting. These changes to our world have demanded changes in the way we teach. Teaching and learning in the second and third decade of the 21st century is no longer about stand-and-deliver methodology. We must realize that educators today are in a tough competition with the attention-grabbing forces our children encounter on a daily, moment-to-moment basis.

The most significant changes I've observed in the neo-millennials (children born post-2000) is their relentless need for stimulation and their shortened attention span. Advances in technology allow students to rapidly access information and contact others through virtual realities, resulting in their spending little time digging into text. Skimming and quickly picking out topics and ideas of interest to gain "just enough" knowledge from the Internet, they randomly overview text rather than following the linear fashion of reading from upper left to lower right. This "in time" learning mode has had a significant effect on the way teachers must engage, educate, motivate, and support children of the 21st century.

Self-Regulation for Learning: Not a New Idea

For over four decades, the topic of self-regulation has been studied in the field of psychology. Never before has this topic taken on greater significance than today in our classrooms. Popular media has propelled the topic through the use of words such as: grit, determination, stick-to-it-ness, mindset, drive, and self-control. Books such as *How Children Succeed* (Tough, 2012), *Mindset: The New Psychology of Success* (Dweck, 2006), *Drive: The Surprising Truth About What Motivates Us* (Pink, 2009), and *Talent Is Overrated* (Colvin, 2010) all make the point that what matters most in succeeding is the ability to avoid distractions, stay focused on tasks through completion, and develop a sense of autonomy in learning.

In his revealing book, *Visible Learning: A Synthesis of Over 800 Meta-Analyses Relating to Achievement* (2009), John Hattie states that achievement increases when students can focus on learning rather than performing, set goals that stretch them, monitor their own learning, accept feedback as a guide to success, and calculate their accomplishments based on criteria rather than on comparison to others. Students who "possess high rather than low efficacy in learning, and effect self-regulation and personal control rather than learned helplessness" are far more likely to be successful in school and beyond.[1]

1. Hattie, J., 2009, p. 47

Using both popular texts as well as research tomes, such as *Motivation and Self-Regulated Learning: Theory, Research and Application* (Schunk & Zimmerman, 2012); *Handbook of Competence and Motivation* (Elliot & Dweck, 2005); and *Handbook of Self-Regulation: Research, Theory, and Applications* (Baumeister & Vohs, 2004), I've compiled a comprehensive look at self-regulation and its implications in the classroom.

Self-Regulation in the Classroom is written for educators to gain a deeper understanding of the theories behind self-regulation, to learn what it looks like in the classroom, and to discover how to foster students' development of autonomy in learning. The ideas, strategies, and processes in this book provide a framework for schools, administrators, and teachers to guide students toward greater levels of success and narrow achievement gaps.

The book addresses the learning needs of *all* students, from those who need more supports to the most advanced learners. The book includes ideas for assisting students who live in poverty to those who come from strong economic backgrounds. I truly believe that when students can self-regulate, they can and will achieve great things.

Self-regulation for students who may not be reaching their potential. Students living in chronic poverty or in difficult home situations often lack role models of effective self-regulation, which causes them to struggle in school or fail to reach their potential. This book provides ways to assist the neediest students by focusing on the modeling/observing level and then the purposeful practice level, which prepares them for future learning opportunities. Directly teaching and modeling the strategies of self-regulation can be highly beneficial for students who may not have had prior positive learning experiences.

Self-regulation for advanced students. My 25 years' experience of working with advanced students showed me the importance of teaching self-regulation for learning to students who easily met academic requirements. Many of these students find elementary school a breeze, with nothing too challenging to stretch their affect or cognition. By the time they reach middle school, classes may become more challenging and complex, requiring them to call upon internal strengths to maintain high levels of achievement. This is the period in school when underachievement by advanced-level learners becomes a critical issue. Many of these underachieving students haven't learned when and how to use the skills of self-regulation to manage complex tasks. Some find their way to high school, prepared for even more complex study.

However, some advanced-level learners languish in their underachievement, mistakenly believing themselves to "not be gifted after all." My contention is these students have not learned how to use or rely upon their self-regulatory capacity when the going gets tough. Therefore, reinforcing the strategies of self-regulation with advanced-level students on a regular basis is critical to their success in secondary school, postsecondary opportunities, and beyond.

Self-regulation for all students. All students can value from learning and using self-regulatory strategies. As Bill Gates states at the beginning of the introduction, we learn best from learning how to deal with our failures. Many students fear failure, as if it defines them completely. Being able to reflect on failure as a learning opportunity, being resilient both emotionally as well as cognitively is a powerful tool in this ever-changing and complex world. Having an awareness of the concept of self-regulation and the ability to regulate affect, behavior, and cognition toward success is critical for all students.

About This Book

The opening chapters of the book clarify the definition of self-regulation and how it applies in the learning context. For students to reach their potential they must possess traits that allow them to focus, avoid meaningless distractions, use the proper thinking tools, and maintain a confident attitude. Before we can guide students to success, they must achieve "self-regulation FOR learning" (SRL). SRL happens in four stages over a lifetime, sometimes moving forward and sometimes moving back, all in approach of learning autonomy.

Getting students to engage in tasks helps facilitate the development of self-regulation, so the book then presents four phases of engaging in learning and a review of how we learn best. Based on neurological studies and learning research, there are specific requirements all students need and want when learning.

In the remaining chapters of the book, the four stages of developing self-regulation merge with the four phases of engaging in learning to provide practical, evidence-based practices that will support you in guiding your students to greater levels of autonomy in learning. The main goal of this book is to provide teachers with up-to-date research, solid theory, and doable practices to increase student achievement, thus narrowing the achievement gap. Additional goals include:

- To clarify the theories that are foundational to SRL
- To define how students engage in learning
- To demonstrate ways to foster learner confidence
- To offer ideas for developing greater capacities for thinking
- To assist in goal formation
- To keep students focused and on task
- To develop lifelong scholars
- To teach learners how to learn from learning
- To put it all together as a doable district, school, or classroom plan

Chapter 1 is an overview of the theories about SRL presented through the lenses of various experts in the field. For educators to implement effective practices, they need a solid foundation of the theories and the supportive research. The chapter defines self-regulation as a three-dimensional, learned process through which the teacher guides the learner to balance affect, behavior, and cognition (the ABCs of learning).

Chapter 2 takes the reader through the process of developing SRL and spells out the four stages: originate, intervene, support, and release. Knowing how these stages are developed offers teachers a way to view students in a progressive manner, one in which the student's maturity, academic exposers, early parent/family modeling, and sustained growth are taken into account. Having a tone of progressiveness in the classroom assures students they can achieve when they have had the models, supports, practice, and autonomy to reach their highest potential. Also included in this chapter are biographical sketches of students and analyses of how the development of self-regulation applies to their individual experiences.

Chapter 3 offers assistance for learners in developing greater SRL through the context of engaging in a task. Research suggests that there is a cyclical pattern for engaging in learning (EiL). This chapter defines the four phases of EiL and broadly identifies actions within each phase. Additional comprehensive strategies are broken down into doable actions and activities in subsequent chapters (4–9). The chapter guides readers through the use of a cross matrix of the phases of EiL and the stages of developing SRL; it shows the actions teachers and students perform. The Cross Matrix is useful for teachers in planning lessons, differentiating learning tasks, and assessing student growth. Students can use it to monitor their development and to focus on the process toward success.

Chapter 4 is a guide through the early stages of learning by building student confidence. Before learning can happen, students must feel confident in taking actions toward learning. This chapter identifies and provides supports in shaping students' confidence and emotional strength. A critical component in learning is knowing how a learner feels about the learning situation. Neuroscience research suggests that a learner's emotional state, or how one feels, has a significant effect on what he or she pays attention to in the learning space. This chapter also shares ideas for igniting students' interests and building value in learning. Useful ideas for moving students from pessimism to optimism, necessary for achieving SRL, are provided. Also included in this chapter are ideas for motivating students by developing their self-efficacy through a supportive learning environment.

Chapter 5 provides ways to develop students' habits of thinking. It explains cognition—the multiple levels of thinking—and metacognition—the thinking about our own thinking, which includes how we view ourselves as learners and how to approach dealing with problems. Additional ideas about the metacognitive process are given in Chapter 9. In this new century, it is more important that we teach students how to think rather than what to think. Stand-alone and content-infused strategies provide support for the development of thinking in your classroom.

Chapter 6 is about setting goals. Goals are set within a hierarchy, moving from who we want to be (the ideal self) to those goals that balance the ABCs of learning, to learning and performance goals. Expanding on the SMART goal framework, the SMARTS/S goal framework includes self-regulatory aspects. Strategies for providing feedback to students about their development are included along with suggestions of apps to help incorporate technology in goal setting.

Chapter 7 provides ways for students to manage the goals they have set. Today's students are perhaps more distractible than ever before. Teachers and parents need tools to assist students in "paying attention" and avoiding distraction. This chapter will provide numerous ideas, strategies, and techniques for assisting students in managing goals both inside and outside the classroom. Other topics in this chapter cover how to manage time, keep organized, manage stress, and overcome the self-imposed feelings of boredom through creativity.

Chapter 8 offers ideas for shifting from the practice of homework to the essential tool of home study. Few topics in education cause as much consternation as homework. Although little research or evidence supports homework, children must learn how to study outside of the classroom. This chapter shows how teachers can maintain a productive learning environment that nurtures study habits and study skills. It provides useful ideas and tips for parents and others to encourage study outside the classroom.

Chapter 9 focuses on the critical nature of reflection and relaxation in learning. People learn more from reflecting on an experience than from the experience itself. This chapter provides various formats for the reflection process. Students who are over-scheduled have high stress levels, so I have included ideas for teachers and parents to help children de-stress through relaxation techniques.

Chapter 10 puts it all together! This chapter offers a framework for classroom practice that can be expanded upon for school-wide implementation. Included are ways to assess the development of self-regulation and a way for students to identify how they like to learn and stretch themselves to become autonomous learners.

Lastly, all of the reproducible forms (and some of the Figures) in the book exist in digital form as customizable PDFs for your personal use and sharing. See page xi for the website link to download these forms.

How to Use This Book

Using this book as a foundation of self-regulation and engagement in learning can assist you in developing autonomous self-directed learners. Read Chapters 1–3 to familiarize yourself with the theory and research on self-regulation and engaging in learning. From there, depending on the level of your students' self-regulation development, you may choose individual chapters to address critical needs. For example, if you are working with students who chronically underperform, you could read Chapter 4 on fostering student confidence. If you are working with more advanced students, you could head to Chapter 6 on goal setting.

Whether you are a classroom teacher or a building- or district-level administrator, this book will be a valuable resource. What's more, *Self-Regulation in the Classroom* can also be used by your professional learning team or as a book study with your staff. To that end, I've created a guide with questions and activities for each of the chapters for PLC or book study teams. You can download this free guide at freespirit.com/PLC.

Finally, I'd love to hear how this book has helped you in your classroom. If you have stories or questions for me, you can reach me through my publisher at help4kids@freespirit.com or visit my website www.nrich.consulting.

Richard M. Cash, Ed.D.

CHAPTER 1

Self-Regulated Learning for 21st Century Students

If we give our children sound self-love, they will be able to deal with whatever life puts before them.

—bell hooks

However direct or convoluted the route you took to reach your present role as an educator, imagine how different that journey would have been with endless streams of texts, emails, and captivating YouTube videos vying for your attention. Not to mention having the option to stop along the way to take smartphone photos, post updates to your Facebook page, and check your friends' Twitter feeds. The sheer amount of information and the easy access to it that our children have present educators with a problem previous generations didn't have. Although teachers always have had to work to get students' attention and engage them in lessons, the competition for their mental energy has never been greater.

Responding to a continuous overload of information keeps learners distracted, and gathering information in random ways may not be the most effective way to foster deep thinking. When students focus their attention, they can move information from working memory to long-term memory, which assists in the development of conceptual thinking, creativity, and critical reasoning. To use the full potential of their minds, students must learn to filter distractions and interruptions and to think deeply and critically.

Likewise, some children live with the ready availability of such things as money and food whenever the impulse strikes for short-term satisfaction. A large number of our students are caught in the clutches of "instant gratification." The famous Marshmallow Study conducted at Stanford in 1972 by Walter Mischel showed how important self-regulation is to achieving success in life. *Self-regulation* (also known as self-control or self-discipline) is the control of conduct based on goals an individual has set for himself or herself.[1] Mischel offered four-year-olds a marshmallow but told them that if they waited for him to return from running an errand, he would give them two. The children had a range of success in delaying gratification. After about 13 years, Mischel found that children who are able to wait for a marshmallow reward (delay gratification) through various affective, behavioral, and cognitive methods perform better in life. Those who waited for the marshmallows were more self-reliant and confident, more motivated when working on projects, more academically successful, better at concentration and planning, more eager to learn, and still able to delay gratification. These are the characteristics of self-regulation. Those who ate the one marshmallow were more easily upset by frustrations, were more likely to negatively respond to stress, scored 210 points lower on their SATs, and were still unable to delay gratification.[2]

In his 2011 book *The Shallows: What the Internet Is Doing to Our Brains*, Nicholas Carr writes that early peoples were more likely to survive and carry on the gene pool if they were able to shift their attention quickly to

1. English and English, 1958.
2. Mischel et al., 1988.

understand their environment. Later, when print became a popular medium for the accumulation of knowledge, we learned to focus for longer periods of time. And today, we skim and scan the Internet, taking us back to quickly evaluating the environment and long periods of distraction. Historically, Americans have prided themselves on a national character comprised of independence, resourcefulness, persistence, inventiveness, determination, and dependability. No matter how high- or low-born, success was a viable goal for those willing to persist. Now, the United States leads the world in percentage of students who drop out of college. So, in light of the information overload and easy access to short-term gratification in today's world, how do we instill in our students the need for purposeful learning, persistence, self-control, and a healthy regard for failures as learning opportunities?

This chapter will show the importance of self-regulation for learning (SRL) in helping your students attain their academic goals. SRL will help learners develop resilience and autonomy, learn to reflect on experiences, and consider multiple ways to solve complex, ambiguous problems. Using the books' SRL strategies model, students learn to balance their feelings, behavior, and cognition. As they coordinate these three foundations of SRL, they find greater motivation and enjoyment in learning. Mastering the skills of self-regulation involves the traits and dispositions shown in Figure 1.1.

A Model of Self-Regulation for Learning

A topic of interest to social scientists for several decades, "*Self-regulated learning* (or *self-regulation*) refers to the process by which learners personally activate and sustain affects, behaviors, and cognitions that are systematically oriented toward the attainment of learning goals."[3] SRL is a process in which the learner manages and controls his or her capacities of affect (feelings), behavior, and cognition (thinking)—the ABCs—to engage in learning, and improve achievement and performance. Figure 1.2 shows how the three dimensions are interrelated.

In reality, the three dimensions of SRL are tightly interwoven and, in successful learners, work in tandem. One without the other two or two without the other one create an imbalance in the learning process. For example, if you feel estranged in a situation (perhaps at a party where no one else looks like you, speaks like you, or comes from a similar background), you might spend the majority of your time thinking about how different you are and might behave in a reserved manner, not meeting as many new people as possible. This is an example of how one dimension (feelings) can derail the other two

Figure 1.1 **Traits and Dispositions of Self-Regulated Learners**

Self-regulated learners . . .

- Take responsibility for learning.
- Maintain engagement in learning.
- Welcome challenges.
- Learn from intrinsic motivation.
- Are performance-oriented.
- Set challenging goals.
- Monitor and assess the goal process.
- Utilize a repertoire of learning strategies.
- Modify or adapt learning strategies.
- Expend effort.
- Establish a productive home learning environment.
- Seek help when necessary.
- Are persistent and determined.
- Find personal value, relevance, and interest in learning.
- Find satisfaction in learning.
- Use failure as a learning tool.
- Use effective study habits.
- Make choices in learning based on personal interests or preferred ways of learning.

3. Schunk and Zimmerman, 2012.

Figure 1.2 **Self-Regulation for Learning Model**

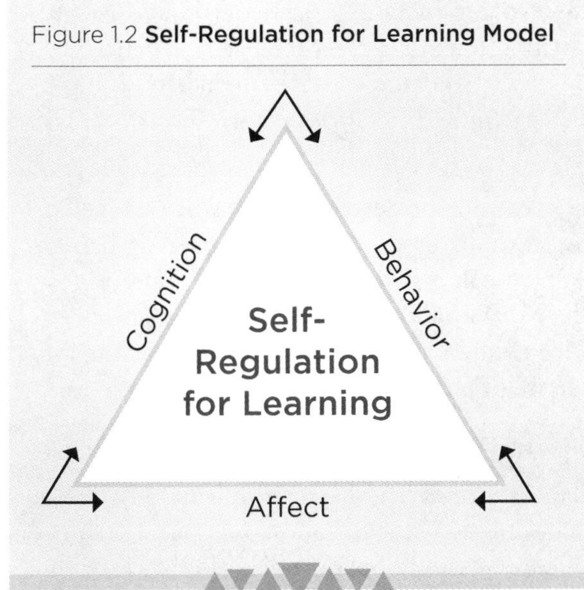

(cognition and behavior) to be less productive. Following, the three dimensions are defined as separate but intertwined entities.

A Is for Affect

How a learner feels about a situation determines the focus of his or her attention, drive, and motivations. Affect is defined as how we feel, or our conscious awareness of our emotions. Emotions are a chemical reaction within our limbic system (the primitive midbrain area that controls emotion and memory) triggered by internal and external stimuli.

Emotional responses (feelings) develop in this basic manner:

1. **Interaction** with an event, environment, object, sensation, or thought
2. **Attention** to the interaction either consciously or unconsciously
3. **Interpretation** of the attention given to the interaction based on prior experience or on another person's reaction
4. **Reaction** (instinctual or conditioned) to the interpretation

Example 1: A toddler learning to walk lets go of mom's hand and falls to the ground (interaction). The child's first reaction is of mild pain from the fall (attention). The toddler may not scream in pain because the fall was not serious. However, if mom's reaction (interpretation) is one of fear and she screams, the child then interprets the fall to be more than a mild pain and begins to cry out in fear mirroring mom's response (reaction).

Example 2: A new student enters the classroom (interaction). The teacher and other students warmly welcome her to the class (attention). The new student feels a sense of belonging (interpretation). She is more likely to open up, be willing to take intellectual risks, ask for help, and feel accomplished throughout her time in the class (reaction).

How we regulate or manage our emotional responses has a significant effect on our learning. Researchers have found that when people consciously use positive behaviors (such as going for a walk or bike ride) and positive cognition (such as reflecting on how to improve a situation) rather than focusing on negative effects, they are able to overcome negative feelings more rapidly.[4]

Additionally, studies suggest that there are physiological changes in our brains when we feel good, causing us to think more clearly and effectively.[5] Negative feelings can actually have a negative effect on our thinking process. These research studies inform us that when we focus students' attention toward a consciousness of their feelings and provide them with specific behavioral and cognitive strategies to adjust those feelings, they are more likely to achieve success.

For example, Mateo, an average fourth grader, tried to learn to convert fractions to decimals. His group partners all learned the process quickly. The comments they made as they tried to help him ("Why can't you get this?" and "You're so slow") made him feel bad about his abilities. His teacher, Mr. Anderson, met with Mateo to help him and quickly perceived his feelings. Instead of focusing Mateo on practice drills, he sent him on a walk to the water fountain (physical behavior) and told him during the walk to think about something other than math, such as how his soccer game went or what he planned to do after school. When Mateo returned to class, he had overcome his negative feelings and, with encouragement from his teacher, set to work

4. Dillon and LaBar, 2005.
5. Hidi and Ainley in Schunk and Zimmerman, 2008.

again, understanding the process more quickly than before and ready to continue positively to learn new math processes.

B Is for Behavior

For purposes of this text, behavior is defined as the actions we perform that are initiated, sustained, changed, or developed based on both internal and external factors. Behaviors can be both conscious and unconscious. For students, having a solid grasp on what to do and a positive belief in their ability to do it can powerfully impact their attainment of goals. Learning certain behaviors that are more effective than others and then repeating those behaviors will create what is known as habits of learning.

Academic Behaviors

Academic behaviors typically are those that are useful in school and career success. The behaviors can be categorized into five interactive categories:

1. **Determination:** the level of commitment one puts toward initiating, sustaining, and achieving a desired outcome. Student behaviors include using self-talk, seeking help, attending to details, and overcoming obstacles.
2. **Interest:** the personal attention or curiosity one uses to engage in school, others, and goal attainment. Academic behaviors include driving to learn more about a topic, making connections to material or others, and redirecting one's attention when distractions occur.
3. **Work habits:** the strategies and techniques one uses to learn new information. Student behaviors related to work habits include setting time limits on studying, using organization strategies, and planning and monitoring goals.
4. **Communication and collaboration skills:** the effectiveness one has with others to achieve a common outcome. Student behaviors include speaking and listening strategies, cooperation and negotiation, as well as ethical use of technology.
5. **Goal focus:** the process one goes through to set, manage, and achieve a realistic goal. Student behaviors include knowing strengths/limitations, controlling impulses, and using reflective practices.

As students develop and practice the behaviors, eventually they become habitual. Chapters 4 and 6 will provide more specific strategies for the behavioral dimension of self-regulation. Meanwhile, the following figure details the four phases of behavioral change.

Four Phases of Behavior Change

Based on research of how people modify their behaviors to become habitual, Figure 1.3 shows the process and how to apply it in the classroom. The arrows at the bottom of the graphic show that as learners progress through the strategies and phases and the behavior becomes habitual, they are developing skills.

PHASE 1: ATTENTION

When the student recognizes a need for a change in behavior, he or she starts the change process. In some cases, students are not aware that their behaviors are unproductive, inefficient, or unaligned with success. To help students become aware of the need for a behavior change, help them find value in their efforts to achieve the goal or find meaningfulness in the tasks. Meaningfulness is when the students recognize that the task or strategy has an immediate application and completing it can lead to a positive feeling. Help your students find relevance in the need for a change of behavior by encouraging and building their self-beliefs.

At this phase and the next, ensure students know the difference between a strategy implementation and skill development. A strategy is a discrete, conscious action, whereas a skill is automatically using a set of strategies to accomplish a specific task. In other words, strategies are small and skills are big. Strategies are effortful, while skills are effortless. Students who are aware of the strategies that develop into skills know that being able to face greater challenges requires expending much effort upfront. Being able to articulate specific steps in solving problems is most critical

Figure 1.3 **Four Phases of Behavior Change**

1. ATTENTION	2. REWARD	3. MAINTENANCE	4. HABIT
› The student recognizes a discrepancy between current state and desired state. › Student perceives outcome as worth the effort. › Student finds meaningfulness in the goal.	› Student finds initial/immediate success in adopted behavior. › Student feels a desire to continue the success. › Student's confidence is gaining strength. › Student needs continual reinforcement of the applications of the behavior. › Student can overcome obstacles due to continual reinforcement.	› Student desires the behavior change and is willing to persist. › Student recognizes the impact of the new behavior. › Student can handle setbacks or obstacles with less reinforcement. › Student is able to recognize when there is a need to shift or adjust a behavior.	› Student feels confident in abilities and application of strategies. › Student is automatic in implementation and autonomous in performance.
Student needs: › confidence › support › belief in self › direction › specific details to strategies	**Student needs:** › sustained support › continued direction › guidance › descriptive feedback	**Student needs:** › willingness › desire › committment › effort › practice › refinement	**Student needs:** › self-evaluation › maintenance

STRATEGY IMPLEMENTATION → SKILL DEVELOPMENT

Adapted from Rothman, Baldwin, and Hertel, 2004.

as students enter middle school and high school when situations become more complex.

Strategy example: working backward
Skill being developed: problem solving

Strategy example: using pictures to understand the story
Skill being developed: comprehension

Students must build their confidence to perform the tasks required of them. Therefore, at this phase students will need support in building their self-beliefs and self-efficacy toward doing well. They will also need direct instruction on the specifics of the strategies and how to apply them. Students who struggle or are less self-directed will need more hands-on experience with the strategies, concrete representations of the outcomes, and step-by-step implementation tools.

PHASE 2: REWARD

This phase of the change process offers immediate rewards for performing the behavior. When implementing a new behavior, it is critical for the student to see or feel instant gratification. Even though we are trying to change this need for instant gratification, we must also recognize that our students are used to receiving rewards quickly. During this phase, slowly wean your students away from needing the continual extrinsic reward toward more intrinsic feelings of success. Move from "you are doing well" to "how does it feel to be making progress toward your goal?" Build your students' self-confidence through descriptive feedback that focuses on their growth. You will begin to see your students overcoming obstacles and mistakes with more resilience as they become more intrinsically motivated.

As students move toward the third phase, they will need sustained attention toward detail and continued direction toward success. The most effective technique at this phase is the use of descriptive feedback, which is specific to the learning target, ongoing, and defines what the student is doing well and where the student needs to focus attention. One of the major outcomes of descriptive feedback is the student's move from the desire for extrinsic reward to the impact of intrinsic feelings of accomplishment. Moving from extrinsic desires to intrinsic joy is what will move the student toward habit formation.

PHASE 3: MAINTENANCE

At this critical maintenance phase students have now seen the positive outcomes from their behavioral changes and wish to continue their drive toward success. Because they are consciously aware of the behaviors they are using and know when there is a need for adjustments or shifts, students are able to handle setbacks and errors. However, this phase can also lead to students' moving backward toward wanting immediate rewards as is indicated by the circular arrows in Figure 1.3. If a student encounters more failures than successes in the maintenance stage and is unable to adjust or is unwilling to modify behaviors, return to the immediate reward phase to move the student back toward maintenance.

During maintenance, students must dig deep inside themselves to find their willingness and desire to continue to achieve. Discuss with students how they feel and what they are thinking during this stage. Assist them in developing a plan to continue the effort and practice required to sustain success. Also, encourage students to refine their behaviors to fit different situations as they arise.

PHASE 4: HABIT

The final phase in the process is habit. A behavior becomes a habit when students have sufficient confidence to unconsciously apply strategies during tasks. Even when the task becomes complex or learners stumble in the learning process, students readily act to achieve success. Students are now autonomous in performance—moving from strategy implementation to skill development.

Once students habitually perform a behavior or skill, they should continually evaluate the implementation. Students should learn not to expect that the skills will always be useful in their first application. They should expect to practice, self-evaluate, and continue to maintain their beliefs in themselves.

C Is for Cognition

The dimension of cognition plays a significant role in SRL as students reflect on experiences, consider the multiple ways to solve complex and ambiguous problems, and communicate ideas to others.

Basically, cognition is the conscious act of thinking. Over the past century, the word *cognition* has become a common term to mean anything that is a mental process from simple or subtle processes (such as awareness of sensory input, movement at will, and recalling factual information) to very complex or abstract levels (such as critical reasoning, interpretation, and creativity). We can increase our cognition through the experiences of learning, whether it's repetition, practice, or discovery-based. However, for our purposes, we will be looking at cognition from the perspective of the varied thinking processes students use in the classroom.

This section will discuss metacognition (thinking about thinking), infra-cognition (broad, general thinking), and metaphysical cognition (existential, philosophical thinking). An important factor of SRL is the ability to move from the reflective process of metacognition to the structured thinking tools of infra-cognition and ultimately, to use knowledge beyond the self in metaphysical thinking.

Figure 1.4 **Levels of Cognition**

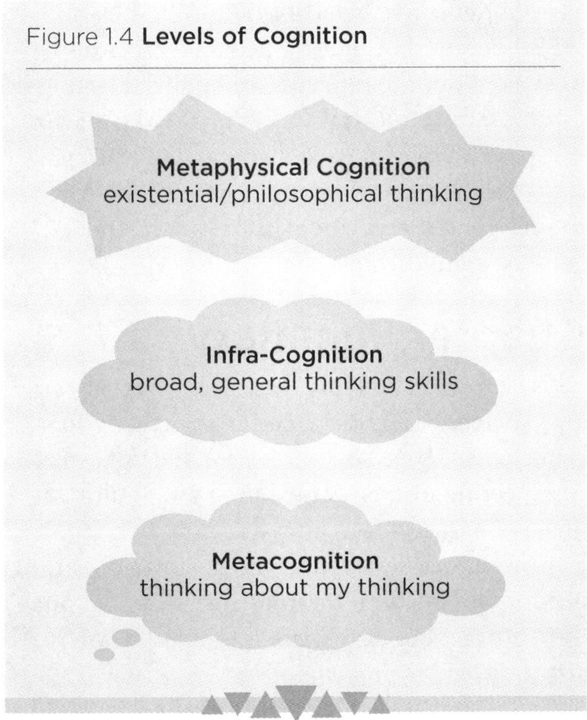

Metacognition

Metacognition is "thinking about our own thinking." This close thinking is the reflection process we all go through every day as we ponder recent and past occurrences. This active control over our higher forms of thinking enables us to engage in a more effective learning process. Metacognition includes the mental actions of planning how to approach a task, monitoring comprehension, and evaluating progress toward completion.

In some cases, metacognition has been used as an interchangeable term with self-regulation and executive functioning. In general, metacognition can be thought of as overseeing and controlling the cognition (thinking) process. Metacognition can be broken down into three subcategories of knowledge:[6]

- **Personal knowledge:** where and how you learn best. Do you prefer to work in a quiet room alone or are you more productive in a group where ideas flow freely?
- **Task knowledge:** knowing what kind of problem needs to be solved. Do you work best with very linear types of problems (algorithms) or are you better with abstract, undefined situations (real-world-type problems)?
- **Strategy knowledge:** knowing what to do and when. Do you know the specific strategies to solve problems and when to apply those techniques?

Central to learning is the awareness of personal strengths and limitations, knowing how to approach and solve problems, and proficiency with effective strategies to successfully complete tasks. Students can learn metacognition and how to apply it to be more effective learners. For more on the learning of metacognition, see Chapter 5.

Infra-Cognition

Infra-cognition is the perennial or "grand" thinking processes. Just as in gardening, the term "perennial" in this instance means to live for many years. Perennial thinking has been used for generations and is more than the survival thinking of how to acquire food, shelter, and water. It is complex, critical, and creative thinking processes. These processes are "grand" because they are bigger than metacognition (personal thinking). As we progress through the 21st century into the neo-millennial era, thinking must advance beyond knowing the right answer to knowing multiple pathways to solving complex, ambiguous problems without simple solutions.

Incorporated in infra-cognition are the general academic skills essential for success in and between content areas. This includes techniques specific to the discipline, such as the strategies for editing (in a writing class), as well as general skills of analysis, such as breaking an idea or a problem into sub-components to identify similarities and differences among the parts. Chapter 5 offers strategies to increase students' efficiency with infra-cognition.

Metaphysical Cognition

Metaphysical cognition is the most sophisticated level of cognition. In general terms, metaphysics is philosophical abstract or theoretical thinking about the nature of being, causality, truth, and the world in which all exist. Metaphysical thinking is the mental process that occurs when we have a deeper understanding of content and can connect ideas across subject areas to interpret the world around us.

6. Flavell, 1979.

Dorothy M. Emmet, a British philosopher, defined metaphysical thinking as analogical thinking, a form of reasoning in which similarities between two or more objects or ideas are compared to come to one point.[7] Emmet divided analogical thinking into two categories:

Coordinating analogies: when ideas from one subject domain are used to understand or interpret another content area (example: using the phrase "big bang theory" to describe ideas of how the universe came to exist).

Existential analogies: when ideas from experiences are used to explain or make judgments about reality or our being (example: "Time is the fire in which we burn," from Delmore Schwartz's poem, "Calmly We Walk Through This April's Day").

Balancing the Three Dimensions of SRL

Attainment of peak levels of academic performance requires students to balance affect, behavior, and cognition. Keeping students strong in all three dimensions or learning how to adjust one dimension to support the others is an essential tool for learning and success.

Without a strong affect (the motivational beliefs that one can achieve), students will not focus their behavior and ignite their cognition. Without effective behaviors (study and learning skills), cognition is not refined and affect tumbles. Without the reflective, thoughtful cognitive aspects, affect (motivation) wanes, and behavior instigates helplessness. Self-regulated learners can adjust the coordinating system of the ABCs to find greater enjoyment, motivation, and autonomy in learning.

Chapter Summary

This chapter gave a brief historical overview of how society has transformed from striving for achievement based on hard work and persistence to expecting instant gratification and multitasking. With this shift in how students perceive the learning process, we must understand the critical need to direct attention toward self-regulation for learning: the interrelated dimensions of affect, behavior, and cognition (the ABCs). Affect, or our feelings, is the conscious reaction to the emotional response to the internal and external world. A four-step process for behavior change enables students to move from using strategies to skill development. Cognition is a multilayered way of reflecting upon, thinking about, interpreting, and communicating complex ideas. Self-regulated learners fluidly balance these ABCs to be productive and successful, recognizing that when one dimension is out of balance, they can use the other two to create equilibrium.

7. Emmet, 1945.

CHAPTER 2

The Process of Developing Self-Regulation for Learning

Education is not a product: mark, diploma, job, money in that order; it is a process, a never-ending one.

—Bella Kaufman

To be a lifelong learner, one must possess or develop motivation and drive to take personal responsibility and control of acquiring new knowledge and skills. These attributes are characteristics of self-regulated learners. As defined in Chapter 1, self-regulation for learning (SRL) is managing and controlling one's affect (feelings), behaviors, and cognition (the ABCs) to achieve worthy goals. People who possess tenacity, discipline, and focus (sometimes called "grit") most likely have had to meet challenges as they learned new things. As they develop competence in learning and applying new ideas, they develop a positive personal identity and self-esteem. This chapter explains the process of developing the attributes of SRL and offers strategies and techniques for moving students from one stage of the process to the next. Following discussions of the stages are biographical sketches of two different learners along with analyses of the students' levels of SRL and sample recommendations to improve or refine their achievement.

Research Says: It's a Process

As students balance the three dimensions of SRL (the ABCs), they must adjust for adversity, obstacles, and complexities in an ongoing, fluid sequence. The most efficient learners recognize that affect, behavior, and cognition need continued attention, adjustment, and alignment. These students show they are resilient in difficult situations, possess a sense of determination, and recognize the need for patience in getting a job done well—critical attributes our future leaders will need to rely upon to solve problems.

Barry J. Zimmerman, a leading social cognitive researcher, states that a person self-initiates adjustments throughout the learning phase of SRL.[1] Affectively, a person feels stressed during performance, recognizes the feeling as stress (cognition), and knows he or she needs to alleviate the stress through relaxation-type actions (behavior). If using a learning strategy such as outlining a chapter (behavior) is not successful when it comes time to discuss information in class (cognition), the student needs to learn or employ a new strategy (behavior) to be better prepared for the next day's discussion. If, after a class session, the student realizes he or she has little understanding of the concepts defined and worked on, then the student will need to plan for techniques (such as a mnemonic) to remember information for the next session (cognition). These are the conscious actions that self-regulated learners undertake to continually achieve at the highest level.

Students who struggle, are disengaged, or find little relevance in the academic setting lack the awareness of the process and techniques of SRL. Many issues exist that prevent students from becoming more self-regulated as learners, including:

1. Zimmerman, 1989.

- insufficient support inside and outside school
- conflicting cultural/economic/historical/societal beliefs
- self-doubt/self-criticism/lowered expectations
- stereotyping by others
- inadequate modeling of appropriate school behaviors
- inadequate educational resources to increase self-regulation
- lack of awareness by educators of differences in students' background knowledge, culture, home life, learning preferences, economic status
- lack of persistence, motivation, desire, drive
- fixed mindset verses a growth mindset

Mindset

In 2006, Dr. Carol Dweck, a leading researcher in the field of psychology, theorized that all people observe and interact in the world through lenses of "mindsets." These mindsets are either fixed or growth. People with fixed mindsets believe intelligence, abilities, and talents are fixed traits that cannot be changed or enhanced. Their belief systems are supported through documentation, such as test scores or others' reports on performance. Individuals with fixed mindsets measure their successes based on the evaluation of others. Students with fixed mindsets have difficulty admitting to mistakes, taking on challenges, developing resilience, and understanding the need for effort to complete tasks.

Individuals with growth mindsets, on the other hand, are aware of their strengths and limitations, know that their abilities can be improved through practice, and understand how dedication, hard work, and effort greatly affect achievement of success. Students with a growth mindset learn to persevere until tasks are completed.[2] During the origination stage, it is critical for teachers to model the growth mindset for students.

The Key Stages of SRL

Self-regulation for learning requires an array of tools and strategies to attend to, adjust, and align the ABCs for optimal performance. For students to be successful, they need to pay attention to their feelings, behaviors, and thought patterns and learn to adjust them when meeting a challenge. Self-regulation develops in stages, from simple to complex. The stages are fluid and not always associated with the age of the learner, rather they are more dependent upon expected outcomes or performances. The process of developing SRL initially is interactive and gradually shifts from a need for external support and guidance to a more proactive, internal perspective. Eventually, the learner achieves the capability to routinely apply the strategies of the ABCs toward successful outcomes.

SRL Stage 1: Originate

Teachers *originate* the learning of SRL by having students observe others (1) managing emotional reactions, (2) using behaviors to achieve an outcome, and (3) analyzing information. At this stage, it is essential for teachers to model effective self-regulation strategies. Novice learners often cannot discern positive from negative affect, behavior, and cognition and need continual examples of strategies to manage them. Students from homes where parents or guardians use ineffective or negative strategies can bring those strategies with them to the school setting. Chapter 3 discusses this issue of "preventative" (survival-related) verses "promotional" (learning-oriented) strategies.

ROLE MODELS

Teachers and other adults routinely model specific strategies to help students attend to, adjust to, or align with the ABCs. When applying SRL, the role model talks specifically about how he or she feels, behaves, and thinks during the lesson. Role models can increase learners' motivation by talking about the rewards the role model receives from being successful (such as earning good grades or acknowledging they feel good about what they are doing) or by sharing how they redirect their focus when they are not achieving success.

2. Dweck, 2006.

Example: When teaching a new literary strategy, seventh-grade English teacher Mr. Warnert first directly describes the strategy, shows what it looks like in an author's writing, and discusses how it enhances the meaning of the author's work.

Then Mr. Warnert describes his experience of using the literary strategy in his own writing. In a demonstration of writing, he "thinks out loud" as he writes a short essay using the strategy. He shares his feelings (affect) of frustration about having to stop to think about how to spell a word. He tells what he does when he hits a mental block, such as taking a break by going to get a drink of water (behavior). He describes stopping to reflect on his progress (cognition). Mr. Warnert also shares that he has enjoyed producing a quality piece of writing; he talks about feelings of satisfaction when others find his prose informative and of feeling accomplished when he has overcome difficult situations. He encourages his students to also use the "think aloud" strategy when approaching a new strategy, working through difficult situations, and reflecting on accomplishments.

At this stage, the learner must perceive some connection to the role model. The closer the student's personal connection to the role model, the more likely his or her motivation will increase to achieve the role model's status.[3] If students perceive no connection to the role model, especially if the model is a teacher, they are less likely to be motivated to pay attention. This is why it is critical for teachers to build a strong connection with their students.

Also, using higher performing students as academic role models for lower performing students generally does not increase achievement. When using students as role models for each other, they should be within a similar zone of proximal development—having similar skill attributes or efficacies, a willingness to be stretched, and a connection with each other apart from ability (such as gender, ethnic background, or socioeconomic status).[4]

MODEL POSITIVE SELF-TALK

Sharing one's feelings, thoughts, and actions in an affirmative manner can build confidence to continue. Using statements such as "I will do well on this test by reducing my anxiety, staying focused, and thinking clearly" can have a profound effect on learning. Although students use self-talk in each of the subsequent stages, it is critical for the teacher to model it routinely during the origination stage.

During the development of an action, a technique, or a strategy, students use self-talk to identify what they are doing well and where they need to focus their efforts for improvement. Self-talk is a way to get students to verbalize the cognitive process. Self-talk is different from general or substantive conversation in the classroom; it is the verbalization of the "running commentary" in the learner's mind while working through a problem. One form of talk students can use is "thinking out loud." Another form is repeating what has been written, for example, directions, an equation that has been completed, or a passage in a text. This type of repeating can help students "hear" what they are to do or process.

Positive self-talk can also help struggling learners and learners who fear failure (like many gifted students) approach new learning tasks. These learners need to use phrases like, "I'm going to do my best on this task" or "Even though I didn't do so well last time, I'm going to try again, because I know I can do better." Positive self-talk helps reduce stress and improve attitude toward self and others. Share the following self-talk tips with students:

- Really listen to yourself—say the directions over and over again until you understand what to do or steps to complete.
- Use self-talk to guide your learning—ask yourself questions to secure your accuracy, identify flaws in reasoning, ensure evidence supports your thoughts, reframe the ideas, keep the situation in perspective, or adjust your feelings.
- Use positive self-talk—after making a mistake, adjust the way you think and then speak about it ("Well, I've learned I won't do that again!"). Staying positive can change the way you feel, behave, and think about learning.

3. Zimmerman and Kitsantis in Elliot and Dweck, 2005.
4. Vygotsky, 1987.

ENCOURAGE SOCIAL FEEDBACK

Learning is enhanced when it becomes social. Students who work together or who are encouraged by their peers are more likely to apply strategies to develop skills. At the origination stage, building the collaborative skills in the room is vital to the students' future growth.

INDUCTIVE AND DEDUCTIVE THINKING

Teaching students the various types and strategies of thinking supports their development of complex thinking skills. Inductive thinking is "going with your gut feelings about the information you have received." Whereas, deductive thinking is "taking into account all the facts presented with the information."[5] As Figure 2.1 indicates, graphic organizers can assist students in building their thinking skills.

SRL Stage 2: Intervene

In the *intervene* stage, teachers provide interventions at the right time and place to move students beyond just copying actions. Learners emulate or copy the patterns the model has performed. Even though learners may be able to do some aspects of the ABCs, they need continued trial and error to perfect the strategies. Discriminate intervening, such as descriptive feedback, must be neither too much nor too little, too often nor too far between. Intervention must hit what is called the "Goldilocks principle": Just right. Close attention to the implementation of the ABCs is critical at this point.

During this stage students may also directly copy what the model has presented. Some teachers fear students "just copying and not creating their own work." However, research does not support this contention.[6] In fact, the act

Figure 2.1 **Strategies for the Key Stages of SRL**

	Affective	Behavioral	Cognitive
Stage 1 Originate	› Discuss how feelings affect learning. › Discover/pique interests. › Build confidence through modeling positive self-talk.	› Introduce specific strategies. › Model step-by-step applying the skill and correcting mistakes. › Encourage social feedback.	› Introduce using graphic organizers to document thinking. › Introduce inductive and deductive thinking.
Stage 2 Intervene	› Encourage self-talk about feelings. › Encourage discovery of interests.	› Model corrections for individuals. › Design group work for support.	› Provide time to reflect. › Suggest using thinking strategies.
Stage 3 Support	› Encourage making affirmations about emotions.	› Focus on deliberate practice. › Focus on strategy implementation rather than on overall outcomes.	› Encourage verbalizing what is working or not working (self-review).
Stage 4 Release	*Monitor students':* › Maintaining a positive outlook on learning through intrinsic drive. › Fluidly adjusting emotional responses.	*Monitor students':* › Self-monitoring until aware of excellence. › Seeking help when necessary.	*Monitor students':* › Automatically implementing grand thinking skills. › Focusing metacognition on mastery.

5. Cash, 2011.
6. Rogoff et al., 2003.

of copying (or parroting) is extensively used in many cultural groups for learning shared values, expectations, and traditions. Mimicry represents the learner's desire to perfect the task or skill. Additionally, group or social support is necessary for learners to move from the copy-and-do stage to the next level. Being part of and making contributions to a community bolsters emotional resilience and confidence. When learners can share experiences, they are more likely to be able to support each other in expanding their thinking and decision making. The group mindset must be one of collaboration.

INTEREST FINDING

As students begin to feel more confident about themselves, they begin to build or identify areas of interest. Interest is a driving, sustaining force in learning that keeps us focused and attentive. Finding topics of interest or using students' interests in the learning process helps them feel connected to the information they are studying.

REFLECTION

Self-reflection on the learning process is important and leads to changing direction or recognizing success. At the intervention stage, offer students structured ways to reflect on their performances, such as those presented in Chapter 9. Teach students how to use the strategies and provide time for them to reflect on their work.

SRL Stage 3: Support

Practicing the tasks and skills within a supportive setting is a critical factor at this stage. Students should, in their own words, explain the process the model went through to create or complete a task. A student's reframing of the process guides the teacher in providing the amount and kind of support or structure the student will need as he or she continues to practice and refine the skills.

DELIBERATE PRACTICE

Deliberate practice is a useful strategy to employ at the support stage. Initially coined in the field of athletics, deliberate practice is a framework of skill improvement to reach expertise. In this process the learner breaks down the larger skill into discrete, conscious parts and identifies the parts that need improvement. Then, the learner focuses on those specific strategies or steps that need work and repetitively practices them.

The teacher's guidance and continual feedback are extremely important during deliberate practice. To prevent deliberate practice from becoming tedious, the teacher should vary the practice assignments, model using the skill in various levels of complexity, and limit the amount of time a student practices. If you play an instrument or a sport, you have experienced deliberate practice. A musician working on a complex piece will focus on one measure at a time, breaking it down note-by-note and playing it over and over again. The musician starts playing at a very slow rate and gradually increases the speed until he or she can play that section at the piece's appropriate tempo. Hand out copies of the reproducible "10 Steps to Deliberate Practice" on page 21 and discuss with students.

FOCUS ON SPECIFIC STEPS

Another strategy learners use in this stage is to keep their focus on the specific steps rather than on the overall outcome of the tasks. When learners focus only on the final outcome, they can become overwhelmed and frustrated by making ineffective adjustments. When students implement deliberate practice on defined obstacles or know specifically what to correct to reach a set standard, they are more likely to achieve proficiency.

SRL Stage 4: Release

After sufficient practice, learners reach the final stage of self-regulation, and teachers release students to full autonomy. At this stage, learners confidently apply strategies and are able to decide which strategy to use and when to implement it. Because they self-monitor and are aware of the standards of excellence, they are ready to make adjustments as necessary. Each time they make successful adjustments, they are intrinsically motivated to continue to strive. At this stage, they become more performance-oriented rather than process-focused. Setbacks do not deter their efforts. Autonomous learners adapt their performance based on various cues from others.

At the release stage, learners develop and apply their own style to their performances. Even though the support of others is greatly reduced, students still need to be reinforced with social support such as offers of congratulations or praise for a job well done. However, self-regulated learners initiate seeking help, are aware of the most effective resources, and only require support for brief periods of time. Affectively, the self-regulated student focuses on the intrinsic nature of learning. The feeling of success is maintained through a positive outlook.

Self-regulated learners know how to adjust emotional responses to fit the context and are able to avoid spending too much energy on negative feelings. Though errors or mistakes may happen, they don't let the limitations control their emotional responses. Self-regulated learners also use metacognitive action as a tool for mastery. As tools are applied to learning, these learners evaluate and justify their proficient use. Even though limitations may be uncovered at this stage, the self-regulated learner is able to automatically implement thinking tools to overcome or focus in on improving the limitation.

The four stages to achieving autonomous self-regulation of learning, though developmental, may not always happen in sequence. Learners may stall at a particular stage, need to move backward, or jump quickly from one stage to the next. Each learner's progress to autonomy will be different. However, teachers and other adults in the student's life should identify where in the sequence the learner is performing and what obstacles may be impeding movement to the next stage, and continually reinforce the learner through the balancing of the ABCs. Research has found that "individuals who master each skill level in sequence will learn more easily and effectively."[7]

Putting the Stages into Practice: Biographical Sketches

Following are two general biographical sketches of students at different stages within the SRL model. Each is briefly described and then suggestions are made for moving the child to greater autonomy.

Tommy, Grade 8, Age 13

In middle school Tommy is well liked by his peers and teachers. Although he performs below average in his classes, most of his teachers believe he is not working up to his potential. Once a week in elementary school, Tommy attended a gifted and talented pull-out class where he engaged in projects of interest on topics not covered in the regular classroom. His middle school doesn't provide optional programs for students identified as gifted and talented. Typically, teachers offer these students an additional project or ask them to do a different type of assignment than the other students. The reasons for Tommy's below-average performance are: he does not finish his work in the time allotted, he usually forgets his homework, and he spends much of class time off task.

SELF-REGULATION ISSUES

Affective: Tommy finds little motivation to do what is asked of him.

Behavioral: He is disorganized, takes few notes in class, and doesn't use effective study strategies.

Cognitive: While a bright young man, he is rarely required to ask or answer questions above the application level.

ANALYSIS

During Tommy's early schooling years, he could operate as a somewhat independent learner while attending a gifted and talented pull-out class in which he worked on self-directed projects. However, as he moved into adolescence and middle school, he became disorganized, found little interest in the activities of the general classroom, and began to underachieve. There are two different issues going on with Tommy:

1. In elementary school, Tommy received encouragement to develop self-regulating strategies through interest-based learning. Teachers nurtured his advanced abilities and his desire to go more deeply into the content. Because his middle school offers few interesting options for advancing his knowledge, he has disengaged from the low levels of the content.

7. Ibid.

2. Tommy is in adolescent development! Neurological changes in the adolescent brain cause organization to become a huge issue. Details of where things are and when things are due take a lower priority than socialization and identity development. Erratic behavior is natural for adolescents; their neurological development is similar to that of a preschooler. Teachers can support his learning by using and reinforcing basic strategies, specific and clear directions, and simplistic management structures on a daily basis.

RECOMMENDATIONS

Clearly, Tommy has reverted to the earlier stages of building SRL skills. Based on his prior success with managing advanced levels of content, he likely would respond to more interest-based learning designs. Teachers should construct the activities so they are not perceived as "more work" but rather more engaging, interest-based activities to stretch his knowledge. Within these activities he is more likely to be at the *support* or even *release* stages. Using this approach, teachers will heighten his affect (motivation), align his behaviors (goal setting and work completion) to the task, and utilize his cognition (the need for more advanced levels of thinking). He would also benefit from the direct modeling of organizational, note-taking, and study strategies *(originate)*. Teachers should monitor his use of specific strategies on a daily basis until he is proficient in using the strategy (moving toward *intervene* and *release*). The monitoring should be both in and outside of school—keeping his parents fully engaged in the process. Students in a multiple-home situation may be challenged with learning the different rules/norms of each household and may need more support in developing self-regulating strategies.

Olivia, Grade 5, Age 10

Olivia lives with her maternal grandmother, father, mother, and younger brother and sister. Olivia and her siblings qualify for free/reduced lunch at school. Her father works at a lumber mill and her mother and grandmother run a small childcare center out of their home. In school, Olivia has a few close friends, and her teachers find her to be a focused young lady. She tends to do what is asked of her and follows the directions and norms of the classroom. She scores in the average range on standardized assessments. Olivia likes to read, listen to music, and spend time with her friends. She dreams of becoming a doctor and knows that she will need to work hard to fulfill her dream. She also knows that she must have good grades in high school to qualify for college scholarships because her parents cannot provide much financial support.

SELF-REGULATION ISSUES

Affective: Olivia is driven by a dream of becoming a doctor. She is motivated to work hard and feels good about herself.

Behavioral: Because she believes she can achieve her goal by studying, she studies each night before she goes to bed.

Cognitive: Her teachers provide options for Olivia to stretch her thinking. Because she struggles with advanced-level work, she knows she will have to work harder than some of her peers. She understands that she will not get the right answer every time and setbacks do not deter her from continually trying.

ANALYSIS

Olivia has benefited from her multigenerational family situation. Seeing her parents and grandparent coordinating work schedules and negotiating the struggles of living with minimal means has helped her gain confidence that she, like her role models, has the internal strength to succeed. She has set a long-term goal and continues to stay focused on bettering herself. Though Olivia is an average student, if she continues to apply effort and stay focused, she can put herself in position to achieve her dream.

RECOMMENDATIONS

Olivia exemplifies higher levels of self-regulated learning *(support* to *release)* in the affective domain but could use some assistance with study strategies and direct attention toward thinking skills development. She represents lower levels of SRL *(intervene)* in how to study (behavioral dimension) and different ways of thinking (cognitive dimension). Appealing to her intrinsic drive, teachers could provide her with templates of graphic organizers to help her organize her thinking and focus on the specific objectives to be learned. Her teachers should connect her "I can do this" attitude to the content and habits of studying to increase her levels of self-regulation for learning.

Chapter Summary

This chapter discussed the four levels of self-regulation (originate, intervene, support, and release). Continuing the philosophy of the intertwined ABCs (affect, behavior, and cognition) as a framework for developing autonomously self-regulated learners is critical. The balancing act of the ABCs along the way must be maintained for even development. While the four stages are presented in a sequential manner, this does not mean that every child will develop them in a sequential way. The manifestation of SRL is a nonlinear process that can include cycling and recycling back to earlier stages. Keep in mind that all learners are different and will need individualization in their developmental processes.

10 Steps to Deliberate Practice

Deliberate practice is an essential tool for when you encounter stumbling blocks in learning. Deliberate practice is repetitive and sustained over time. It's important that you don't get overly frustrated or exhausted from the practice. Keep in mind that deliberate practice is not a "quick fix" and at times it may feel arduous, but this practice will make you better! Here are 10 steps to deliberate practice:

1. Break down the desired skill into discrete steps. Either verbalize or write down the steps.
2. Pinpoint the step(s) within the process where difficulty occurs.
3. Identify why the step(s) may be causing an issue.
4. Consider specific ways to correct the issue(s).
5. Focus on one step and do it over and over.
6. After each round of practice, get feedback either by reviewing your own work or having someone else review it.
7. If necessary, vary the technique you use so that you continue to find success—deliberate practice can be tiring, so take a break when needed.
8. Repeat steps 5 and 6.
9. Record your practice in a log, journal, chart, or graph. Review past performances to identify if your practice is working or where it may need adjustment.
10. Celebrate your successes and make plans on how to avoid repeating any mistakes.

CHAPTER 3

Engaging Students in Learning

The object of education is to prepare the young to educate themselves throughout their lives.

—Robert M. Hutchins

The previous chapters discussed the concept of self-regulation for learning (SRL) and the stages of its development. For students to successfully develop SRL, they need to actively engage in learning (EiL). This chapter will merge the four stages of SRL (origination, intervention, support, and release) with the four phases of EiL in a matrix that makes the process accessible to students and teachers.

Factors Impacting SRL

Student engagement in learning hinges on three factors psychologist Albert Bandura theorized as important in the process of developing SRL:[1]

1. How learners feel about themselves (self-belief) and their academic abilities (self-efficacy) will strongly influence their motivation to learn.
2. As students transition into adolescence and the middle years of schooling (ages 10–18), there is a general decrease in their self-beliefs and self-efficacy.
3. Gender variances may affect overall learning, based on prior learning experiences, social pressures, and differing neurological preferences.

See Figure 3.1 Factors Impacting SRL.

Figure 3.1 **Factors Impacting SRL**

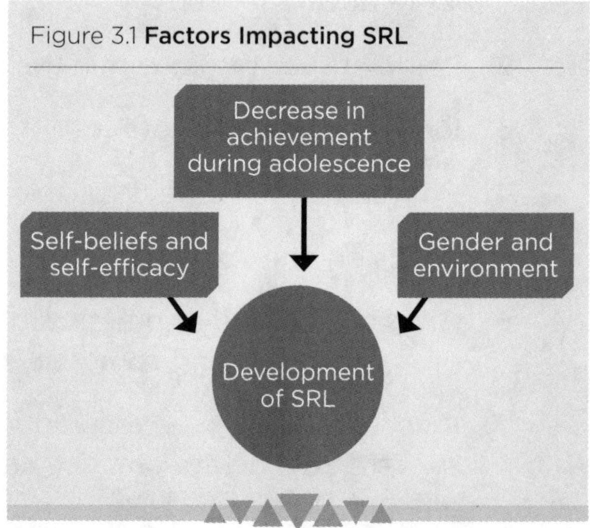

Self-Belief and Self-Efficacy

Self-belief is how people perceive themselves and their level of confidence about their abilities. Self-efficacy is someone's capacity to approach, work at, and ultimately achieve worthwhile goals. Bandura explains the difference between self-belief (confidence) and self-efficacy:[2] Self-belief is a general acceptance of who we are as individuals, whether that acceptance is positive or negative. For example, believing that you are not very good at math and will likely score poorly in class is your self-belief. Whereas self-efficacy is the belief a person has based on prior experiences about how much effort will be required to attain different levels of achievement. Self-efficacy is

1. Bandura 1986, confirmed by Pajares and Schunk, 2001.
2. Bandura, 1986.

more affirmation oriented. When approaching a new task, a student with a high level of self-efficacy will have had previous successes to draw from and would most likely think, "I can do this, because I've succeeded in the past." Both self-belief and self-efficacy are directly related to the acquisition of SRL and improved achievement in school. Strategies to increase both self-belief and self-efficacy can be found in Chapter 4.

Adolescent Changes

Movement from elementary school to middle school, along with a progression into adolescence, signals a shift in the way students think. Generally, adolescence is a significant time in brain growth and development. According to Piaget's theory of human development, students are moving from the concrete to abstract levels of cognition; the adolescent is starting to make connections between personal life experiences and generalizing them to a broader understanding.[3] Adolescents begin developing a more mature thought process, such as critical and logical reasoning, problem solving, and impulse control. However, it's not an easy or quick transition. This can be a period of unpredictable mood swings, shifts in attention, irrational behavior, and a downward trajectory of grades.

Gender Differences

The third characteristic of SRL development identified by Bandura is the impact of gender differences. Debate continues in the scientific community regarding how gender affects learning and behavior. However, through more advanced levels of technology and research, evidence does suggest that the effects of sex hormones on early brain development and the differences in how boys and girls are treated in the environment may vary the way they prefer to learn. Generally, girls may be more inclined to learn through the verbal and auditory (listening) process, whereas boys may prefer the kinesthetic (action) and visual/spatial process. Additionally, hormonal development triggers some gender specific behaviors, such as rage and aggression in boys and nurturing in girls. There does not seem to be evidence that gender differences have an effect on overall intelligence (as measured by an IQ test). We all possess our own strengths and limitations that are specific to us as individuals and not to our gender.[4]

Environment

Our environment, which includes social status, economics, culture, and history, can have a significant effect on our learning outcome. Again, little evidence suggests that any group of people are more intelligent (IQ-wise) than any other. Children from enriched home lives are more likely to do well in school than children not from enriched home lives. With the understanding that our strengths and limitations are natural, the environmental impact on nurturing those strengths and limitations can be substantial. To heighten our strengths, we need challenges, intellectual stimulation, and caring individuals to support us in the face of struggle. To limit the effect of our limitations we need to be nurtured in the learning process, encouraged to stretch, and supported emotionally.

Four Phases of Engaging in Learning (EiL)

How can teachers and schools structure learning to increase SRL? Barry Zimmerman, an educational researcher at the City University of New York, and his colleagues described students developing self-regulation by engaging in learning (EiL).[5] A student goes through four interrelated phases of learning engagement to develop a greater sense of SRL. The four phases are cyclical—each time a student successfully cycles through the phases, they become more self-regulated in their learning (see Figure 3.2).

EiL Phase 1: Fostering Confidence

Before students can engage in a task, they must have a sense of confidence in their ability to successfully perform the task. This can be difficult for some students who have rarely felt confident or successful. In these cases, the teacher must construct activities and structures that will build the students' confidence to perform. This is also

3. Piaget, 1937/2013.
4. Hearn, 2004.
5. Zimmerman et al, 1996.

Figure 3.2 **Four Phases of Engaging in Learning (EiL)**

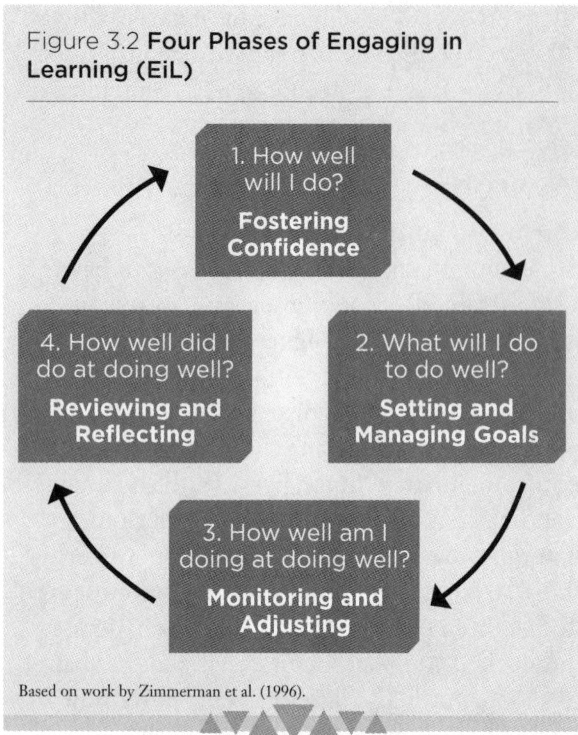

Based on work by Zimmerman et al. (1996).

the phase in which teachers empower students to take control of their own learning.

According to Bandura, when fostering students' confidence, the teacher must have an awareness of the learners' emotional state.[6] As stated in earlier chapters, how learners feel about a situation will determine the focus of their attention. Students need assistance in recognizing their emotional responses to different learning situations and how to adjust their responses to feel more secure in approaching learning tasks.

In the beginning phase of learning, the student needs to reflect on past performances and prior knowledge experiences to step forward into learning. For struggling students, this initial stage may set them on the path to failure because they can't recall positive past performances or prior successes. They don't know what to think about (cognitive), how to act (behavioral), or how good it feels (affective) to be accomplished. This phase is considered the most important stage in learning—getting the students to ground themselves confidently.

Begin to foster the students' confidence in learning by helping them identify their emotional state. By building a positive learning environment where all students are respected and encouraged to do their best, the teacher increases the chances of students feeling good about their experiences.

Building students' self-beliefs to increase self-efficacy is also necessary in the first phase. Self-belief is very much related to the emotional state of the learner. Self-efficacy develops from self-beliefs. When students feel they have the skill development or learning tools to accomplish a task, they are more likely to approach the task with a productive mindset. Students need to learn how to judge their own skill development and task commitment prior to engaging in the activity.

DEVELOPING POSITIVE SELF-BELIEF AND SELF-EFFICACY

An effective strategy to help foster confidence is to have students do a visualization activity prior to starting a task. In this activity students either lie on the floor or sit comfortably at their desks with their eyes closed. Using a soothing voice, ask students to imagine a peaceful, calm place. This place can be their bedroom, the fort they built as a child, walking in the woods, or elsewhere. Next ask them how they feel when they are in this peaceful place. Have them capture that feeling as an example of calmness. Now ask them to think of a time when they were excited about their performance or when they accomplished something that was at first difficult. Again, ask them to capture that feeling of success and remember it. Have students open their eyes and recall the feelings of calm and success. Say, "Those are the feelings you will have when you successfully complete this task."

Other ways to foster confidence are

- Set and maintain acceptable learning behaviors in the classroom.
- Use a nonconfrontational style with your students—don't get into power struggles!
- Use affirmative language rather than punitive language ("Jamal is really focused on the task at hand!" rather than "Sarah, stay on task.")
- Give students time to de-stress—play fun learning games or tell jokes after a difficult task, activity, or test.

6. Bandura, 1986.

- Refuse to engage in public arguments—don't allow students to "get your goat." If a student has a disagreement with you, take the student aside to discuss it.

For intrinsic motivation and self-efficacy to increase, students need specific thinking tools or habits. When students are consciously aware of what it takes to perform successfully, they know they can rely upon themselves to achieve a task. Here is where directly teaching specific thinking habits (such as convergent and divergent thinking) and literacy skills can strongly influence how prepared students feel prior to engaging in a learning task. Craft time in your class day to embed thinking activities where students develop the abilities to think independently.

Finally, providing a classroom structure that continually supports learning development is necessary for students to acquire a positive outlook on approaching difficult tasks and building greater self-belief and self-efficacy. Schools need to be places where intellectual risk taking is the norm, getting "wrong" answers is respected, and divergent ways of gathering information is encouraged. The teacher must be the one to set the standard and uphold values of a positive learning environment and also be a supporter of intellectual risk taking, curiosity, and hard work. Specific strategies and ideas for empowering students prior to learning can be found in Chapter 4. Teaching students the habits of thinking will be found in Chapter 5.

EiL Phase 2: Setting and Managing Goals

Once students feel a sense of confidence to approach learning, they then make a plan or set a goal, which, for many students, can be difficult. Once students finalize their goals, they learn how to manage and achieve their goals (see Chapter 6 for specific examples of goals). Students can use the techniques in Figure 3.3 to help them avoid distractors such as cell phones, websites, and tweets. Chapter 7 will highlight more strategies for maintaining focus during the goal process.

Figure 3.3 **Eight Strategies for Avoiding Distractions**

1. Set time limits for work—do no more than 15–20 minutes of continuous work without a break.
2. Take breaks that are physical in nature—but make sure they are not for more than two minutes. It is beneficial to do something physical—jumping jacks, push-ups, dancing.
3. If you listen to music while you work, make sure that it is peaceful and without words. Our brains have a difficult time processing multiple bits of information. Music with words forces our brain to multitask, which is an inefficient learning process.
4. Ensure that you have appropriate lighting for the work you are doing. If your homework is reading, the more direct the lighting, the better. Sunlight is the best!
5. Study in a cleared space. Get rid of clutter and disorganization—move it off to the side so your brain can focus on the task at hand rather than the mess around you.
6. Change your study location to increase thinking. Studies have found that when you routinely alter your study environment, your brain will increase its ability to remember the studied information. Since you can't always predict where and when you will be required to use the information, changing your environment, even in simple ways, can make what you are learning independent of the location.
7. Whether it's spending an additional five minutes on the computer or eating your favorite cookie, reward yourself when you study the entire time allotted for homework. Even if you didn't complete the work, congratulate yourself for sticking to the study period.
8. Take a moment to reflect on what worked and what didn't work while you were studying. Record what you will do or not do next time. Post those ideas in your workspace as reminders.

EiL Phase 3: Monitoring and Adjusting

Phase 3 of engaging in learning requires students to monitor their progress toward achievement. Using formative assessments is an excellent way to move students from the desire for extrinsic rewards (grades/certificates/trophies/pizza parties) toward the intrinsic desire to achieve. Formative feedback is provided to the student throughout the learning process. The most beneficial type of formative feedback is descriptive, which goes beyond saying "good job" or "work harder!"

Descriptive feedback is:

- Ongoing throughout the learning process.
- Provided to the learner in a timely manner.
- Explicitly focused on skill development and understanding.
- Articulated to the progress toward the goal.
- Specific to the task or performance.
- Incremental (never giving too much at once or too little to make sense).
- Praising the effort over the achievement to develop a growth mindset.

More ideas on monitoring and adjusting are given in Chapter 8.

EiL Phase 4: Reviewing and Reflecting

The final phase of this model is the reflective stage (How well did I do at doing well?). This is when the summative assessment (the final product or end point in the learning) is used to help the student contemplate the effectiveness of their learning strategies and behaviors as well as define their feelings of success.

Teachers can stimulate metacognition with reflection on questions such as:

- What was I thinking throughout the learning process?
- How clearly did I understand what was expected of me during the lessons?
- In what ways did I use self-talk positively or negatively?
- Why would my teacher ask me to consider different points of view?

Students can also reflect through:

- logs or journals
- portfolios of work (both good and poor quality)
- group conversations (from large to small groups)
- coaching sessions with the teacher (two to three students talk about their learning process with the teacher, who offers advice for improvement)

Finally, consider using prompts to get students to reflect more from a growth mindset, such as:

- Write about one thing you learned today.
- Tell a partner about a mistake you made today that taught you something about yourself or made you laugh.
- Sketch something you worked hard at today.
- Share with your tablemates one thing that you were proud of in your learning today.
- Blog about something you would change about your learning today.
- Tweet me one specific goal you will set for yourself tomorrow.

When students are able to believe in themselves to do well; identify what strategies, skills, and resources they will need to be successful; monitor their progress toward the goal; and reflect on what they did cognitively, behaviorally, and affectively post-production, they are more likely to be successful in future learning endeavors. Chapter 9 includes more ideas about the reflective process.

Achieving Success

The term *success* has varied and multiple meanings. Dictionaries will use such phrases as "accomplishing goals," "attaining wealth, position, or honor," or "achieving a favorable outcome." In short, as famed psychologist and author of *Successful Intelligence: How Practical and Creative Intelligence Determine Success in*

Life[7] Robert J. Sternberg describes, success is "in the eye of the beholder." Defining success is like trying to describe a cloud. It's a nebulous term that is difficult to pin down. But, numerous years of research and study on how to achieve success shows three critical factors are the combination of our *personal characteristics* with *ongoing feedback* to accomplish *important and challenging goals* (see Figure 3.4).

PERSONAL CHARACTERISTICS

The first factor of success is the distribution of our personal characteristics. Inert abilities, those measured by IQ tests, have some effect on our success. But as Sternberg found in his studies, abilities, while producing higher test scores, don't always lead to greater successes in life.[8] Aptitude, the acquired capacity to do something, has a greater effect on our future happiness and success. To be successful, then, it's important to recognize the need to adjust, modify, or compensate both our abilities and our aptitudes. Additional characteristics such as motivation, desire, drive, and grit are also necessary to achieve success and will be discussed further in Chapter 4.

ONGOING FEEDBACK

Whether the student's motivational focus is promotional or preventative determines what approaches should be used for ongoing feedback

7. Sternberg, 1997.
8. Ibid.

Figure 3.4 **Success Factors**

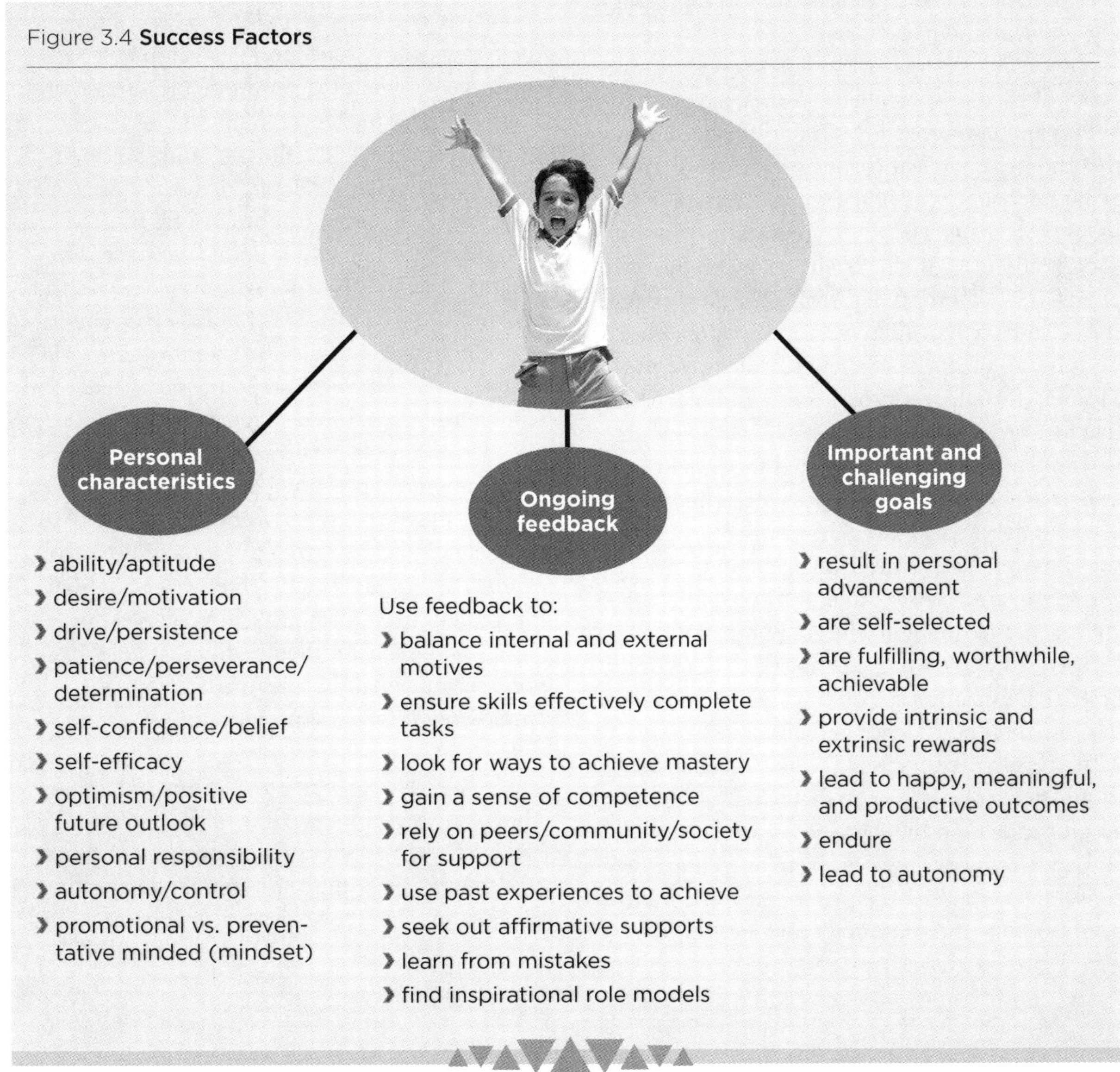

to help the learner achieve success. This feedback balances the internal and external motives to achieve the goal. Feedback also assists the student in recognizing which strategies are working and which strategies need to be adjusted.

Promotional or preventative outlook. The idea of promotional- or preventative-focused minds describes two motivational focuses similar to Dweck's fixed versus growth mindsets.[9] E. Tory Higgins, a prominent psychologist at Columbia University, recognized that our motivational focus can affect how we attain a goal.[10]

Promotional-focused students are those who find learning enjoyable and challenging. They try new things because the novelty engages them, use coping strategies to overcome failures, and use mistakes as learning tools. They value the learning enough to take risks and feel that learning is within their control.

Preventative-focused students feel learning is out of their control. Because they have failed before and perceive the level of difficulty beyond their ability, they fear the learning process and avoid the challenges of the work. Preventative-focused students use handicapping strategies to protect themselves affectively, behaviorally, or cognitively. These students view learning activities as so risky that they are not worth the effort of trying to meet the challenges they present. Figure 3.5 compares promotional and preventative focuses.

Students with a promotional focus tend to think more about what's possible, while preventative-focused students think more about the consequences of individual actions. This "far versus near" vision suggests two differing approaches to giving feedback. For promotional-focused students, using positive feedback can have a significant effect on learning and continue to grow their confidence and outlook. Whereas, with preventative-focused students, feedback should reflect on the work that needs to be accomplished, on the sustained effort required, and on the vigilance necessary to avert negative consequences.[11] More on feedback strategies for promotional- and preventative-focused students will be provided in Chapter 8.

IMPORTANT, CHALLENGING GOALS

The final factor necessary for achieving success centers on goal setting. Students must have the freedom and control to create goals that have value to them. The goals must be fulfilling, worthwhile, achievable, and rewarding. Reward is both an intrinsic and extrinsic force in goal approach. Goal attainment should not only make us feel good, but should also produce an outcome that has an enduring effect on ourselves as well as others. Additionally, well-crafted goals lead students to a greater sense of autonomy in their learning process. A full explanation of goal setting can be found in Chapter 6.

Stages and Phases Matrix for Developing SRL

Now that you have an understanding of how the phases of EiL encourage development of the stages of SRL, the reproducible "Stages and Phases Matrix for Developing SRL—Teacher Form" (page 31) will help you guide your students to reach greater levels of autonomous learning. The matrix can be a useful tool in recognizing where children may be struggling and offers suggestions for actions to take in the classroom.

The matrix may also be useful when working with students whose classroom issues go beyond what a teacher may have the capacity to manage. Most schools have a team of teachers, social workers, school psychologists, special educators, and administrators that meet on a routine basis to discuss individual student issues. The matrix can be used to identify in which stages of SRL the student may be and in which phases the child has the most difficulty. Because SRL does not develop equally across the learning phases, employing different strategies during different times may be necessary.

Using the reproducible "Stages and Phases Matrix for Developing SRL—Student Form" (page 32) helps students become more autonomous in their learning. When introducing the EiL phases, the teacher may distribute one phase at a time, with the four SRL stages highlighted so students can self-select which stage they feel they

9. Dweck, 2006.
10. Higgins, 2001.
11. Halvorson and Higgins, 2013.

Figure 3.5 **Promotional vs. Preventative Focuses**

Promotional	**Preventative**
Learning is in my control	Learning is out of my control
Future oriented	Present oriented
Success driven	Failure fearful
Growth mindset	Fixed mindset
Use coping strategies	Use handicapping strategies
Use mistakes as learning tools	Fear making mistakes
Solution focused	Emotion/survival focused
Adapt to goals as a process toward fulfillment	Adapt to goals set by others to receive reward or avoid punishment
Find meaning and value in learning	Don't find meaning or value in learning
Confront failure	Avoid failure or failure defines them
Avoid coercion	Are easily coerced
Avoid distraction	Distractible
Problem-solving focused	Fear focused
Adaptable to different situations	Inflexible to different situations
Can mesh academic and nonacademic goals	Academic goals compete with nonacademic goals
Mastery oriented	Performance oriented
Consider my goal attainment as personal improvement of well-being	Consider other's goals as a threat to my well-being
Persistent	Give up easily
Seek out social supports	May be aggressive toward help
Apply effort	Withhold effort
Flexible behaviors to learn	Rigid or passive behaviors for learning
I can do this because: › There is a thrill in trying › I enjoy the risk › I'm driven › It's worth the time › It's worth achieving the goal › I like the challenge › I like testing my limitations › I could succeed › Even though I may have failed before, I will try again	I won't do this because: › There is danger involved › It's a risk › I'm afraid › It takes too much time › It's not worth it › It's too hard or too challenging › It's beyond my limits › I could fail › I've failed before and will do so again

are in at each phase of the learning. For example, if you are just beginning a unit, provide each student with the "Fostering Confidence" frames. The teacher can either identify for each student which stage he or she is at or allow him or her to choose it. Have students use the matrix to find which action to take during the opening of the unit. The handout would look like Figure 3.6.

Chapter Summary

This chapter focused on the process of developing SRL. Three issues need to be accounted for during the acquisition of SRL: self-belief and self-efficacy; the transition into adolescence; and the roles of gender, neurology, and the environment. Four phases of EiL were defined: fostering confidence in the learner to perform well, setting and managing appropriate goals, monitoring and adjusting learning techniques, and reviewing and reflecting. Achieving success is characterized by personal responsibility, the need for ongoing feedback, and setting worthy goals to be attained. Finally, the "Stages and Phases Matrix for Developing SRL" forms are provided for teachers and students to scaffold toward greater learning autonomy.

Figure 3.6 **Example of Student Form for Fostering Confidence**

		Stages of Self-Regulation for Learning			
		Originate (Modeling & Observing)	**Intervene** (Copy & Do)	**Support** (Practice & Refinement)	**Release** (Application & Independence)
Phases of Engaging in Learning	**Fostering Confidence**	Find people and things in the classroom that make you feel good about yourself. To do the best job of learning you need to believe in yourself.	Take this time to try new strategies and techniques. Don't be afraid to ask questions of the teacher or others.	You have been doing well with the help of the teacher and others. Now it's time for you to try things on your own. Don't be afraid to make mistakes—this is how we learn. Also, try out different ways of doing things to make it work better for you.	Now you can apply the strategies on your own. While you may need guidance and assistance sometimes, this is your time to work independently.

Stages and Phases Matrix for Developing SRL—Teacher Form

Phases of Engaging in Learning	Stages of Self-Regulation: **Originate** (Modeling & Observing)	**Intervene** (Copy & Do)	**Support** (Practice & Refinement)	**Release** (Application & Independence)
Fostering Confidence	Teacher creates a learning environment that makes all students feel confident to take intellectual and creative risks.	Teachers provide opportunities for students to stretch intellectually and creatively. Students learn about their and others' strengths and limitations.	Students put into practice learning behaviors that employ creative and critical thinking. Teacher supports students with building, activating, or teaching prior knowledge.	Students independently put into practice thinking skills and habits of productive behaviors. Teacher is available as counsel.
Goal Setting	Teacher models how to set goals. Students fill in graphic organizer with teacher.	Teacher provides students with graphic organizer on goal setting. Teacher checks all students' work on graphic organizer.	Students complete graphic organizer or craft their own goal chart. Teacher checks for clarity.	Students set goals independent of teacher. Students seek out help when necessary.
Monitoring the Goal	Teacher models how to monitor goal attainment. Teacher uses pre-assessments to assist students in recognizing strengths and limitations.	Teacher provides immediate descriptive feedback to support students. Students monitor their goals based on formative assessments created by the teacher.	Students use daily practice to guide them in their goal monitoring. Students may also confer with peers or teacher to measure progress toward the goal.	Students use all forms of feedback (assessments, discussions, coaching) to monitor their goal progress. The teacher is available when requested.
Reflecting on the Goal	Teacher provides summative assessment review as a measure of goal attainment.	Teacher allows time for students to discuss and reflect on their learning. Students document their ideas in a reflection log or similar.	Students ask questions of self and/or peers regarding the learning process. Teacher may provide conversation starters. Teacher assists students in gathering materials to quantify and qualify their learning.	Students document their learning in the format that fits best. Based on the goal attainment, students begin to set plans for future successes. The teacher acts as an advisor.

Stages and Phases Matrix for Developing SRL—Student Form

Phases of Engaging in Learning	Stages of Self-Regulation			
	Originate (Modeling & Observing)	**Intervene** (Copy & Do)	**Support** (Practice & Refinement)	**Release** (Application & Independence)
Fostering Confidence	Find people and things in the class-room that make you feel good about yourself. To do the best job of learning you need to believe in yourself.	Take this time to try new strategies and techniques. Don't be afraid to ask questions of the teacher or others.	You have been doing well with the help of the teacher and others. Now it's time for you to try things on your own. Don't be afraid to make mistakes—this is how we learn. Also, try out different ways of doing things to make it work better for you.	Now you can apply the strategies on your own. While you may need guidance and assis-tance sometimes, this is your time to work independently.
Goal Setting	Pay close attention to how the teacher sets goals. The teacher will work through the process with you.	Use the materials and graphic orga-nizers the teacher offers you to help set your goals. Feel free to make the goal your own by using your own ideas.	Now that you have done some practice with help, you should be able to create your own goals. Make sure to check in with the teacher to ensure that your goal is challenging.	You are ready to set your own goals without help. However, you may want to check with the teacher or a peer to ensure your goal is meaningful and productive.
Monitoring the Goal	The teacher will be asking you often to check your prog-ress toward your goal. This is a good thing. He or she can help you adjust the goal when you need to.	Pay attention to the teacher's feedback on your progress. This information will help you continue to grow and be able to reach your goal.	Make sure to check in with the teacher or your peers to see how close you are getting to your goal. Consider which strategies you are using well and which strate-gies should be adjusted.	It is a good idea to contin-ually review the feedback you are getting from the teacher and your peers. Set an appointment with them to help you monitor what you are doing and consider more productive actions.
Reflecting on the Goal	The teacher will be providing you with information about how you did. Use this information as you think about how well you did and how you can get better.	Use this time to talk to your peers and the teacher about how well you did and what you may want to change next time. Ask them to help you with the ideas.	Set up a time to meet with the teacher or a group of your peers to review what you did and how well you feel you performed. Take their ideas into account as you plan your next learning process.	From the data you have collected throughout the learning process, con-sider how well you did. Specifically define what went well and what needs to be adjusted. Document your successes and where you need to make adjust-ments for your next learning process.

CHAPTER 4

Fostering Confidence to Engage in Learning (EiL)

Learning is not attained by chance, it must be sought for with ardor and attended to with diligence.

—Abigail Adams

Prior to developing self-regulation for learning (SRL) through the processes described in the previous chapter, students must feel confident to take on the actions of learning. This chapter will identify and provide support in building and shaping students' emotional strength, self-belief, confidence, and self-efficacy. The chapter merges "Fostering Confidence," the first phase of engaging in learning (see Chapter 3), with all four stages of SRL as it provides strategies for origination, intervention, support, and release.

The Role of Emotion and Feelings

Significant research suggests the emotional state of learners has a strong effect on what and how much they learn. Basic brain research shows that for higher levels of cognition to occur, the learner must move beyond just using the parts of the brain that are wired to ensure survival. This "survival level" of brain function (the fight or flight mode) is in operation when students are afraid (of the teacher, their peers, the content level), feel like outcasts or misfits in school, or lack basic necessities such as food or adequate shelter.

Emotion and feelings play a significant role in behavioral responses, decision making, memory, and interpersonal interactions. Our emotional responses can have both positive and negative consequences. Inappropriate emotional responses can lead to mental instability, social difficulties, and physical illness.[1] Let's do a quick review of the terms *emotion* and *feelings*. Though we often use these terms interchangeably, there are important differences in them that we must help students learn and then manage. Emotions are a chemical reaction within the limbic system (midbrain) that signals the rest of the brain and body to do something. The "do something" can be to pay attention, run, or avoid. The chemical signals are an involuntary response to external stimuli, thoughts, or memories recognized by the brain. These chemical responses, such as the release of stress hormones, make you react faster; other responses can have a calming effect to settle you down. Emotions are all within the brain and a person's feeling of the emotion is involuntary—you feel the emotion that is chemically in the brain; your *response to the feeling* is a separate matter.

The term *feelings* can have multiple meanings spanning from that which is a physical reaction (such as feeling pain when you burn yourself on the stove or get a cut) to subjective reactions (such as feeling bored by a lecture or dull movie). For our purposes, feelings are the external "read out" when you cognitively become aware of the chemical reaction (emotion). This is how we behave or think after the involuntary chemical reaction. Figure 4.1 lists examples of feelings.

1. Gross and Thompson, 2007.

Figure 4.1 **Feelings Words**

POSITIVE FEELINGS

happy	thrilled	interested
satisfied	glad	determined
confident	cheerful	excited
joyful	elated	enthusiastic
delighted	loving	optimistic
animated	inspired	hopeful
content	thankful	eager
ecstatic	lucky	

NEGATIVE FEELINGS

sad	confused	upset
depressed	helpless	pessimistic
discouraged	irritated	bitter
angry	enraged	aggressive
guilty	hostile	indecisive
dissatisfied	insulted	inferior
miserable	sore	frustrated
fearful	annoyed	

While emotions are released in the midbrain or limbic system, feelings are a product of the prefrontal cortex. Because the prefrontal cortex is the most sophisticated level of our brain and is responsible for abstract thought and reasoning, researchers conclude that most of our feelings are learned. They are also natural. Eric Jensen explains that we have an array of emotional responses based on our history of experiences and emotional responses that are natural to us as human beings.[2] Similar to a keyboard, natural human emotional responses range from fear, anger, and sadness (low notes) to joy, surprise, and happiness (high notes). The great classroom challenge is helping students find the beauty of the music in the middle of the keyboard where they will learn emotional responses like patience, cooperation, forgiveness, and empathy—all of which are important for successful learning and for living a fully deep and rich life (see Figure 4.2).

Students will respond to the chemical reaction (emotion) in ways they have done in the past or in ways that are natural. Consider a running toddler who falls near her mother. If the mother responds to the fall with horror, the child will do the same—this is the learned response by the child (it's being modeled for her by her mother). But, if the mother calmly helps up the child, the child's response may be to shed a few tears over the pain of the fall but not likely to react to the feeling of fear. This type of response is the memory-related response to the chemical reaction.

For some students, especially those coming from generational poverty or highly stressful home lives, they have a gap in the learning of those emotional responses. Students who lack these learned responses may be more prone to acting out in the classroom; they may tend to react with impatience and impulsivity. They may be less empathic toward other students and have gaps in appropriate social skills. Plus, they may exhibit a limited range of behaviors due to the modeling they observe in their homes.

To help students develop a greater awareness and range of emotional responses that can support their emotional growth, consider their level of self-regulation for learning (SRL). Analyze which of the four stages (origination, intervention, support, and release) your students need support in and select the types of actions or activities that will best support their learning. Figure 4.3 Activities That Support Emotional Growth suggests activities for the different stages to develop SRL.

Figure 4.2 **The Emotional Response Keyboard**

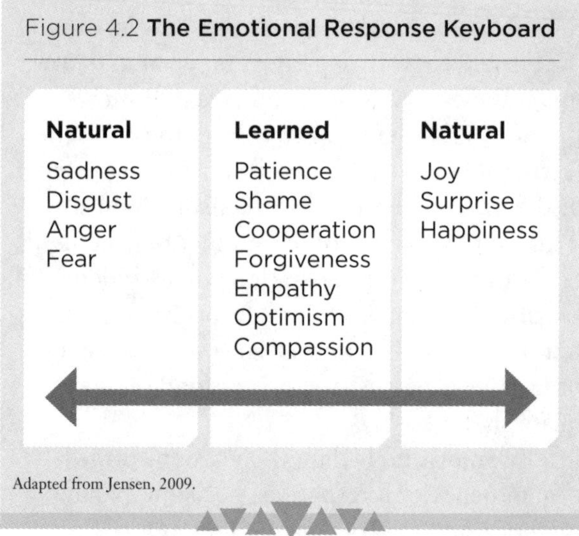

Adapted from Jensen, 2009.

2. Jensen, 2009.

Figure 4.3 **Activities That Support Emotional Growth**

Using Maslow's hierarchy of needs theory, consider the types of activities you use in the classroom to develop stronger and more appropriate emotional responses from your students. Determine developmentally and emotionally where your students are in their need for greater self-regulation. Below are activities linking Maslow's hierarchy of needs to the stages of self-regulation.

Modeling and Observing
Developing a sense of safety in the classroom means:

Predictability in the environment	**Feelings of security**	**Consistency in mood and management**	**Feeling comfortable in the classroom**
› Classroom rules/norms are clear and followed by all students. › Timelines and schedules are posted and accessible to the students. › Lesson objectives are stated clearly and available to students throughout the lessons. › Students are completely aware of consequences and rewards. › When changes occur, students are given time to make adjustments.	› All students know they can take intellectual risks in learning without fear of reprimand by others. › All classroom members use positive and affirming language (sarcasm and put-downs are NOT allowed). › The classroom environment encourages interactions (desks are organized in small groups, students sit facing each other). › All classroom members feel others in the room are supportive and encouraging. › Exceptional student work showing effort and achievement is posted in the room.	› Classroom rules/norms are applied equally and equitably. › Norms are set and understood for classroom discussions, group work, and independent work in which all students' ideas are valued, and intellectual risk-taking is encouraged. › The teacher refers to lesson objectives throughout the learning process. › The teacher is even-keeled when dealing with stressful or difficult situations. › The teacher is organized and displays a sense of confidence.	› Students have places to sit, stand, or stretch out in the classroom. › Lighting is pleasant and appropriate (the lighting is adjustable to the situation—such as when viewing something on a large screen, the general lighting is low; when reading text, the lighting is higher or more natural/sunlight). › Noise is kept to a minimum. › Unpleasant odors are eliminated. › The teacher encourages students to smile by smiling often.

Figure 4.3 **Activities That Support Emotional Growth continued**

Copying and Doing
Develop a sense of belonging in the classroom by:

Learning how to listen	Understanding others' differences	Knowing how to express yourself	Caring for yourself and others
› Teach all students the art and act of listening to each other, such as by paraphrasing others' comments. › Use listening techniques within the content, such as by asking students to repeat the specific details they recall from a lecture or reading. › Discuss the benefits of listening during a discussion or conversation. › Help students clarify the language they use in classroom discussions and conversations. › Demonstrate how looking at and following the speaker with your eyes conveys respect.	› Share the diverse backgrounds of all students in the classroom. › Display artifacts from various cultures and regions of the world. › Present representations of famous people, scientists, mathematicians, artists, and political figures from a broad range of backgrounds. › Have students get to know all the participants in the classroom. › Have students share their strengths through Passion Projects (see the form on pages 47–48).	› Teach students the most appropriate ways to ask for help. › Teach students how to speak to others in ways that are nonconfrontational and polite. › Allow students to share about themselves through varied formats (oral, graphically, pictorial, and in story form). › Provide students choices of ways to demonstrate proficiency, mastery, and competence. › Give students time to talk to each other in small- and large-group discussions.	› Express daily how much you enjoy working with your students. › Share how you care for others in your family and community. › Partner students with a "study buddy" to assist in learning. › Connect your students to other students around the community, state, nation, or globe through an e-pals program or classroom partnership. › Use a classroom pet (goldfish, hamster, lizard) or plants to teach students responsibility and caregiving.

Figure 4.3 **Activities That Support Emotional Growth continued**

Practice and Refinement
Foster individual strength through:

Building self-esteem and confidence	Knowledge of your talents	Maintaining a positive attitude	Sensing individual significance	Setting a vision for your future
› Teach students how to recognize when they are feeling stressed or low. › Use relaxation techniques or yoga to relieve stress or lift students' spirits. › Celebrate successes, no matter how small or seemingly inconsequential. › Teach students how to accept compliments graciously. › Assist students in accepting mistakes as learning tools.	› Give students opportunities to find their talents, by offering different ways to do projects and assignments. › Expose students to different talent areas such as weaving, cultural dances, ventriloquism/puppetry, or game design. › Encourage parents to take their child to museums, art galleries, sporting/community/cultural events, bookstores/libraries, or extracurricular activities. › Invite adults to the classroom to share their special talents and interests. › Display posters or examples of famous people whose talents have improved the world.	› Help students reflect on how their attitude impacts outcomes by having them document when and why things go well. › Post positive attitude attributes such as: – Smiling – Showing kindness to others – Thinking the best of others – Approaching learning with a sense of challenge rather than fear › Teach students ways to shift their attitude by reframing difficult situations (by recognizing the feeling, replacing negative thoughts with positive thoughts, and using positive speak). › Use humor and affirmative language in the classroom to help students feel more positive. › Help students stay organized to increase their sense of control/feeling more positive.	› Highlight students' unique qualities by allowing them time to share their stories. › Offer time in the classroom for students to socialize with each other. › Do not allow negative comments, harassing behaviors, or bullying, EVER! › Help students make connections to the content by relating topics to their talents and/or interests. › Allow students to lead discussions, activities, or classroom procedures to help them take charge of their learning.	› Allow students to talk about their dreams and desires for their future. › To promote optimism, show students examples of people who overcame difficulty to succeed. › Tell students they can do anything they put their mind and effort toward. › Have students document their visions of the future—keep it positive. › Give students information about post-secondary options other than college or university—such as technical, hospitality, or culinary fields.

Figure 4.3 **Activities That Support Emotional Growth continued**

Independence and Application Create a sense of autonomy:			
Reach self-actualization	**Refine individual talent**	**Increasing concentration and persistence**	**Benefiting Others**
› Support students in being their best self—not better than others. › Help students accept their strengths AND limitations. › Assist students in recognizing when they are in control of their life. › Encourage students to continue to learn and grow. › Allow for students to be creative, spontaneous, and challenged.	› Provide students opportunities to showcase their talents. › Focus students on the effort they use to increase their talents. › Allow students to promote their talents through doing projects and assignments in their own ways. › Connect students' talents to career options or entrepreneurial opportunities.	› Challenge students to work on long-term projects that require extended periods of time, such as an end-of-course product or portfolio of work. › Alert students to procrastination and provide them alternatives by using the "Avoiding Procrastination +/-/?" form (see Chapter 7). › Apply study skills of time setting, break taking, self-assessment, and reflection on a routine basis (see "10 Important Study Habits," Chapter 8). › Celebrate the joyfulness in accomplishing a task and achieving a job well done.	› Offer students opportunities to arrange/organize and participate in community development or service-learning projects. › Give students occasions in which they provide support or tutoring to younger students. › Get students involved in leadership and service organizations, such as the student council, neighborhood involvement groups, 4-H, or Girl or Boy Scouts. › Encourage students to volunteer time at the local food bank, library, senior center, or community center.

Igniting Students' Interests

One of the most powerful ways to engage students in learning is to incorporate or pique their interests by offering change, novelty, and opportunities of applying worthwhile effort and attention.[3] In this sense, interest begins in an affective (emotional) way, and over time, to sustain or increase the interest, one must put forth cognitive energy and behavioral regulation. Being interested in a topic or subject can provide the boost needed to overcome difficulties, obstacles, or distractions.

If a student has a particular interest in a subject, the interest allows the student to

- Sustain attention while studying the topic.
- Select challenging courses or topics to study.
- Persist and persevere.
- Achieve higher goals.
- Create value and worth in learning.
- Develop self-efficacy (capacity to perform).
- Increase self-control and concentration.
- Focus on goal attainment.

The development of interests follows a similar pathway to that of the development of self-regulation for learning. First, a student must experience a triggering situation wherein he or she is exposed to the topic of interest. Then the student must interact with ideas that maintain the interest and make it worthwhile. After this point, the student then manipulates the topic of interest to form his or her own direction until the student finally has mastered the topic searches independently for greater ideas and topics.

Example:

1. The teacher triggers students' interest in birds of prey by inviting members of the local raptor center to visit the classroom with some of their rescued birds.
2. To maintain the interest, students research various birds of prey, uncovering some of the gory details of their hunting patterns such as how they were used to hunt.
3. After finding interesting facts about birds of prey and learning how some are losing their habitat to housing construction and population encroachment, one student decides she would like to learn more about how to help protect the bald eagle and owls. This student then decides her main topic of interest related to the trigger topic.
4. Through her research and commitment to the topic, she contacts her local department of natural resources to find ways to protect the birds' habitat, and for information to add to a website to alert the public about the impact of losing bald eagles and owls. Now, she has moved from the external triggering situation, found her own particular topic of interest related to the trigger, and initiated her own study in greater detail.

For more ideas to ignite student interests see Figure 4.4.

Building Value into Learning

The value students place on learning activities will dictate the quality and quantity of their effort and self-regulation toward achievement. The value students place on an activity is more predictive of success than is students' self-belief about being able to do the task. In other words, even though students may have the skills to be successful in a task, if they don't value the task, they may not engage in, attend to, or persist in the activity.

Young students often are excited to find new ideas and try new things. As students mature, they become more aware of their own individual interests, which may be incongruent with the topics of school. They develop their own styles for learning material—sometimes in opposition to how teachers may want the work completed. As students move toward middle and high school, the valuation of engaging in learning becomes a more complex issue. Value in the act of learning is how much a person believes the task is:

- Attainable
- Interesting
- Useful

3. Hidi and Ainley, 2008.

Figure 4.4 **Ideas to Ignite Student Interests**

- Ask questions that stimulate a desire to learn the topic, such as:
  - Why do cycles go around and around?
  - In what ways do systems function and dysfunction?
  - How do we solve difficult problems?
- Form Special Interest Groups (SIGs) in your classroom. The groups could be based on broad ideas (such as sports, the arts, math, science, reading, video games, etc.) or specific to the topic.
- Read articles (either current news, research studies, or historical documents) that relate to the topic under study. Use short articles featuring controversy, ambiguity, and debatable issues.
- Use the problem based learning (PBL) method. PBL is a highly motivational and engaging way to allow students to study a topic through their questions. The process begins with students asking questions. Then teachers frame the lessons to assist in answering those questions and impart critical fundamental knowledge about the subject and topic.
- Incorporate the topics you will be teaching into everyday conversations with students. This can be done by posting questions around the room that stimulate thinking within and across topic areas (Science and geography: What effect might the massive volcanic eruption in Iceland have on your life? Social studies, literature, and math: If you lived during the time of Hamlet, what type of work would you do and how much compensation would you make per year?)
- Play games associated with the topic to reduce students' anxiety. This works especially well in mathematics.
- Set up centers in your room that preview the topics students will encounter. Centers can be physical places within the room with materials and books related to the topic on display or where students can experience activities related to the topic. Virtual centers can show videos, have areas for playing games, present quizzes with feedback on accuracy of answers, or have pages bookmarked on the computer that highlight the topic. You may also want to include career options or post-secondary course work related to the topic. Students can visit the centers when they have time after completing an assignment, at the beginning or end of the day, or on days where it's too cold/rainy/hot to go outside for recess. Students could also take the center home. Consider the transportability of physical centers; have the bookmarks located on your teacher page for virtual centers.
- Expose your students to the topics by showing short videos or television shows.
- Get them excited about the topics by sharing controversies within the field (Literature: Did Shakespeare really write his plays? Math: How can we use math to fool people? Science: Is climate change a myth? Social studies: Should immigration be illegal? Family and consumer science: Is there a problem with food poisoning in school lunches?)
- Take field trips to locations where the students can see the topic in an authentic way. Rather than do the field trip at the end of a unit, do it in the beginning to get students excited about or connected to what they are about to learn.
- Invite experts from the disciplines into your classroom to talk about how they apply the topics in their work life. A critical aspect of successfully bringing experts into your room is that the person should "look like" (have a real-life connection to) your students. Students who live in poverty or come from diverse backgrounds need to see themselves in the experts so they know they too can achieve and be successful.
- Offer students hands-on activities in which they physically engage with the learning materials. Making the content concrete for the student can help them envision themselves in the study. This can include providing artifacts, tools of the study/discipline, or manipulatives to help solve problems.
- Start units with the "big picture." Tell students where you are going, what will happen, and what the expected outcomes will be by the time they finish the unit. Promote the conceptual ideas students will learn instead of what they will do and know. Such as: "Throughout this unit we will be trying to understand what *causes people to revolt*."
- Infuse reading materials that have a high interest value to your students. Texts that are dry and full of information may not engage students into wanting to know more. Try texts written from a first-person perspective or from the viewpoint of students like yours.
- Allow students to work on their own and at their own pace. Some students want to learn new things but prefer to work by themselves. Sometimes working in a group can be stressful or impersonal. Let students work alone but then share their ideas with either a small group or large group.

A vital step in getting students to engage in learning is to help them find value in the learning tasks. Assess your students' level of value for the task, define where they may lack a sense of value, and specifically teach students the value of the learning task.

To assist you in defining the students' valuation of a task, use the chart Steps in Valuing a Task (Figure 4.5). The first step is to ask the students to determine their level of control over the outcome of the task. Students who lack self-regulation in the learning process will often feel out-of-control or believe that the situation/environment or external factors have a greater effect on the outcome. These students often work within the "handicapping" or "prevention" strategies (as noted in Chapter 3). If this is the case, their teacher should help them recognize how actions (internal factors) have a greater effect on task outcomes than do external factors.

Figure 4.5 **Steps in Valuing a Task**

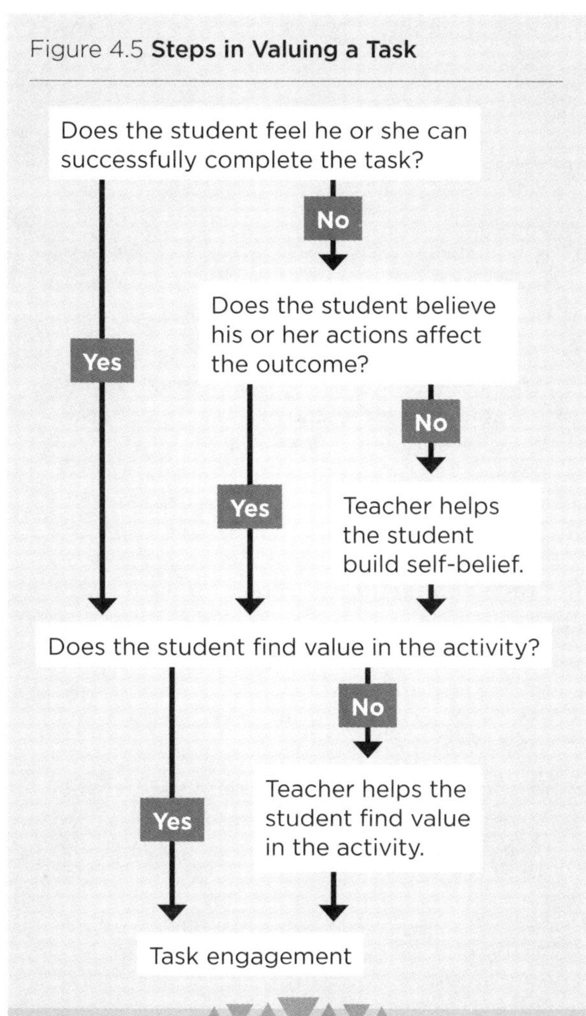

Teachers need to build students' self-belief about their ability to accomplish difficult or complex tasks. Once students have a higher level of self-regulation or sense of control, they identify whether an activity is of value to them (either through the skills they possess, level of interest, usefulness, or worth of the activity). The students who find value in the task are ready to engage in the learning. See Figure 4.6 for ideas for helping students find value to engage them in learning tasks.

Helping Students Build Self-Belief and Self-Efficacy

It is a normal human reaction to have doubts about our abilities and capabilities. To successfully complete a learning task, students must believe they have the internal fortitude to work through challenges toward success. Students who believe they can't do something look for validation of their negative viewpoint. Regardless of the grade they earn, they perceive that they didn't perform well enough. During times when failure is a real possibility, a child with positive self-belief perceives himself or herself as resilient to setbacks, able to overcome obstacles, and willing to try again. Additionally, self-belief is vital to the development of self-efficacy.

Self-belief is developed from inside. Some students come to believe that their self-worth is validated by external rewards, such as grades, diplomas, certificates, pizza parties, and stickers. Although a heavy reliance on extrinsic reward has little effect on learning, it can have an enormous effect on setting a fixed mindset. Teachers can move these students from their habitual negative thought patterns toward greater optimism and satisfying achievement of their goals.

Steps to being optimistic about yourself:

1. Recognize when you doubt yourself.
2. Identify why you doubt yourself.
3. Tell yourself that doubting yourself before taking an action can create a negative outcome before you even begin.
4. Use affirmative self-talk to build yourself up: tell yourself you can do it.

5. Monitor your self-beliefs during the activity—avoid being negative, look for what you are doing well.
6. Reflect on what went well and what you might want to change next time.
7. Start again!

The Motivating Effect of Self-Efficacy and Success

Frank Pajares states, "Findings have now confirmed that students' academic self-efficacy beliefs powerfully influence their academic attainments independent of possessed knowledge and skills, and that self-efficacy mediates the effect of such knowledge, skills, or other motivational factors on myriad academic outcomes."[4] Along with an optimistic self-belief, students must develop a healthy level of self-efficacy. As stated earlier, self-belief is the confidence that one has a certain level of capabilities, whether those abilities are positive toward success (I'm confident I will do well on this exam) or negative toward failure (I'm confident I will fail this math exam). Central to self-efficacy is the reciprocal nature of its development. The dimensions of affect, behavior, and cognition (ABCs) interacting with the environment impact academic results. To develop students with self-efficacy, teachers can approach learners through any of the three dimensions as entry points (see Figure 4.7).

The reciprocal nature of each of the dimensions suggests that affecting one will affect the other two. So, if a child can best be approached through the cognitive dimension of helping him or her recognize having cognitive capabilities to do the task ("you are really good at writing") the behavioral dimension (the skills to be applied) and the affective dimension (feeling good about tackling the task) will naturally fall in line. If the child has a good attitude (affective) about learning (I like school), then behavior and cognition will follow. Similarly, if the student has the behavioral acumen ("you know how to do this"),

4. Pajares, quoted in Schunk and Zimmerman, 2008, p.115.

Figure 4.6 **10 Ideas for Helping Students Find Value in Learning**

1. Construct activities that are meaningful to the students' immediate success. Demonstrate how the activity is directly linked to either a past activity or something that will be coming very soon in their learning process.
2. Activities should be connected to the student either through their interests, daily life, current events, past experiences, and other topic areas.
3. Learning tasks should have a reality or authenticity to them so students don't feel like they are doing busy work rather than work that leads to a valuable outcome. The more real the activity can be the more likely the students will engage in the task.
4. Offer students choices, either in the way of doing the activity or in which activity to do. When students have a sense of control over their learning, they are more likely to value the effort required to do the activity.
5. Keep the learning environment vibrant. Our classrooms should reflect a joyful learning space, one of community, collaborative efforts, and authentic outcomes.
6. Use creative activities to show students that there may not always be one right answer or one right way of doing something.
7. Post the learning objectives in a way that students clearly know what to do and what will come from the activity. Using student friendly language, such as "I can . . . " or "I will . . . " statement starters, keeps the learning focused on the student rather than on the teacher. Additionally, make sure to post the three levels of knowledge (factual, procedural, and conceptual) for each lesson.
8. Keep lectures short—10 to 15 minutes. After each chunk of lecture, have students reflect on the information through discussing, writing, or drawing a picture of what was said in the lecture portions.
9. Provide students with high interest, provocative issues related to the topic. These can be in video or writing (such as a true-to-life article) format.
10. Use graphic organizers, pictures, and images of the final product or performance to motivate students to want to learn more about the topic or activity.

Figure 4.7 **The Reciprocal Nature of Self-Efficacy and Success**

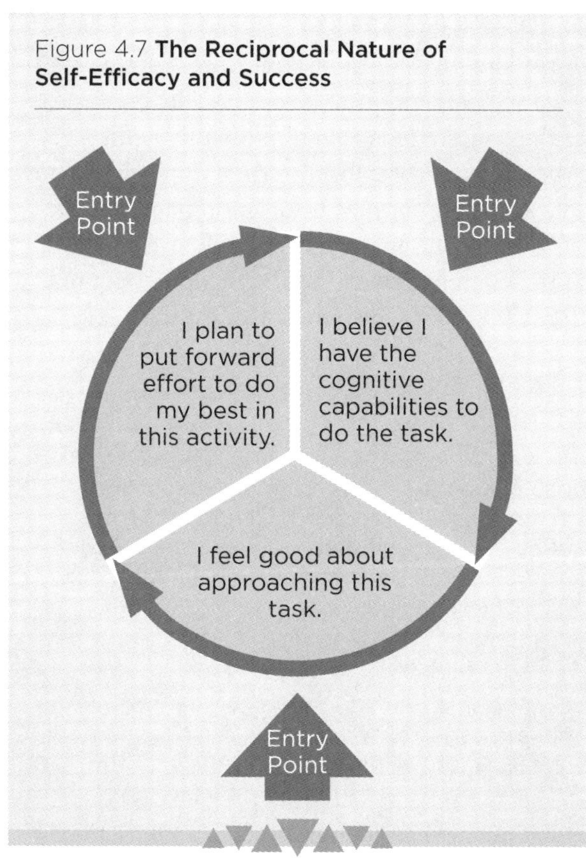

then cognition and affect will come together. Decide how to approach your learners to find the right entry point to bring the other two dimensions into sync.

Four Factors Impacting Self-Efficacy

Four factors influence the development of self-efficacy.

1. Mastery experience. The first and most powerful factor is the learner's previous accomplishments in school. Mastery experience includes past performances in school, how well the learner felt about the experiences, and how much those experiences led to continued positive outcomes. As stated previously, success breeds confidence, which breeds success. The premise behind mastery experience is that each time the learner feels or acts successfully it propels the learner to be successful the next time. Mastery experience can influence both short-term accomplishments as well as long-term course or career endeavors.

Mastery experience is how students *interpret* the outcomes of their efforts. Regardless of the grade or measured level of attainment on a task, it's how a child feels about or construes the achievement. Imagine two students receiving a grade of B on an exam. The grade in and of itself has little significance or meaning. An advanced-level student used to getting A's on most assignments will find the B to be upsetting. Whereas a student used to getting Cs on most assignments will find the B to be a boost to his or her confidence and a victory.

2. Vicarious experience. The second factor in developing self-efficacy is viewing others doing similar work. *Vicarious experience* is the social comparison a student makes when doing a task. Students continually observe others performing and judge themselves against others. Remember in school when teachers handed back a test or an assignment and you would look at your score with some feelings of either accomplishment or sadness? When you compared your neighbor's score to your score, you either felt better or worse about your score. The feelings had little to do with the score's validity; the feelings were connected to your comparison of yourself to your classmates.

Vicarious observations of others' performance outcomes can have an effect on learners' confidence to perform. Students with a growth mindset are more likely to use the observations of others as ways to persevere through an action or realize what not to do when they perform. Students with a fixed mindset are most likely to observe others only to find the flaws in the way the other student performs, or recognize they may not be able to perform to the same standard.

3. Social persuasion. The intentional or unintentional messages sent to students from parents, teachers, peers, or others unrelated to the child is the third factor of developing self-efficacy. Social persuasion can either assist us in putting forward greater effort or giving up. Keeping the messages positive in the classroom impacts the achievement of students' academic performance.

- Use affirmative speak that promotes the effective ways to perform a task.
- Highlight students working positively toward a goal rather than making punitive remarks ("I like how this team is working so

closely together to complete the task" rather than "Stop goofing around and get back to work.").

4. Student attitude. How students reflect their emotional state can affect the level of their self-efficacy. Positive *student attitude* enhances self-efficacy. As in developing self-belief, an optimistic outlook has a positive influence on achievement. As stated in earlier chapters, how a student feels about a learning situation determines the focus of their attention. A child's negative perception of himself or herself or fear of the content level can diminish self-efficacy. Students' interpretation of their emotional state acts as a filter for new information and production. Students' attitude toward their capabilities in the content acts as the Pygmalion effect or the self-fulfilling prophecy toward their level

Figure 4.8 **Four Factors in Developing Self-Efficacy**

To assist students in developing greater self-efficacy toward achievement, consider the four influencing factors.

Mastery Experience

- Provide students with activities where they can be successful. Ensure the activities are not too low or too high. Use the Goldilocks principle of creating activities that are "just right" where the student is stretched but has the supports necessary to achieve success.
- Value attempts at difficult tasks. Even though a student may not have been completely successful at the task, praise him or her for taking on the challenge.
- Praise students' efforts rather than their abilities or accomplishments. Not only will this help in changing from a fixed mindset (I can only achieve as much as I have in the past) to a growth mindset (If I work hard enough I can do it), it will also develop greater self-efficacy.
- Celebrate successes, no matter how small or seemingly insignificant. Students need to feel successful to be able to apply behaviors and cognition in future pursuits.

Vicarious Experience

- At times, flexibly group students with their like peers to talk about how hard they have to work at certain tasks, at other times with their unlike peers to discuss useful strategies each used to be successful.
- Provide students with other student examples of quality work and work strategies.
- Bring in role models to the classroom who have been successful. Ensure your role models represent or "look like" your students. For the vicarious experience to be useful, students must see themselves in the role model.
- Use characters in literature or personalities in the media to represent vicarious examples of how to achieve sustainable success. Avoid using "reality" performers; they are false examples of success.

Social Persuasion

- Give your students both verbal and nonverbal messages of "you can do this." Being the cheerleader will provide students with the drive to persevere through difficult tasks.
- Post positive messages in your room that articulate working toward achievable goals. Messages such as "hang in there," "push yourself," "stick to it," and so on, can keep kids going.
- Use affirmative speak with your students. Avoid using punitive language. Statements such as "I really like how this group is working together to finish the task" have a greater effect than "Your group needs to get back on task."
- Have students talk to each other about the strategies and techniques they are using that are working or not working. This type of community-building networking can offer a safe place for kids to hear from each other ways to improve their learning.

Student Attitude

- Help students identify when they fear failure. Assist them in turning the negative attitude toward one of success.
- Teach students that mistakes are opportunities to learn, not an indication of their limitations.
- Model an optimistic outlook for your students. Ensure they know you believe in them and their abilities to succeed.
- Engage students in learning by providing humor and a joyful learning environment.

of achievement. If a child fears failure, he or she most likely will fail. If the child enjoys the intellectual risk and is willing to be challenged, he or she is more likely to succeed. Discuss the importance of failure, developing resilience, and learning from it. For more strategies for building positive student attitude, see Figure 4.8: Four Factors in Developing Self-Efficacy.

A Supportive Learning Environment for Success

Another factor in student success and engagement in tasks is a supportive school environment. According to John Dewey, renowned progressive educator, education is the interaction between the learner and the context, which includes the physical, social, cultural, and psychological environments.[5] The teacher has a powerful role in creating and maintaining an effective learning environment. Four elements of an academically safe and welcoming classroom and school are:

1. Establish, elicit, and increase interest and enjoyment in the classroom.
2. Assist students in overcoming motivational problems.
3. Point out and redirect unproductive behavior.
4. Create relevance, value, and meaningfulness in the learning.

Figure 4.9 provides strategies for creating a classroom with the four elements.

5. Dewey, 1926.

Figure 4.9 **Fundamentals for a Supportive Learning Environment**

1. Establish, elicit, and increase interest and enjoyment:
   - Create a classroom environment that encourages interests.
   - Use interest centers.
   - Seek out students' interests in the learning process.
   - Get students interested in what you are teaching.
   - Make sure each student feels safe, welcomed, and has a sense of belonging.
   - Celebrate risk taking.
   - Use inclusive language ("our classroom").
   - Make learning fun.
   - Laugh EVERY day; show your students your fun side.
2. Assist students in overcoming motivational problems
   - Use language that is noncontrolling ("I've noticed you are having some difficulty getting started. Is there anything I can do to help you generate ideas?")
   - Provide students with relevant, descriptive feedback ("It appears that you are struggling with the strategy we learned. Let me help you put this new strategy to practice.")
   - Help learners focus on what they CAN do ("I'm always impressed with how well you do at adding figurative language to your writing.")
   - Assist learners in thinking of options when they struggle ("When I struggle, I ask questions of others or I try to think about how I can have fun with the information.")
3. Point out and redirect unproductive behavior:
   - "I can see how this activity may not be your favorite thing to do, and talking to your friends may seem more important at this time. However, this is time for me to help you become a better writer. Tell me what I can do to assist you in getting your ideas out."
4. Create relevance, value, and meaningfulness:
   - With students, determine the relevance of the strategies they are using ("How or when might you use this idea?").
   - Give immediate reasons why students will value from the learning tasks ("The nature of this task will require you to focus your attention on what we are doing.")
   - Tell students how they will use the strategies in the very near future ("In a few minutes we will try this strategy to see how effectively it can help us in solving the problem.")

Chapter Summary

Developing students' self-regulation for learning requires them to engage with the content and feel confident enough to participate in the learning activities. This chapter demonstrated the critical nature of students' feelings about learning and their focus toward engaging. Nurturing students' emotional strength can open wide the door to their ability to learn. Educators have long known that one of the most effective ways to engage students is by connecting topics of study to their personal interests. To be successful, students also need to find value in the learning. They must find the subject doable, interesting, useful to their future growth, and worth their time and energy. Confidence in learning begins with self-belief, which leads to self-efficacy. The reciprocal nature of the ABCs (affective, behavioral, and cognitive) enables students to move from "I can do this" to "I will do this." Knowing where students are in their ABC development provides teachers with the appropriate entry point for sustained learning. Finally, how teachers construct, manage, and ensure a joyful learning space all have an enormous effect on students' willingness to engage in new learning.

Guidelines for Creating a Passion Project

1. Passions are those things you love, greatly enjoy doing, and have a good storehouse of knowledge about. Clearly explain your passion and why others would want to know about this topic:

____

____

____

____

____

____

____

____

____

2. Meet with the teacher to find an appropriate unit project that can be replaced by your passion project.

   Teacher meeting date:_______________________________

   Unit project to be replaced by the passion project: _______________________________

   Due date for the passion project:_______________________________

   Signature of teacher:_______________________________

   Signature of student:_______________________________

3. Construct your passion project for presentation to the class.
   - Think of an interesting way to present your passion project (PowerPoint, speech, role play, charts/posters, etc.).
   - In your presentation, tell the class:
     - How you became involved with the topic
     - How you came to know your topic
     - Why you enjoy your topic
     - What makes your topic interesting
   - Provide the class with information that could stimulate them to investigate this topic.
   - Offer the class a list of resources, websites, books, or other materials that could get other students started on your topic.

4. Your passion project will be graded based on the rubric attached. Your grade on the passion project will replace the grade on the unit project.

continued ➡

Rubric for Passion Project

Category	4	3	2	1
Preparedness	Student is completely prepared and has obviously rehearsed.	Student seems fairly prepared but might have needed a couple more rehearsals.	Student is somewhat prepared, but it is clear that rehearsal was lacking.	Student does not seem prepared to present.
Enthusiasm	Student's facial expressions and body language generate a strong interest and enthusiasm about the topic in the audience.	Student's facial expressions and body language sometimes generate a strong interest and enthusiasm about the topic in the audience.	Student's facial expressions and body language are used to try to generate enthusiasm, but seem somewhat faked.	Student makes very little use of facial expressions or body language and did not generate much interest in the topic in the audience.
Content	Student shows a full understanding of the topic.	Student shows a good understanding of the topic.	Student shows a good understanding of parts of the topic.	Student does not seem to understand the topic very well.
Resources	Student provides a wide range of resources (at least 10) including websites, text, and artifacts.	Student provides a range of resources (at least 8) including websites, text, and artifacts.	Student provides some resources (at least 5) including websites and text.	Student provides few resources (less than 5), which include websites and text.
Connection to Content	Student makes exceptional connections to content including math, science, social studies, language arts, the arts, physical education, and/or other areas of study.	Student makes some connections to content including math, science, social studies, language arts, the arts, physical education and/or other areas of study.	Student makes few connections to content including math, science, social studies, language arts, the arts, physical education, and/or other areas of study.	Student makes no connections to content.

Adapted from *Advancing Differentiation* by Richard M. Cash, Ed.D., Free Spirit Publishing Inc., 2011. Used with permission.

CHAPTER 5

Developing Habits of Thinking

It seems to me that education has a two-fold function to perform in the life of man and in society: the one is utility and the other is culture. Education must enable a man to become more efficient, to achieve with increasing facility the legitimate goals of his life.

—Martin Luther King Jr.

The advances of new and more rigorous local and national standards require our students to do advanced levels of thinking and performing. As preparation for college and careers, the new standards require students to perform inquiry, read in the content areas, and write to convey arguments and show evidence and reasoning. Students must be able to readily use critical reasoning, creative thinking, problem solving, and decision making. This "end point" is the connection of Release and Reflecting in the "Stages and Phases Matrix for Developing SRL" (see Chapter 3). For students to reach their goals, they must have solid grounding and practice in developing habits of thinking. This chapter will explain the different kinds of thinking and skills and provide strategies for strengthening each.

Structure of the Mind

Thinking is a mental process often referred to as cognition. The brain processes thinking on three levels. (1) The unconscious mind is primitive; it operates on instincts that enable a person to survive. The unconscious mind holds the information or memories we acquire that form our beliefs, patterns, and realities that then drive our behaviors. (2) The subconscious mind stores information that is recalled or declarative in nature, such as phone numbers or home addresses. Having subconscious recall of processes, not having to consciously think about certain actions, allows us to multitask, such as driving a car while talking to the person seated next to you. (3) The conscious mind is our awareness of the moment; it is directed and controlled thought. This most sophisticated part of cognition is the part we use to assist our students in developing effective strategies for greater self-regulation for learning (SRL).

The act of thinking can be considered along a spectrum (see Figure 5.1). At one end of the spectrum is convergent thinking, thinking through a set of logical steps based on factual information. At the other end is divergent thinking, the thinking where many ideas are generated, creating new and imaginative ideas. Students must employ both types of thinking to be effective problem solvers, thus the overlap in the center of the spectrum in Figure 5.1. Well self-regulated students know when it is efficient to use mostly convergent types of thinking, when it is appropriate to use divergent idea generation, and when it's necessary to use the combination of the two to solve problems.

Metacognition: Thinking About One's Thinking

The act of metacognition, the awareness of one's thoughts and actions, happens within the conscious part of the mind. Metacognition includes the ability to know (factually) and understand information (conceptually) and be able to perform (procedurally) specific tasks. Metacognitive

Figure 5.1 **The Spectrum of Thinking**

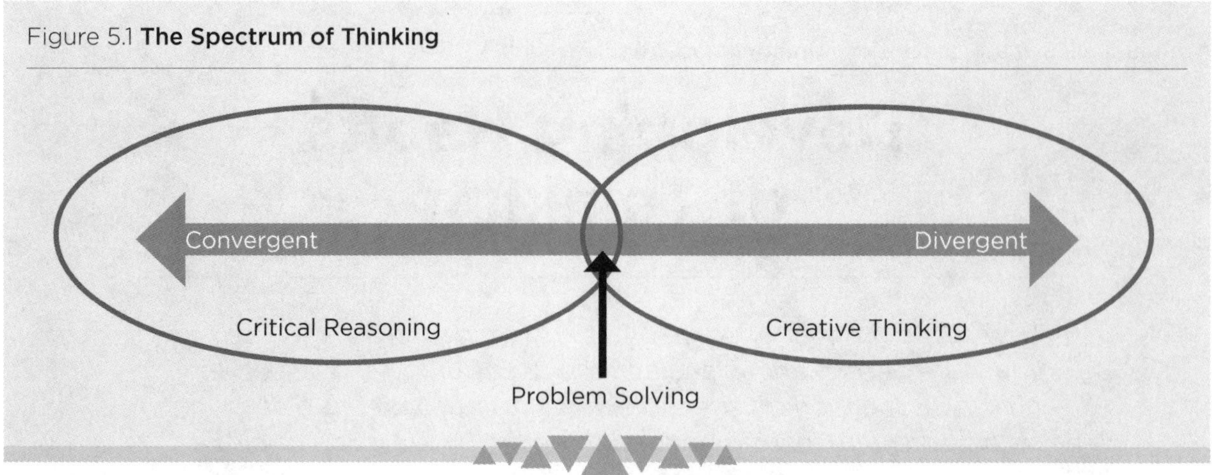

ability controls and regulates our thinking processes, such as study habits and memory capabilities. This part of the mind holds our personal knowledge about our self-beliefs and awareness of confidence. Successful learners engage in metacognitive activities daily to develop the strategies of cognition toward self-regulation. Robert Sternberg defined six general steps in the metacognitive process: problem recognition, problem definition, formulation of strategies to solve the problem, resource allocation, monitoring problem solving, and evaluating the outcome.[1] See Figure 5.2.

Infra-Cognition: Grander Thinking Tools

A level up from metacognition is infra-cognition. When students specifically use their creative, critical reasoning, problem-solving, and decision-making skills, they are engaged in infra-cognition. As with the development of any skill, the learner first uses it as a strategy—a discrete, conscious action. Using a step-by-step process, the learner specifically defines what they are doing, what should come next, and what the end result should be. The conscious application of the strategy is critical in the development of a skill. If learners know what to do and why, and if they repeatedly practice the act, it will become automatic. Some students will need more practice to develop the skill. The goal is for students to identify what and when to use specific strategies and when they need to switch out or adjust a strategy to be more successful.

Students must view information through a variety of lenses to understand that knowledge is subjective and open to inquiry. For students to successfully reach higher levels of thinking, it is essential they be actively inquiring and self-directed in the classroom. They must engage in learning through creativity and critical reasoning.

Creativity: Igniting New Ideas

Students use creative thinking, a divergent thought process, to generate multiple options for solving problems. Students can strengthen their creativity by cultivating these characteristics:

- Flexibility in ways of doing and acting
- Ability to change and adapt quickly
- Ability to link ideas together in ways not often considered
- Questioning attitude
- Playfulness
- Ability to generate numerous workable solutions
- Welcoming errors as opportunities
- Valuing the process over the product
- Tolerance for disorder, discord, ambiguity, complexity, risk, and cognitive dissonance
- Willingness to put effort forward to come up with original ideas

1. Sternberg, 1997.

Figure 5.2 **Strategies for Developing Metacognitive Ability**

Metacognition is most commonly defined as thinking about your own thinking. To encourage students to develop a greater awareness of their thinking process, employ any of these strategies on a daily basis.

For the Originate Stage of SRL

- Model behavioral self-talk, such as: "As I think about this problem, I remember that we learned a strategy yesterday that I may be able to apply to this situation."
- Model overt observation talk, such as: "When I look at this book cover and its title, they make me think that this story may be about the conflicts that young people go through to become independent."
- Model the balancing of affect during learning, such as: "When I'm stuck on something, though I might get frustrated, I take deep breaths and tell myself, 'I can do this.'"
- Directly model the step-by-step nature of a thinking process.

For the Intervene Stage of SRL

- Talk to students about which strategies they are consciously using while working through a task.
- Observe students as they work, looking for signs of stress or struggle (such as knitted brows, looks of frustration, or off-task behaviors) and be ready to provide them with some affirmative self-talk.
- Ask your students inferential questions to help you identify their levels of metacognitive thoughts, such as: "As you work through this task, tell me which strategies you are using or have used."
- Assure students that thinking strategies are general and may work in some cases and not work in other cases.

For the Support Stage of SRL

- Praise your students when you observe them using metacognitive strategies.
- Ask your students to share their effective metacognitive strategies with their teammates.
- Have your students rate the effectiveness of their metacognitive strategies throughout the executing of a task.

For the Release Stage of SRL

- During coaching or consulting periods, ask students to reflect on which strategies they found to be the most helpful in completing tasks.
- Facilitate discussions between students about the most appropriate strategies to use when addressing complex tasks.
- Have your students generate questions to ask each other, themselves, or the teacher about how they use the metacognitive strategies to continue to be successful.

Additional ideas:

- Encourage group discussion about the pathways students might take to solve problems.
- Routinely ask students to explain how they got to a solution or migrated through a problem.
- Construct group discussions on the actions students take to solve complex problems.
- Support students in finding multiple ways to solve problems—especially in unconventional ways.
- Offer students opportunities to rate their levels of metacognitive effectiveness.
- Debrief students at the end of a task to review their thinking process.
- Provide students ample time to think and talk about metacognitive strategies. This can be anywhere from a few minutes to a few days.
- When teaching a specific metacognitive strategy, apply it to both content-based and authentic situations.
- Remember to use the ABCs when having students do metacognitive reflection: "How did that make you feel?" "What behaviors did you use that were useful or not useful?" "What thinking tools did you use to accomplish the task?"
- For young students, provide a graphic organizer for them to document their metacognition (see "Graphic Organizer for Young Students: Metacognition"). Older students can document through writing (see "Graphic Organizer for Older Students: Metacognition").

Structuring Creative Thinking

One of the best ways to structure creative thinking in your classroom is to use the four elements of creativity: fluency, elaboration, originality, and flexibility.[2] Following are ideas that can be used as "sponge activities" (when you have a few minutes left in a lesson, before lunch or recess, or at the end of the day), warm-ups to more strenuous thinking activities, or as "brain breaks" (when you know your students need a little mental downtime).

FLUENCY

Fluency is the ability to generate a lot of ideas or alternate solutions. An example of a fluency activity is List All, which allows students to think freely about crafting a list of items. Give students two minutes to generate as many items as possible that are:

- colorful
- other ways to say terms such as "good morning" or "thank you"
- names for the class goldfish or skeleton
- questions you have about science/math/history/consumer science
- questions you would ask a character in a book
- questions you would ask an author/important figure from history/the surgeon general/your great-great-great-grandmother
- ways to solve a major or minor conflict
- ideas to slow climate change
- characters Shakespeare created
- influential mathematicians
- parts of a cell
- problem-solving strategies
- paired
- compound words
- three-syllable words
- words without an "e"

ELABORATION

Elaboration is the ability to provide extensive or extended details. It helps students push beyond the limits of the borders. Students' ability to elaborate on ideas or topics may show their deeper understanding of the content and can improve their motivation to learn more about it. Activities that can stimulate elaboration are:

- Make changes, additions, or adaptations to a board game to make it more challenging.
- Create a short tune that will set the mood for reading *The Three Pigs*, *Romeo and Juliet*, or *Call of the Wild* (use any book title).
- Create a children's picture book to explain line and slope/angles/measurement/data and statistics.
- Using numbers only, give someone directions from your school to Times Square in New York City.
- A burglar has broken into the First National Bank of Extraopolis and stolen all of the nation's wealth. The burglar used only three items to break in (a three-foot step stool, a wine glass, and toenail clippers). How did she do it?
- A burglar has broken into the First National Bank of Extraopolis and stolen all of the nation's wealth. Exactly what was stolen? If you are really courageous (or a good sleuth), put all the items into three categories (such as monetary, artistic, and militaristic). You are free to create your own categories.
- Which year of your life has been the heaviest/lightest/fairest/meanest/fluffiest/ . . . ? Why?
- Which nonliving item in the school is the sweetest/most sour/tiniest/most obnoxious/ . . . ? Why?

ORIGINALITY

Consider originality as the taking apart of old ideas and putting them back together in a new way. Originality is often considered the most difficult of the creative thought realms—it is certainly critical for solving 21st-century problems.

2. Torrance, 1979.

- Create a new use for your laptop, smartphone, pen, or desk.
- Create a new ending, beginning, or character for a well-known fairy tale or story.
- Come up with the most unusual occasion for writing a love letter to someone.
- Design a new way for students to enter the classroom without having to use the doorway or windows.
- Create a new title for the Bill of Rights.
- Come up with a way to "sell" math to someone who fears it.
- Using two types of sports (such as soccer and baseball), create a new game that could be played in the snow.
- Using only biodegradable products, come up with a new smartphone, computer, or laptop casing.
- Create new ways to receive text messages, email, or other social contacts.

FLEXIBILITY

Flexibility, the ability to look at things in different ways, is a vital tool in the creative process. Seeing things from various perspectives helps students develop deeper understanding and strengthens their ability to apply information. Consider posting flexibility challenges on the board, in a prominent area of your room, on your class website, or in student journals. Examples include:

- Create a metaphor that describes our classroom/the school/our city/our state/ . . .
- Give reasons why you might forget your homework.
- Give reasons why someone would be angry/happy/sad/delighted/confused/ . . .
- Generate a list of reasons why people travel/migrate/immigrate.
- List uses for your computer power cord (other than providing power to your computer).
- List reasons why people don't:
  - revolt/disagree/fight/conflict/organize/believe.
  - shop for new clothes.
  - get angry/mad/sad/happy/terrified.
  - own a computer/smartphone/other technology.
  - work together/talk to each other/work in teams.
  - have pets/children.
- List reasons not to:
  - solve a problem.
  - modify genes/seeds/chemicals/ . . .
  - use statistics.
  - understand an author's point of view.
  - know how to spell/communicate/interpret/ . . .
- Explain what would happen if:
  - there were no airplanes.
  - it snowed/rained every day.
  - you were invisible for a day.
  - there were no flowers.
  - all books were banned.
  - science/music/history/the arts/ . . . were not allowed to be taught.
- Imagine grouping everything in your desk into three categories; what are the categories and why did you choose them?
- Categorize the conversations you had yesterday and identify the category with the most conversations.
- In what ways is water (replace water with any other noun) unsafe/scary/enticing/forgiving/disrespectful/ . . .

SCAMPER

Another way to incorporate creativity into the classroom is through this activity. Each letter of SCAMPER stands for an action students take related to the content under study.

S=Substitute
C=Combine
A=Adapt/Adjust
M=Modify/Minimize/Maximize
P=Put to other use
E=Eliminate
R=Reverse/Revise

SCAMPER language arts example:
For a unit on *Tuck Everlasting* by Natalie Babbitt,[3] the story of a young girl who encounters a family of immortals:

Substitute the concept of immortality with compassion; how does this change the focus of the story?

Combine events in the book using the characters of Mae, Winnie, and Jesse as categories. How do they compare/contrast?

Adapt the time the story took place to today. How might this change the outcome?

Minimize the effects of the water to 20 years. How does that change the story?

Put the water to another use. How does this change the story?

Eliminate the arrival of the constable. What impact would it have on the story?

Revise the plot so that Winnie was the one to attack the man in the yellow suit. How would this change the story?

SCAMPER geometry example:[4]

Substitute cartoon or anime characters for the names of polygons.

Combine art with geometry; construct an artistic three-dimensional tetrahedrons and other solids out of poster board and tape.

Adapt the triangle area formula to create formulas for squares, rectangles, and parallelograms.

Modify the parallel postulate to allow for more than one line parallel to another line through a given point.

Put triangles to work as tools. Investigate inherent characteristics of different triangle types to invent a tool that has a useful purpose.

Eliminate the words in the Pythagorean theorem: use skit/pantomime, sketches/paintings, or any other medium.

Reverse the order of the steps in a two-column proof. Work backward from what you intend to prove.

SCAMPER physics example:[4]

Substitute light for friction; write a story about a NASCAR race.

Combine formulas for motion with a popular song: replace lyrics with symbols for distance, speed, and time.

Adapt the units of velocity (meters per second) into comparable units of food and activities. How many servings of fruit did you eat today per number of steps you took?

Modify Newton's Second Law of Motion (force is mass times acceleration) so there is no acceleration. Describe how life changes for humans.

Put sound to another use. Study sonic properties and hypothesize devices that could make life easier or do work for us.

Eliminate the names of Newton's Laws of Motion; rename them after actors or singers.

Reverse the order of the colors in the light spectrum and re-create a famous still life or landscape.

SCAMPER social studies example based on the American Revolution:

Substitute the leadership qualities of George Washington with those of Dwight Eisenhower.

Combine events leading up to the American Revolution into categories (political, economic, social).

Adapt/Adjust: What if electricity had been invented at the time of the American Revolution? How might the events have been different?

Maximize: What if the war had lasted for 20 years?

Put to other use: What impact would Canada have had if it entered on the side of the colonies in the American Revolution?

Eliminate: If the Treaty of Paris had never happened, what would have been the outcome?

Reverse: How would the world be different today if the British had maintained control of the colonies?

3. Babbitt, 1975.
4. Provided by John Cash, high school math and physics teacher, Washington, D.C.

Helping students develop strategies that support creative thinking can engage them in the learning process. Providing them with different ways to approach the learning and finding the "what ifs" in the content gives them freedom to come up with new ideas while digging deeper into the content.

Critical Reasoning

To evaluate information through a critical lens is to view it devoid of personal interpretation and emotion. To critically analyze information, learners must judge it against set standards, rules, and procedures. Critical reasoning is a shifting between probing persistence and open-minded flexibility. Students who lack critical reasoning skills often rush to conclusions, accept first answers, or insist on instant gratification. These students must learn to develop a tolerance toward ambiguity and to defer judgment. Critical reasoning therefore requires the development of self-regulation for learning.

Traits of Critical Thinkers

Linda Elder and Richard Paul of the Foundation for Critical Thinking define critical thinkers as having the traits of:[5]

Independence: After listening to others and reasoning through the various arguments, independent thinkers then do their own thinking. Questions they ask:

- What did the others in the group say?
- Am I making a decision based on what others are saying?
- Have my thoughts been changed by the way others are thinking?
- Did I allow others to do the thinking for me?
- Would I still make the same decision after what I heard from others?

Integrity: Good critical thinkers use the Golden Rule of "Do unto others as you would have them do unto you" in coming to solutions. They ask:

- How did I treat others in the decision-making process?
- Did I treat them the way I would like to be treated?
- Was I respectful to others' ideas?
- Did I model good thinking strategies for others to follow?
- In what ways did I show respect to the others in the group?

Humility: Some students, especially very bright students, tend to think they know everything. Good critical thinkers understand that they can't know everything and do rely on others to support their thinking. They ask:

- Did I try to be the "know it all"?
- Did I allow others to have their say?
- How do I know what I know is true?
- Did I question others about how they know what they know?
- How did I respond when someone knew more than me?

Confidence: Confidence is being aware of what you know, but it is also being secure when mistakes and failures happen. Questions confident students ask:

- How did I react when there was a disagreement?
- Did I question myself on what I thought or knew?
- How did I dig deeper into the arguments?
- Is my information relevant to the arguments?
- Is my information accurate?

Perseverance: Learners with perseverance work through difficult problems until they find a workable solution. Perseverance is a worthy trait for facing 21st-century challenges. Questions these learners ask:

- Did I work through to a solution?
- What did I do when things got tough?
- How did I feel when I hit a wall?
- What thinking techniques (creative or critical) did I use when I got stuck?
- Did I take charge of my own affect, behavior, and cognition?

Fair-mindedness: Similar to integrity, fair-minded thinkers allow others to take the

5. Paul and Elder, 2014.

stage, allow others to have right answers, and even allow others to lead in decision making. Questions they ask:

- Did I keep others in mind when making decisions?
- Was everyone involved in the process?
- How do others feel or think about the decision?
- Did I consider all the issues when making this decision?
- Was the decision self-serving or in the best interest of all?

Courage: Sometimes a critical thinker will be in the minority and may come to conclusions that are not preferred by the majority. Students with courage learn to say things or act in ways that are right but not accepted by the masses. Questions they ask:

- Did I speak up even though my ideas may not have been popular?
- How did I question my own beliefs?
- When I did speak up, was I respectful of others?
- If my ideas were not popular, why were they not well-received?
- What can I do in the future to ensure I am courageous when I have unpopular views?

Empathy: Thinkers must also take into account the emotional effect (affect) of the decision-making process. Taking how people feel into account makes one a powerful thinker and leader. Questions these learners ask:

- How do others think and feel about the process and decision?
- Did I show respect for other points of view?
- In the decision-making process, did I consider the best interests of all?
- In what ways did I incorporate the ideas of others into my decision?
- How will my decision affect others?

A Problem-Solving Process

Teach students to methodically approach problems they face at home and in school.

Figure 5.3 **Problem-Solving Process**

1. Define the problem in your own words. This helps you know what kind of solution the problem requires.
2. Order the information from most relevant to least relevant. This helps eliminate the clutter of information. An effective way to do this is through a graphic organizer (see the reproducible handout "Most to Least Important" on page 64).
3. Look for what is missing, what is not stated; look for what is assumed or not assumed. Many problems have missing information, over-stated information, or assumptions. A good critical thinker unpacks the problem by analyzing the difference between what's important and what's not important; what is missing from the information and that which is not clear. Use the graphic in the reproducible "Clarifying Information" to assist students in clarifying the information.
4. Consider what the outcome should look like, should solve, or should accomplish. This is also a helpful step in gathering multiple solutions to a problem.
5. Select the best solution to fit the problem. After crafting numerous solutions, select the one that makes the most sense and will be the most effective in solving the problem.

Approaching problems with a calm assurance that grows from the knowledge that they have the tools, process, and courage to overcome challenges is key to learners developing self-reliance (see Figure 5.3).

Zoom Out Strategy

Using a work of art or picture, show students a small portion of the work on day one. Each subsequent day, show a bit more of the picture. (See Figure 5.4). Each day ask the same questions. Make sure the image is interesting enough to get students talking about it. Consider using images directly from the class content, such as graphs in math, book covers in English language arts, propaganda posters in history, weather images in science, and building structures in engineering. Once you have selected the images, use the Problem-Solving Process discussed in Figure 5.3

or structure the activity with questions based on Bloom's taxonomy:

Bloom's taxonomy questions for day one:

- Recall: What's happening?
- Understanding: Why is it happening?
- Application: What can be done to solve the situation?
- Analysis: What makes this situation similar or different from ______?
- Evaluation: What would be of concern to others not seen in this picture?
- Synthesis: Remove one item from the picture, how does it change your perception?

On subsequent days, ask the same questions and listen for changes in the original answers.

Socratic Questioning Strategy

Socratic questioning is using a series of questions to challenge the accuracy and completeness of students' thinking. Such as:

Clarification

- Can you say that again?
- What do you mean by that?
- How does your argument relate to what we are discussing?
- Why are you saying what you are saying?
- Are you saying . . . ?

Identifying assumptions

- What assumptions are you making?
- Why do you believe that?
- Do you agree or disagree with others' assumptions?
- Explain how you arrived at that assumption.
- Can you verify your beliefs?

Checking reasoning

- Why do you say that?
- How do you know that?
- What reasons do you have for your ideas?
- Where did your answer come from?
- Would your reason be enough to change other people's minds?

Figure 5.4 **Zoom Out Images**

Day 1

Day 2

Day 3

Day 4

Day 5

Citing evidence

- Where is the evidence to support your answer?
- How did you come to this idea?
- What supports do you have?
- Who else might support your claim?
- Is that a fact or an opinion?

Fishbowl Strategy

A small group of students sits in a center circle (the fishbowl) while other students sit in an outer ring of chairs. The fishbowl students wrestle with a question or topic while the outer-ring students document the lines of thinking and how the fishbowl students participated using the traits of critical thinking.

Prior Knowledge: Support for Success

One of the issues struggling learners face is a lack of or inconsistency with their prior knowledge of the content. Prior knowledge is based on past experiences that provide a grounding for new information and is key to getting students to invest in their learning. This also includes the past practice and development of strategies and skills that support the development of new strategies and skills, including the acquisition of language or vocabulary. Prior knowledge can be built, activated, or organized depending on the students' past experiences.

Building Prior Knowledge

Some students may have had limited to no experience in a content area, therefore building fundamental knowledge to begin the learning will be important. This can be done through

- Showing overview video clips of the topic.
- Using picture books or "fact" books to develop a base understanding.
- Providing various websites that can introduce or offer information about the topic.
- Bringing in an expert from the topic area/discipline.
- Showing products created by last year's students.
- Using analogies to connect a past topic to the new topic.
- Offering mini-lessons (two to three minutes) to introduce concepts or skills.

Activating

Some students have had experiences in the content but may have forgotten them or have a hard time remembering them. To activate a student's prior knowledge, consider:

- Use a KIQ (Know, Interested in, Question) Chart. Create a chart with three columns: What I *know*, find *interesting*, and have *questions* about. This strategy makes students aware that they don't know everything about a topic and nobody knows everything about a topic. See the reproducible "KIQ Chart" on page 66.
- Start a unit by using an anticipatory set/action. This is a simple activity that can encourage students to become interested in the ideas surrounding the topic. Ideas for anticipatory sets:
  - To introduce parts of speech: tape sentences on the floor and label each word with its part of speech. Let students try to figure out the coding [(The (A) big (ADJ) wolf (N) ran (V) quickly (ADV) through (Prep) the (A) woods (N)].
  - To start a discussion of evolution, use artifacts, such as a fossil bone; to begin a unit on the constitution, use a quill pen; to start a baking unit, use a flopped cake; to start a unit on Newton's laws, view a YouTube video of skateboarders.
  - Tell a story about a personal experience that highlights the key point of an upcoming lesson or unit.
  - Use an analogy to compare what is being learned to something the students already understand. When introducing atoms, use Legos to show small things make up big things or use a drink mix to demonstrate how solute and water make up a solvent.
  - Use current events to highlight the importance of learning new information. For example, have students list

the various effects the California water drought (cause) has had on everything from the economy to social concerns.

- Use mystery to engage the students in an upcoming lesson by crafting a crime scene investigation (CSI) or "who done it?" scenario.
- Put objects related to the lesson in a bag and have students pull out the items and try to guess the topic.
- Play music related to the unit. Consider using music to introduce math, science, history, or literature themes. For a geography unit, play music from the region to be studied and ask students to imagine what types of food the music suggests. For a physical education class, play a piece of music that allows students to repeat rhythmic moves of the skill they are developing.
- Show pictures of people famous in careers related to the unit content. For example, use a diverse group of scientists who have made discoveries.

› Use an anticipation guide to set up the unit. Anticipation guides give students a sample of what's in the unit, a chance to clear up any misperceptions they have about the topic, or an opportunity to share what they already know about the topic. (See Figure 5.5 for an example of an "Anticipation Guide" and the reproducible form on page 67.) Note that not all the statements should be true in an anticipation guide. Plus, the statements should highlight the main concepts or ideas from the unit.

› Have students do some prereading on the topic to get them interested, show the controversies associated with the topic, or discuss current news that makes the topic relevant to the students.

› Through directed readings you can arrange students into subgroups of "experts" on different parts of the topic. For instance, in the mathematic study of linear equations, have students read how chefs, street and yard maintenance workers, party planners, and car sales personnel may use linear equations to improve performance.

› Mind maps are graphic organizers that help students manage their thoughts about a topic of study. To create a mind map, students put the topic in the center and attach to it smaller bubbles labeled with the subheadings of the topic. See Figure 5.6 as an example.

Organizing

When students do have prior knowledge, they may need help organizing it to make sense for new learning. Before beginning a unit of study, have students graphically represent what they already know or remember about the topic. Ideas include:

› Key points list (See "Key Points" reproducible form and Figures 5.7 and 5.8).

› Mind maps (see Figure 5.6).

› Master notebook or file system (see Chapter 7).

› Ideas notebook

- Students can create a Web page or carry with them a small notebook to jot down their ideas about what they would like to learn or cover during a unit of study. Many smartphones have a "notes" application that could be used for this idea.
- Select websites for students to browse to pique their interest. Allow them to burrow down into subtopics or pick an area that they would like to investigate independently.

Chapter Summary

This chapter defined thinking as moving from metacognition to infra-cognition. Metacognition, or thinking about your own thinking, is a valuable tool in becoming self-regulated as a learner. Keeping yourself aware of what you are feeling and how you are behaving can keep you on track toward success. Infra-cognition is the grander thought process we all go through to solve problems. By using divergent (creative thinking) and convergent (critical reasoning) techniques, students are better prepared to handle the complex nature of changing standards and the issues of the 21st century.

Figure 5.5 **Anticipation Guide Example**

TOPIC: THE ROCK CYCLE

Prior to beginning this unit of study, take this survey to find out what you already know about the topic. This is NOT a test—it's simply a way for you to uncover what you do and do not know about this unit. Keep this form with you throughout the study, so you can validate what you do know and adjust what you don't have completely correct.

Statement:	I believe this to be true/false because:	What I learned:
1. Rocks come in three main types: sedimentary, metamorphic, and igneous.		
2. The differences in the types of rocks are based on how old they are.		
3. Paleontology is the study of rocks.		
4. Rocks are the building blocks of the earth's lithosphere, asthenosphere, mesosphere, and core.		
5. Most rocks visible today formed in or on continental or oceanic crust.		
6. Igneous rocks are formed from the cooling of magma.		
7. Sedimentary rocks formed at the bottom of the ocean.		
8. Metamorphic rocks formed through high pressure and/or high temperatures.		
9. All rocks are classified based on their color and size.		
10. The reason it's called a rock cycle is because rocks begin as igneous, then become sedimentary, then metamorphic.		

Figure 5.6 **Mind Map Example**

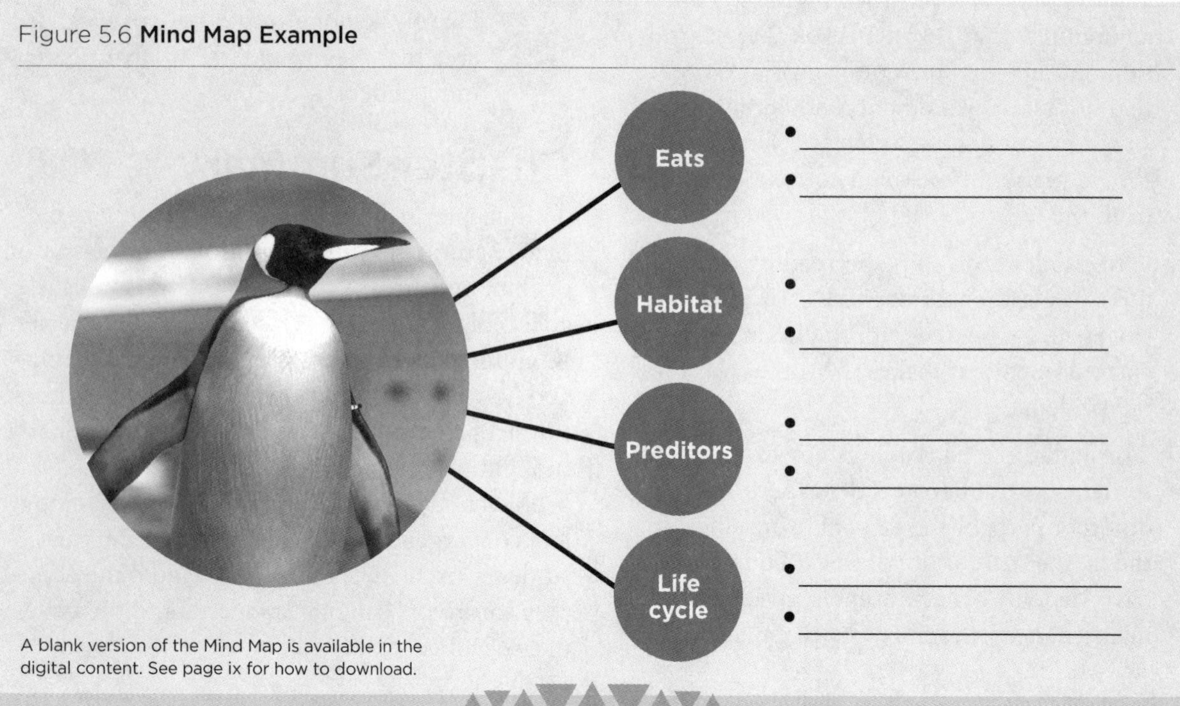

A blank version of the Mind Map is available in the digital content. See page ix for how to download.

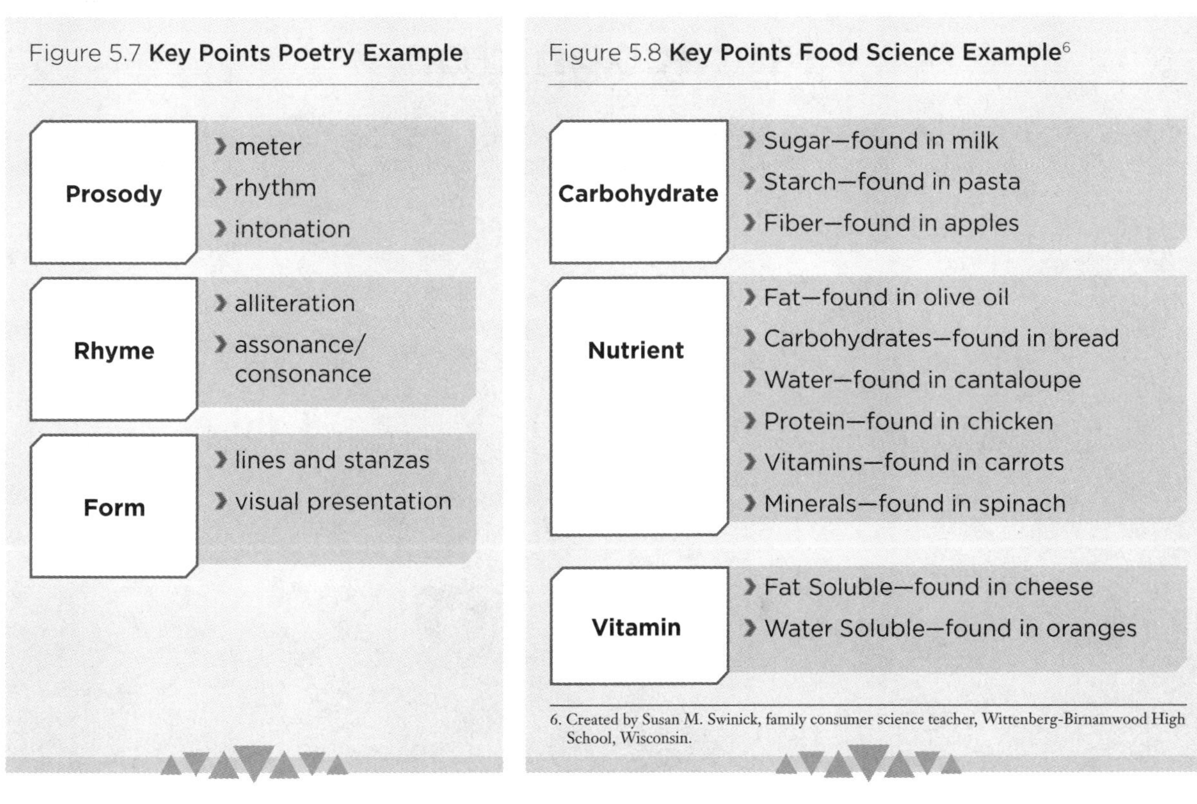
Figure 5.7 Key Points Poetry Example
Prosody
meter
rhythm
intonation
Rhyme
alliteration
assonance/consonance
Form
lines and stanzas
visual presentation
Figure 5.8 Key Points Food Science Example[6]
Carbohydrate
Sugar—found in milk
Starch—found in pasta
Fiber—found in apples
Nutrient
Fat—found in olive oil
Carbohydrates—found in bread
Water—found in cantaloupe
Protein—found in chicken
Vitamins—found in carrots
Minerals—found in spinach
Vitamin
Fat Soluble—found in cheese
Water Soluble—found in oranges
6. Created by Susan M. Swinick, family consumer science teacher, Wittenberg-Birnamwood High School, Wisconsin.

Graphic Organizers for Young Students: Metacognition

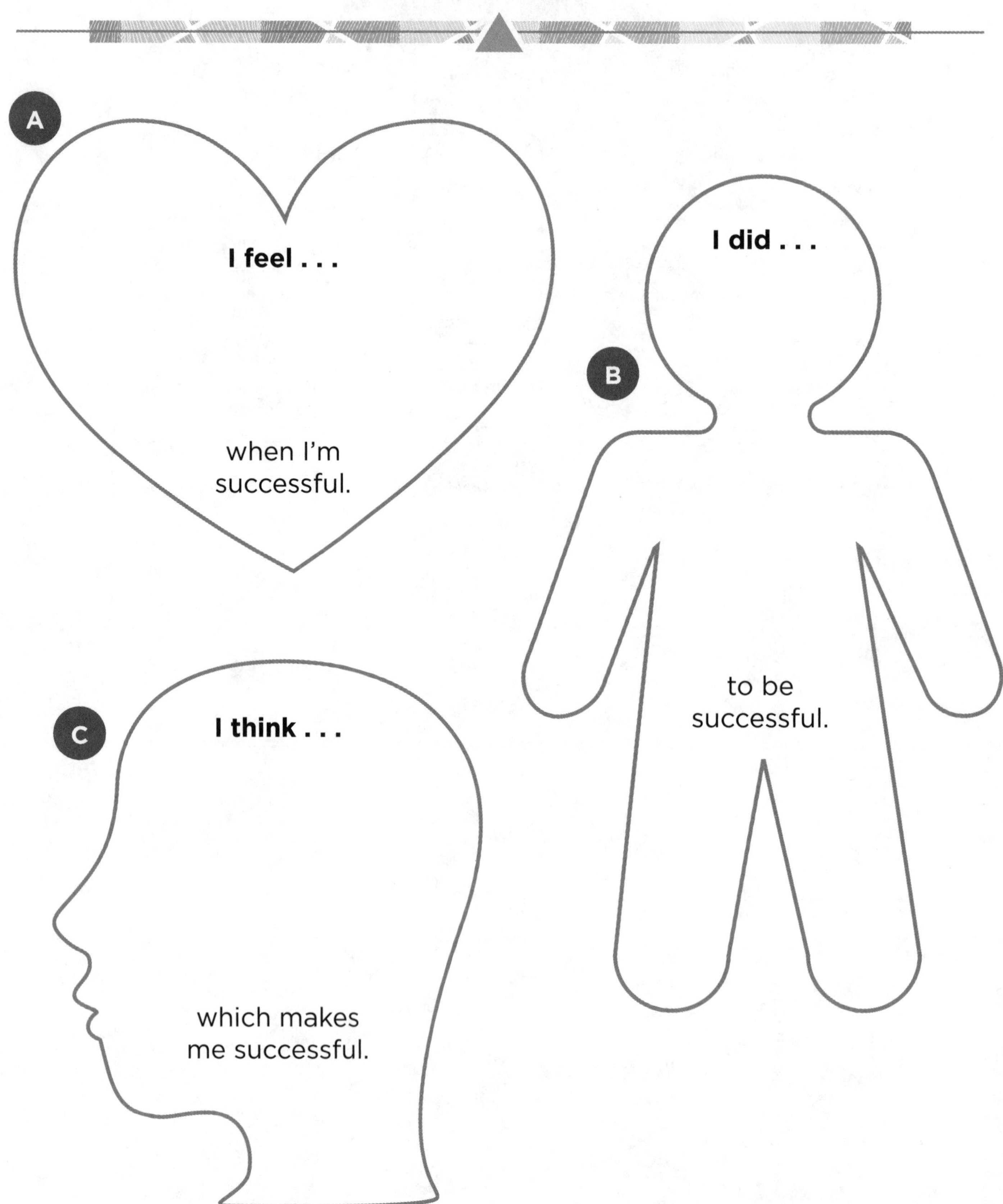

Graphic Organizer for Older Students: Metacognition

A) My affect throughout this task:

Before the task ________________________________

During the task ________________________________

After the task ________________________________

B) My behaviors throughout this task:

Before the task ________________________________

During the task ________________________________

After the task ________________________________

C) My cognitive process throughout this task:

Before the task ________________________________

During the task ________________________________

After the task ________________________________

Most to Least Important

Clarifying Information

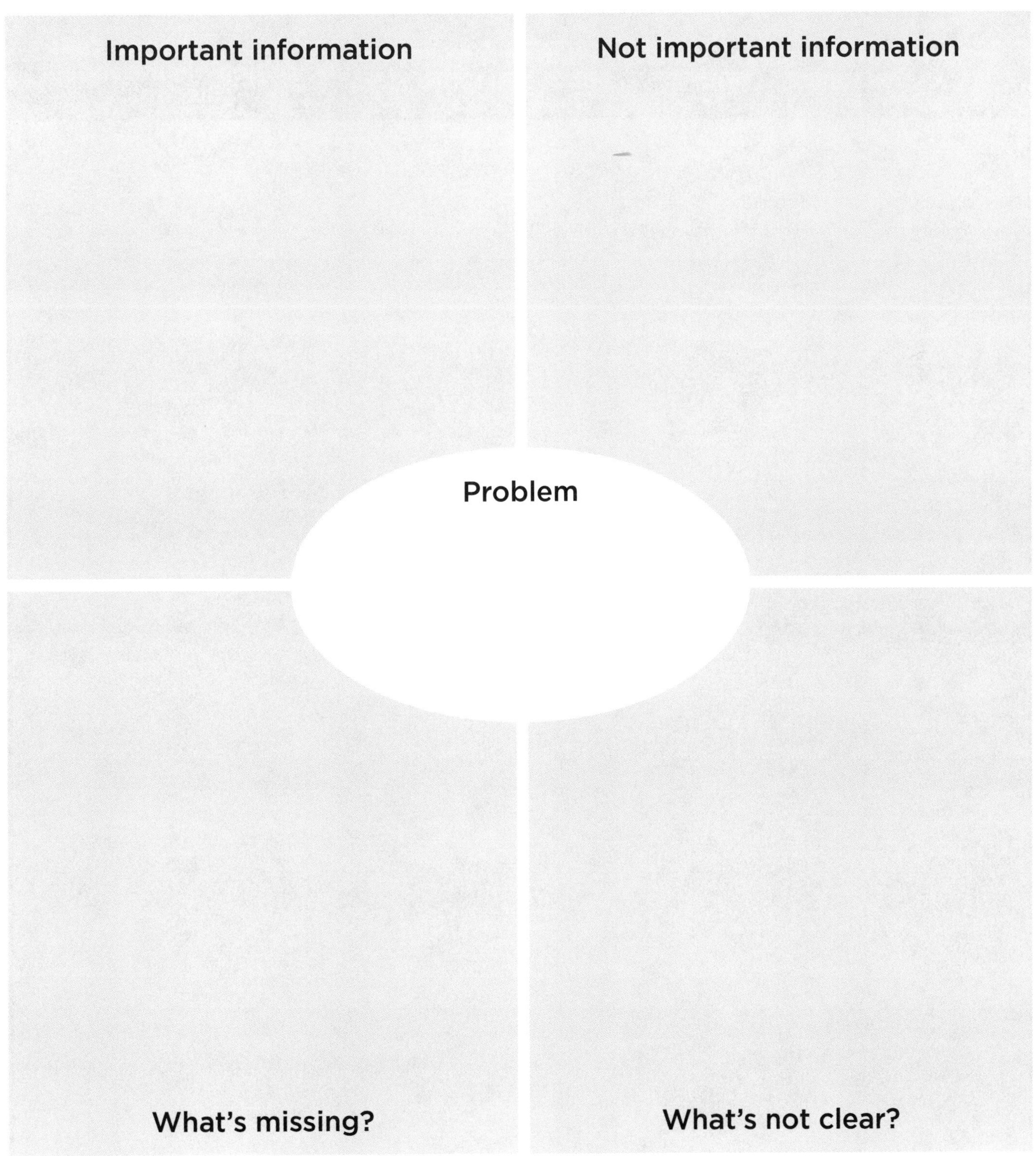

KIQ Chart

What I KNOW about this topic	What I find INTERESTING about this topic	What I QUESTION or don't know about this topic

Adapted from *Advancing Differentiation* by Richard M. Cash, Ed.D., Free Spirit Publishing Inc., 2011. Used with permission.

Anticipation Guide

Topic:____

Prior to beginning this unit of study, take this survey to find out what you already know about the topic. This is NOT a test—it's simply a way for you to uncover what you do and do not know about this unit. Keep this form with you throughout the study, so you can validate what you do know and adjust what you don't have completely correct.

Statement:	I believe this to be true/ false because:	What I learned:
1.		
2.		
3.		
4.		
5.		
6.		
7.		
8.		
9.		
10.		

NOTES:

Key Points List

CHAPTER 6

Setting and Achieving Goals

What we find is that if you have a goal that is very, very far out, and you approach it in little steps, you start to get there faster. Your mind opens up to the possibilities.

—Mae C. Jemison

This chapter discusses how to incorporate the ABCs of self-regulation (affect, behavior, and cognition) into goal setting, monitoring, and reflecting—all phases of the engaging in learning process (EiL) described in Chapter 3.

Setting goals is a significant factor in achieving self-regulation for learning (SRL). A goal is either something a person aspires to accomplish or a desired outcome. The person setting the goal must understand what is realistic to accomplish, which outcomes are doable. Students who haven't encountered much classroom success usually have difficulty understanding what outcomes are attainable and appropriate, so goal setting can be quite challenging for them.

Numerous studies show the impact goal setting has on learning and learners. Edwin Locke and Gary Latham found that setting goals was a critical factor in enhancing performance.[1] However, just setting a "do your best" goal had little effect on performance. Achievement is most positively affected by students and teachers setting challenging goals that are relative to the students' levels of abilities and achievement. Researchers have found that rather than the specificity of the goal, it is the appropriate degree of difficulty that leads to success. Students who set the most challenging (yet achievable) goals out-performed by over 250 percent their peers who set easier goals.[2]

As John Hattie states in his seminal work *Visible Learning*, "Any school with the motto 'do your best' should immediately change it to 'face your challenges' or 'strive to the highest.'"[3] Through Hattie's reviews of studies on student goals, he found that students with goals tended to be more self-energized, motivated, and directed toward being successful. Goals can advise the learner about what success can be (affective), the level of effort required to reach the goal (cognitive), and the appropriate actions necessary to achieve the goal (behavioral). Students developed greater self-efficacy and confidence with each goal attainment. These findings held true even for students identified with special needs.[4]

Learning Orientation

Before students can set goals, teachers should be aware of their students' disposition toward learning. Psychologists have found that two factors are essential in learning: achievement orientation and goal approach. Achievement orientation is how a learner interprets and responds affectively, behaviorally, and cognitively to a task. The theoretical framework of achievement orientation suggests students consider how they feel about themselves (confidence), the value of the task, and how well they think they will do in the task. The students' focus is on either mastery or performance.

1. Locke and Latham, 1990.
2. Wood and Locke, 1987.
3. Hattie, 2009.
4. Fuchs and Fuchs, 1986.

Students focused on achieving mastery are characterized by exerting high levels of effort, desire to succeed, and adaptability in applying strategies to overcome difficulty. These students tend to be more intrinsically motivated, are persistent, and demonstrate a growth mindset. They are willing to take on challenges they may perceive to be beyond their capabilities, and they find challenges stimulating and recognize failures as learning opportunities.

On the other hand, performance-focused students believe their abilities propel them to success and they measure their achievement against others' achievement. Performance-oriented students try to be better than others. They avoid challenges where there may be a risk of failure or where they may not outperform others. They may fear tasks that are unfamiliar or that have an unknown outcome, such as open-ended tasks. Performance-oriented students also see their failures as evidence that they lack the abilities to succeed.

Additionally, awareness of students' goal orientation, how much they value accomplishment or achievement, is also critical in knowing what direction to take with students in learning. This theoretical framework suggests two constructs toward goal setting: approach or avoidance. Approach-type learners strive to develop their skills and abilities to become more successful. Whereas avoidance-type learners prefer to maintain their levels of acquired abilities through routine practice that may not challenge them or help them develop a new skill. These learners "avoid" undesirable outcomes or any activity where they might be perceived as incompetent or lacking knowledge. Typically avoidance-type learners have acquired a level of accomplishment they feel is "good enough."

Figure 6.1 shows how achievement orientation and goal orientation connect to become *learning orientation.* Four types of learners can be identified in our classrooms:

- Mastery approach learners work hard to achieve their personal best.
- Mastery avoidance learners are comfortable being "good enough."
- Performance approach learners compete to be better than others.
- Performance avoidance learners fear being defined by their failures.

The graphic in Figure 6.1 provides general characteristics related to the learners. The goal is to move all students toward master approach learners. In the goal-setting process, consider where students are in relation to the type of learners they are and how to encourage them to move toward the mastery approach.

The Hierarchy of Goals

The order or hierarchy that goals are framed within makes them both effective and interactive. The use of the term *hierarchy* in this case is not to suggest that some goals are more important or influential than others. *Goal hierarchy* signifies that subordinate goals influence and interact with superordinate goals to achieve both types of goals. Subordinate goals tend to be more extrinsically validated and motivating, while superordinate goals are far more intrinsically motivated. Through this constant interaction, all goals work within a feedback loop that makes adjustments to the goals above or below. The feedback loop within the framework is explained later in this chapter.

Framework of the Goal Hierarchy

An important aspect of learning is to identify goals worthy of achieving, plan a way to achieve those goals, and then upon completion, consider ways to improve performance. Figure 6.2 is an outline for assisting students in setting goals that are interrelated, self-regulated, and focused on influencing various realms of life. The interactions between and among goals within all levels leads to a fuller more complete life. The process of engaging in goals at any level will lead to engagement of all other goals. The following sections describe each level of the goal hierarchy (shown in greater detail in the figure).

Ideal Self Goal

According to humanist psychologist Carl Rogers, the ideal self is the person you would like to be.[5] This person is a creation of your life experiences, including interactions with role models, society, and school. Typically, the interpretation of the

5. Rogers, 1951.

Figure 6.1 **Learning Orientation**

Orientation	Characteristics
Learning Goal Orientation (Mastery Approach)	**Sets achievement goals based on personal best** Enjoys the learning process Strives to achieve at high levels Has a growth mindset Seeks help when needed Is a deep learner Is intrinsically motivated to succeed
Learning Maintenance Goal Orientation (Mastery Avoidance)	**Sets achievement goals based on not being wrong or not understanding** Uses the learning process to maintain skills and abilities Fears failure Has a fixed mindset Avoids seeking help Is a surface learner Is less intrinsically motivated
Performance Approval Goal Orientation (Performance Approach)	**Sets achievement goals based on being better than others** Uses the learning process for positive reinforcement and feedback Puts effort forward when assured positive reward Avoids tasks in which he or she may fail Avoids seeking help Is a surface learner Is extrinsically motivated
Performance Evaluation Goal Orientation (Performance Avoidance)	**Sets achievement goals based on not being evaluated as incompetent** Causes many problems in school Does not enjoy learning; avoids engaging Fears failure Has a fixed mindset Avoids seeking help Is a surface learner Is extrinsically motivated

ideal self is defined in a set of characteristics or positive qualities we are committed to achieving or the negative tendencies we would like to avoid or manage.

Examples of positive qualities to achieve:

- compassionate
- courageous
- courteous
- creative
- dedicated
- dependable
- diligent
- kind
- loyal
- purposeful
- resilient
- sensitive
- thoughtful
- trustworthy
- wise

Possible negative tendencies to avoid:

- authoritarian/bossy
- disloyal
- distractible
- helpless
- impatient
- inconsiderate
- inconsistent
- inflexible
- insincere
- late
- mean-spirited
- selfish
- thoughtless
- uncooperative
- unforgiving
- uninviting

When guiding students toward creating the ideal self goal, teachers must take into account the age and experiences of the child. Jean Piaget, the renowned developmental psychologist and

Figure 6.2 **Goal Hierarchy**

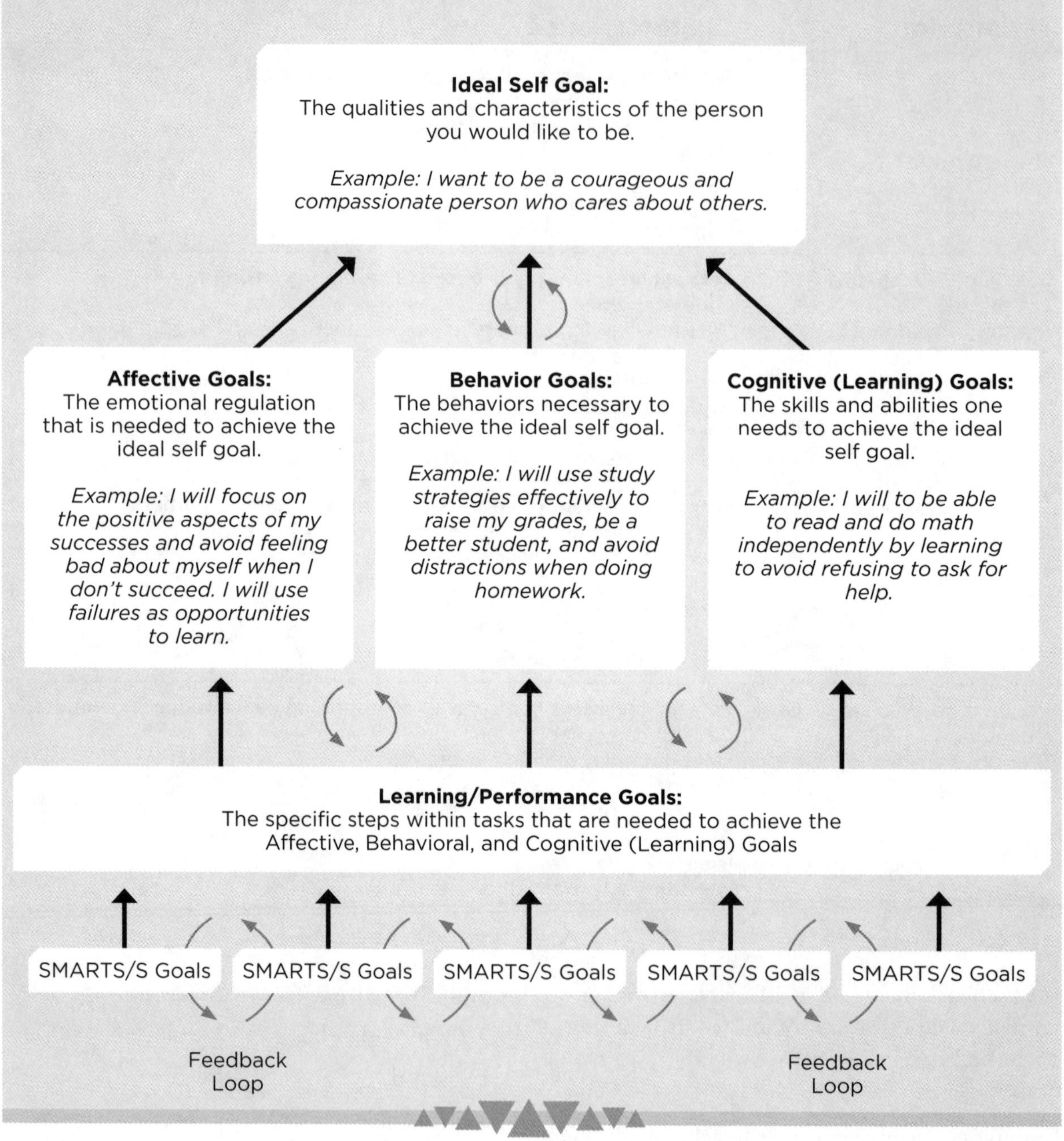

Ideal Self Goal:
The qualities and characteristics of the person you would like to be.

Example: I want to be a courageous and compassionate person who cares about others.

Affective Goals:
The emotional regulation that is needed to achieve the ideal self goal.

Example: I will focus on the positive aspects of my successes and avoid feeling bad about myself when I don't succeed. I will use failures as opportunities to learn.

Behavior Goals:
The behaviors necessary to achieve the ideal self goal.

Example: I will use study strategies effectively to raise my grades, be a better student, and avoid distractions when doing homework.

Cognitive (Learning) Goals:
The skills and abilities one needs to achieve the ideal self goal.

Example: I will to be able to read and do math independently by learning to avoid refusing to ask for help.

Learning/Performance Goals:
The specific steps within tasks that are needed to achieve the Affective, Behavioral, and Cognitive (Learning) Goals

SMARTS/S Goals | SMARTS/S Goals | SMARTS/S Goals | SMARTS/S Goals | SMARTS/S Goals

Feedback Loop

Feedback Loop

philosopher, developed the theory of cognitive development in children.[6] The theory is defined in four stages:

1. **Sensorimotor stage (birth to two years old):** behaviors lack a sense of thoughtfulness or logic. The child moves from reflexive responses to interacting with the environment. It is a developmental time of gaining mental representations of the real world.
2. **Preoperational stage (age 2 to approximately age 7):** this is an egocentric time of life. The child views the world from his or her own eyes, unable to recognize that others have different points of view or perceptions of how the world works.
3. **Concrete operational stage (approximately age 6 or 7 to approximately age 13):** at this stage children begin to develop logic and reasoning. Their thought processes

6. Piaget, 2013.

start to become more adult-like and mature in development. Inductive reasoning, drawing inference from generalized experiences, is a common thought process. Deductive reasoning, predicting outcomes from experience, is still limited at this time. Children in this stage may have difficulty generating logical solutions.

4. **Formal operational stage (approximately ages 11 to 15–20):** intelligence is demonstrated through the use of symbols to represent abstract concepts. Children can use hypothetical and deductive reasoning to solve problems. This is the stage when abstract thinking, metacognition, and more sophisticated problem-solving techniques blossom.

Consider students' cognitive abilities in each stage as you guide them in setting goals.

Kindergarten–first grade, preoperational stage: Teachers construct the broad class or grade-level goal—all students continually strive for the same goal. Example: "We want to be kind and helpful people."

Grade 2–late elementary/early middle school, concrete operational stage: Teachers assist students in crafting the vision of what the ideal self looks like. Use examples of people the child knows personally (such as parents, teachers, faith leaders, and caregivers); characters from literature, movies, and television shows; or local personalities. Keep the role model as close to the child and use as many concrete examples as possible because developmentally, abstractions (such as using historical leaders/figures) may be difficult for them to comprehend.

Middle school and beyond, formal operational stage: In most cases, students at this age will be in the Support and Release stages of self-regulation (see Figure 2.2), so students can craft their own ideal self goals. Within their personal circle and through academic and other media, students will have encountered numerous role models. These students are also ready to consider characteristics of historical or prominent figures as they craft their goal. Students still in the Origination or Intervention stages of self-regulation will need more teacher support in finding appropriate role models and examples upon which to base their ideal self goals. See Figure 6.2 and "Graphic Organizer for Creating Ideal Self Goals: Secondary Grades" on page 84 for more- or less-direct formats in guiding students to create this goal.

ABC Goals

The level below the ideal self goal in the goal hierarchy contains the ABC goals involving affect, behavior, and cognition. In Figure 6.2, note that each ABC goal is stated with what the student will do and what the student will avoid. When developing ideal self goals, there are things we want to achieve and tendencies we should avoid. Researchers report the goals we want to achieve, such as "I want to get an A in my math class this semester," have a positive valence or an attractiveness toward doing an activity, which leads to a greater level of intrinsic motivation.[7] Tendencies we want to avoid, such as "I want to avoid negative peers who may speak poorly about school" have a negative valence that can lead to fear or anger. However, ideal self goals can have a powerful effect on students who need to focus on managing negative aspects of their lives to become more motivated learners.

As noted psychologist Dr. Carol S. Dweck states in her groundbreaking text *Mindset: The New Psychology of Success*, "Success is about being your best self, not about being better than others; failure is an opportunity, not a condemnation; effort is the key to success."[8] This is the philosophy students should adhere to when crafting their ABC goals.

Affective Goals

Affective goals are for maintaining a positive outlook on learning and avoiding a negative feeling about failures.

Primary grades. Primary students should construct a classroom or grade-level goal that focuses on the enjoyment of learning and how to manage feelings when things don't go the way they expect. An example of a classroom affective goal may be: "We will have fun while learning and know that mistakes help us get better." The goal

7. Elliot and McGregor, 2001.
8. Dweck, 2006.

is created with the preoperational stage understanding in mind—students are mostly egocentric and may not be able to accept their feelings of failure while others are enjoying success. Note the community nature of the goal for this age of students.

Intermediate grades. For intermediate students setting affective goals, the focus should be on the egocentric nature of this age. Again, the emphasis should be on creating the approach-avoidance type of goal and formed as an "I" statement, such as "I will focus on the positive feelings when I find success and learn from my mistakes so I can improve."

Secondary grades. Generally, secondary students will have had more life experiences to draw upon in forming their affective goals. Adolescence is a precarious time of life, especially in emotional development. Executive functioning, located in the frontal lobes of the brain, and emotional regulation, located in the limbic system or midbrain, are under a great deal of maturing during adolescence. Therefore, it is essential that students craft the affective goals in the approach-avoidance design. Those students who have had previous modeling and support in affective self-regulation may be more emotionally mature. These students will need less assistance in creating effective goals. Those students who have not had prior positive modeling and support may be less mature. Students with less positive emotional support or more negative school experiences may not be able to view the world positively. Plan on giving these students more direct support in goal design, especially in framing the goal in an optimistic manner. An example of a secondary affective goal would be: "I will focus on feeling confident in myself and learn to accept mistakes, errors, and failure as opportunities."

Behavioral Goals

Behavioral goals are focused on the actions, mannerisms, and interactions one has in and with the environment. There is evidence that links our affect (how we feel) directly to our behaviors. In the case of behavioral goal setting, students focus on their actions and interactions in school and at home that impact their achievement. As with affective and cognitive goal setting, we use the approach-avoidance framing.

Primary grades. With primary students the focus is on the community effort of getting along with others and following directions. Teachers frame the behavioral expectations with students to give them a sense of ownership of the goals. State the classroom or grade-level goal in terms students can understand. Avoid using terms that are vague, indirect (such as "respectable" or "persistence"), or abstract. Use more direct and precise terms (such as "continue to try even when it's hard"). Although, it is extremely important to use the approach-avoidance design to direct and redirect young children's behaviors, note how at this age both the approach *and* the avoidance parts of the goals are stated in positive terms. An example of a primary classroom/grade-level goal would be: "We will be nice to each other and make sure our voices are off when someone else is speaking." Research on student behavior suggests that forming affirmative norms or goals can have a significant effect on how positively students will behave in the classroom setting.

Intermediate grades. Intermediate students can set behavioral goals both for the context of the classroom and their out-of-school lives. A typical goal at this age could be "I will follow the norms of the classroom and avoid disrupting others." Keep the goals as affirmative as possible; students can use the term *avoid* in setting goals at this grade level.

Secondary grades. Behavioral goals may have a great impact on young adolescents following the norms of the classroom and school and on their overall motivation and engagement. Goals should challenge students to avoid distractions and not give up when the going gets tough. A behavioral goal for secondary students could be: "I will self-test each night after my study period and use the rule of 20:2[9] to avoid getting distracted or mentally exhausted."

Cognitive Goals

Cognitive goals are those skills and abilities necessary to achieve the higher level ideal self goal. These are the goals that are most specific to the

9. For every 20 minutes of continuous studying, spend up to two minutes doing something different (such as taking a walk, looking at social media, listening to a song, etc.).

learning acquired in school. Cognitive goals will also include the levels of thinking from meta-cognition and infra-cognition. Generally, cognition refers to thinking. Thinking takes on many forms: attention, memories, decision making, evaluating, or judgments. Thinking can be introspective (an inward examination of your conscious thoughts and feelings, oftentimes called reflection) or the surface attention of processing our environment.

Metacognition in goal setting involves students reflecting on their own thinking processes to achieve goals. Other examples are (1) setting a goal to use mnemonic strategies ("Every Good Boy Does Fine," which equals EGBDF, the musical notes on the treble staff and FACE, which are the musical notes in the spaces on the treble staff), (2) remembering factual or declarative knowledge, and (3) goals regarding how to complete an activity (also known as procedural knowledge).

Infra-cognitive goals challenge students to think conceptually through generalizations and principles. For example, when students are studying about the water cycle, they should be raising their thought beyond "what" is a water cycle (factual/declarative) to the abstraction of "why" cycles function or dysfunction.

Primary grades. Cognitive goals should be set in broad, general terms for early problem solving and conceptual relationship building. It's advisable to construct class-level goals in the early primary years and to construct individual cognitive goals by the late primary years. An example of a class-level cognitive goal is: "We will use the 4 Question Process in math to solve problems, and I will ask for help when I need it." The 4 Question Process is (1) what's the problem, (2) will I use +/- to do the problem, (3) did I do the problem correctly, and (4) did I review the problem?

Intermediate grades. Setting individual cognitive goals supports the development of independent thinking. Ask students to think about what they do well and in which content areas they would like to do better. Focus on the approach-avoidance framework of goal statements. At this age students may form goals such as "I am good at reading and will continue to push myself to read more complex text. Because I have a harder time in math, I will avoid giving up when things get difficult, and I will ask for help."

Secondary grades. Secondary students also should focus on the areas in which they succeed and struggle. Cognitive goals should be specific to thinking and questioning techniques. Help students frame their goals toward deeper reflective thoughts and overarching thinking strategies (such as critical reasoning and decision-making tools). An example is, "I will use deductive and inductive reasoning to solve complex problems, while avoiding the simple declarative responses."

Learning/Performance Goals

Now the learners are ready to define what they will do to do well in learning. Goal setting, management, and reflection are the critical elements at this stage. The quality of the goals a student sets prior to a learning activity will have an effect on their motivations to learn. As defined by Barry Zimmerman, quality goals can have four motivational effects on the learner.[10]

1. First, a goal can focus the student on the *choices of* and *attention toward* tasks that are relevant to achieving the goal. The specificity of the goal can assist students in tuning out irrelevant information or chores. This also helps students retain information most directly related to the task at hand.
2. Second, a quality goal statement helps students know where and when to exert higher levels of *effort*.
3. Third, students who set quality goals learn *persistence*; they are willing to work longer toward achieving their goal than those students who set poorly framed goals or no goals at all.
4. Finally, students who set quality goals achieve a greater sense of *self-satisfaction*, which has a sustaining effect on future goal setting, monitoring, and attainment. Feeling successful can lead to a greater sense of confidence, which leads to more success.

10. Schunk and Zimmerman, 2008.

Setting Quality Learning/ Performance Goals

Learning or performance goals are related to the students' learning of the content in a unit of study. Prior to setting these goals, students need to know what they should understand (conceptually), be able to do (procedurally), and know (factually). Frame this information in the daily lesson objectives and the overall unit plan. Secondary teachers can state this in the course syllabus, and elementary teachers can do a mini-lesson (brief introduction) or overview of the entire unit with the objectives clearly stated.

Be specific about the outcomes of the lessons and unit. Students should be able to define the expectations or the reasonable "take-aways" from the total unit of study. This clarity will help them align prior experiences to future learning and notice the importance of information learned in prior lessons and its impact on what is to come.

Setting goals for unit-level learning can be somewhat difficult; there may be too much to consider, or students may not have a good handle on what should or could be learned. In this case, guide students toward a list of specifics to accomplish or toward what is possible during the learning process. Avoid having students focus too closely or narrowly on what the possibilities might be for the unit. Remember, the subject matter is a launching point for students to continue their learning, whether on topics of interest, important materials, or thinking skills essential to their future growth.

SMARTS/S Goal-Setting Method

Have students use the SMARTS/S method of setting goals. This format provides students with an explicit way of framing their goals for greater attainability. The more focused students are in stating their goals, the more likely students will be to reach their goals. Note in the following framework, included in the specific and measurable nature of the goals, are the consciousness of the goal, the flexibility toward adjustments of the goal, and the direction toward greater skill development.

When working with young students, set goals as a collective group effort. Young children may not have the developmental maturity to individually set these types of goals. However, if the teacher sets class SMARTS/S goals and models the daily attention toward meeting the goals, eventually children will learn how to set their own goals. Once students have had practice setting learning/performance goals as a group, they are more likely to set their own SMARTS/S goals without much prompting. Start off using the graphic organizers in this chapter ("Creating Ideal Self Goals: Primary, Intermediate, and Secondary Grades" on pages 82–84) and eventually allow students to create their own methods for stating and monitoring their goals.

SMARTS/S Goals Framework

Quality goals are those that follow the formula of SMARTS/S.

Specific: The more specific the goal is, the more likely the student will be able to gauge progress toward achievement of the goal. Students should avoid general goals because they are harder to measure and less likely to be achieved.

> *Good example:* I will read 10 pages of *To Kill a Mockingbird* this evening before 8 p.m.
>
> *Poor example:* I will read as many pages as possible of *To Kill a Mockingbird* this evening.

Measurable: The learner states the measurement and criteria of achievement in the goal so the learner can track progress, make adjustments to the goal when needed, and exert more effort to hit the target. Measureable goals answer the questions of "Where?" "When?" "For how long?" and "By how much?"

> *Good example:* I will complete at least 5 math problems correctly during study time in class.
>
> *Poor example:* I will attempt to solve some math problems by the end of math class.

Achievable: The achievable quality of the goal is continually, consciously perceived by the student ("I can do this as long as I work hard.").

> *Good example:* Yesterday, I was able to correctly use one verb during Spanish class. Today, I will correctly use three verbs during my Spanish class.

Poor example: I will learn more verbs in Spanish class.

Realistic: The goals students set for themselves must be within their reach (skill-wise). This is when the teacher's knowledge of the students' abilities is critical in helping shape quality goals. If a student overestimates his or her abilities, he or she may set a goal that is unreachable. The goal should also be something that the student personally wants to achieve. Setting goals based on others' perceptions or desires for the student results in goals that are less likely to be achieved and goals that may even be conflicting.

Good example: I want to have a better understanding of the causes and effects of the Civil War, therefore, I will read at least 10 pages of the text during study time and be able to identify at least 3 causes of the Civil War.

Poor example: My parents want me to get an A in my U.S. History class, therefore, I will work as hard as possible during this semester.

Timely: Students should write short-term goals that build toward their long-term goals. Frequent, thorough feedback on progress guides students toward success. They use the feedback to correct or modify study habits.

Good example: My short-term goal is to be able to do 5 problems correctly by myself during this math period so that I can achieve my long-term goal of getting at least 90% on the final exam.

Poor example: I want to get at least 90% on the math final exam.

Strategies to Success (S/S): The most sophisticated level of goal setting includes building from strategies (discrete conscious actions) to skills (automaticity). Students can learn to effectively apply a strategy and can tell you what they are doing and why they are doing it. When students become skilled, they pull from a vast array of strategies to solve problems and complete tasks. As an example, a student who is working at the strategic level in reading must make a conscious decision about which strategy to use when dealing with unfamiliar vocabulary, such as analyzing root words, sounding out phonetically, looking the word up in the dictionary, or doing an Internet search. Students who are working at the skill level do not need to stop and consider the individual strategies, they read with fluency and automatically apply strategies along the way. Students who work automatically free up cognitive functioning to focus on more sophisticated aspects within the text. Skilled readers are outcome-oriented, whereas strategic readers are process-oriented.

Students with a higher degree of self-regulation are more outcome-based in their learning. They learn in a more holistic manner, seeing the outcome of proficiency in a subject as the goal. Students with a lower degree of self-regulation are more likely to focus on the process of achieving a performance. These students learn through setting specific manageable steps that lead to the outcome of greater learning proficiency. In the goal-setting process students should set both performance (strategic) and outcome (skill/learning) goals. Teachers support students in setting goals by teaching them numerous strategies on a daily basis and demonstrating how practicing the strategies leads to greater skill development and learning.

Good example: I will use one of the six strategies for solving a math problem during this math period so that I can improve my abilities in mathematics this semester. (The six strategies for solving a math problem: Draw a picture, work backward, guess and check, look for a pattern, make a list, and make a table).

Poor example: I will get better at math by solving more problems correctly.

Teaching the Goal-Setting Process

The process of teaching goal setting should be done incrementally beginning with S and progressing through the remaining letters M A R T S/S. As you can see from Figure 6.3, teachers can determine at which stage of SRL the individual student begins. The teacher then guides students through the various stages within each of the strategies embedded within SMARTS/S goal setting.

Example: A group of students in your fourth-grade classroom has had little educational practice with setting goals. These students will work at the origination stage of specific goal setting, using the teacher-demonstrated goal. In Figure 6.3, this is located in the Specific row and the Origination column. Another group of students has had significant work with setting specific (see the Release column of the Specific row) goals and can set their own goals, however they are at the Origination stage of the Measureable row of the figure. Students will progress through the matrix at varied rates, so the teacher should be prepared to differentiate the goal-setting process for students. Within this chapter you will find graphic organizers to assist in the differentiation process.

Giving Feedback

Feedback is essential in the development, maintenance, and achievement of goals within the hierarchy. The feedback loop is a process to control or regulate approaches toward achieving a goal. Through feedback, students maximize their potential, raise their awareness of strengths and limitations, and identify actions to improve performance. In setting goals, they use the feedback loop to adjust, modify, quit, or restart an action. Feedback at all stages of the goal-setting process is essential for moving between the higher level goals (ideal self) to the lower goals (SMARTS/S). It can be informal (such as a general conversation with a student or between students), or formal (as in formative or summative assessments). This type of feedback usually happens after students have completed goal setting.

Positive or Negative Feedback

Motivationally, students react differently to positive and negative feedback. Positive feedback increases students' motivational drive toward their goal. They feel validated in their attempts and efforts; it can increase their sense of self-efficacy and help them maintain their focus on future achievements. Using positive feedback can encourage a child to invest more effort in the pursuit of the goal. Feeling successful builds students' confidence to achieve more sophisticated or complex goals.

While positive feedback can have a useful effect on motivation, negative feedback often has a harmful impact on motivation. Negative feedback can lower confidence or encourage disengagement. In some cases, negative feedback can be considered as punishment and may elicit avoidance-type behaviors. Students who receive negative feedback are more likely to lower their expectations of success, thus supporting a fixed mindset of failure.

We should consider all interactions, whether direct or indirect, to be acts of feedback to students. Direct acts would be those that are purposeful in helping students attend to their goals, whereas indirect acts may be the nonverbal communications that students sense from the teacher and others. These actions typically happen during the actions or learning or goal pursuit. Considering that a vast majority of our communications are through nonverbal channels (such as the look in our eyes; approving or disapproving looks on our faces; smiling, nodding, hand gestures, and so forth), teachers must always be aware of what they may be unintentionally communicating as feedback to students.

Intrinsic and Extrinsic Rewards

Motivation to achieve goals can be conceived as the combination of the intrinsic and extrinsic reward system. Intrinsic reward is the personal satisfaction one receives when doing a job well. While extrinsic rewards are those that come from outside of the individual, such as certificates, money, diplomas, trophies, and ribbons. When students focus on extrinsic reward they are more likely to compare their achievement levels to others, measure their self-worth against others, and detract their attention from what was to be learned. Ultimately this undermines their own well-being.[11] Students who are more intrinsically motivated do a better job at deep thinking, perform higher academically, manage their time more efficiently, have more focus, and have lower dropout rates.[12] Using positive feedback can shift those extrinsically motivated students toward more intrinsically motivated learners.

Feedback in the goal system is best when learners find value in the information, especially when they respect or find the source to be

11. Lens and Vansteenkiste in Schunk and Zimmerman, 2008, p. 159.
12. Ibid.

Figure 6.3 **Stages of Goal Setting**

SRL Stages for Goal Setting	Origination	Intervention	Support	Release
Specific	Teacher demonstrates how to write specific goals.	Teacher provides graphic organizer for setting specific goals. Teacher checks student's work.	Student writes specific goal using graphic organizer or format of his/her choosing. Teacher checks for clarity.	Student writes specific goal. Teacher provides assistance when requested by student.
Measurable	Teacher demonstrates different measurements of goals and shows students which measurement is best to use.	Teacher guides students to choose the right measurement for the goal. Students complete a graphic organizer based on teacher recommendation.	Student decides which measurement will be used to quantify their goal. Teacher checks for accuracy.	Student selects measurement for goal. Teacher provides assistance when requested by the student.
Awareness	Teacher demonstrates how he or she consciously thinks about his or her personal growth possibilities when setting a goal. Teacher continually speaks about trying to meet the goal.	Teacher provides a student time to think and talk about what is possible by the end of the task/goal period. Students are provided a graphic organizer to write out their thoughts.	In small groups, students decide what they think they can achieve by the end of the task/goal. Individually students craft their goal with support by the teacher or peers.	Individually, students select what they believe to be achievable by the end of the task/goal. Students craft their goal with assistance from teacher or peers when needed.
Realistic	Teacher demonstrates how to create a goal that is realistic. Students are told about the "Goldilocks Principle" (It's just right!)	Teacher provides students with feedback about their strengths and limitations and directly assists them in creating a "Just Right" goal.	Based on past performances, students select a realistic goal. The teacher reviews goals for "Just Rightness."	Students set their own challenging goal. Teacher is available if necessary to provide feedback.
Timely	Teacher shares short-term goals and how they build to long-term goals. Students follow teacher example.	Teacher provides a graphic organizer for short-term goals that build to long-term goals. Teacher assists students in crafting the goals.	Students set short-term goals to address teacher designed long-term goals. Teacher reviews short-term goals for accuracy.	Students set their own long-term goals with supporting short-term goals to support success. The teacher is available for counsel when needed.
Strategies to Success	Teacher defines the difference between strategies and skills. Teacher demonstrates how strategy autonomy leads to skill development. Students note the strategies they are learning.	Teacher provides students with a list of several strategies that have been learned. Students select which strategies will assist them in meeting their goal.	Students define strategies that can be used in the task/toward goal achievement. Student defines the skill that needs improvement in goal statement. Teacher checks for accuracy.	Students state which skills will be addressed in the goal and can list various strategies toward achieving that goal. Teacher is available for counsel when necessary.

credible. If your students feel you are supportive of their efforts, care about them as learners, and promote a healthy attitude toward their success, they are more likely to "hear" what you have to tell them as they move toward their goals.

Goal Feedback Loop

As soon as students set a goal, they must consider the discrepancy between where they are at and the desired end point. When they realize the dimensions of the gap, they can plan to take appropriate actions to close it. Figure 6.4 is a diagram of the goal feedback loop, using the acronym G-MARC.

The parts of the feedback loop are:

Goal: What is the desired outcome or end point?

Monitor: In the first cycle of the loop, the child considers what is necessary to achieve the goal (such as resources, motivation, time, effort, etc). In subsequent cycles of the loop, the student performs a gap analysis to find out how near to the goal he or she is getting.

Adjustments: Is there a need for more or less of the resources, time, effort, etc?

Result: What is the result of the adjustments?

Consequence: Did the child achieve the goal? If not, begin the process again by monitoring or performing a gap analysis. When the goal is achieved, the cycle ends.

For feedback to be valuable, it must be:

Specific: Provide students with specific information about how to monitor, adjust, or make improvements. Ambiguous or subjective information does not provide the student with a clear direction toward the goal.

Audience Appropriate: Give "just the right amount" of feedback to students in language they understand. Using terminology with which the child is unfamiliar or for which he or she has no frame of reference can cause confusion. Too much feedback all at once can be overwhelming and may lack a clear direction to guide the child in taking the next step.

Relevant: Focus feedback on direction toward the goal. Irrelevant information will only confuse the student and may lead him or her away from the goal.

Timely: Give feedback as close to the action or performance as possible. To affect changes in learning, students need feedback relatively quickly to make adjustments or corrections. Delayed information on an action or performance may not be "heard" or responded to. Remember, feedback does not always have to

Figure 6.4 **G-MARC Feedback Loop**

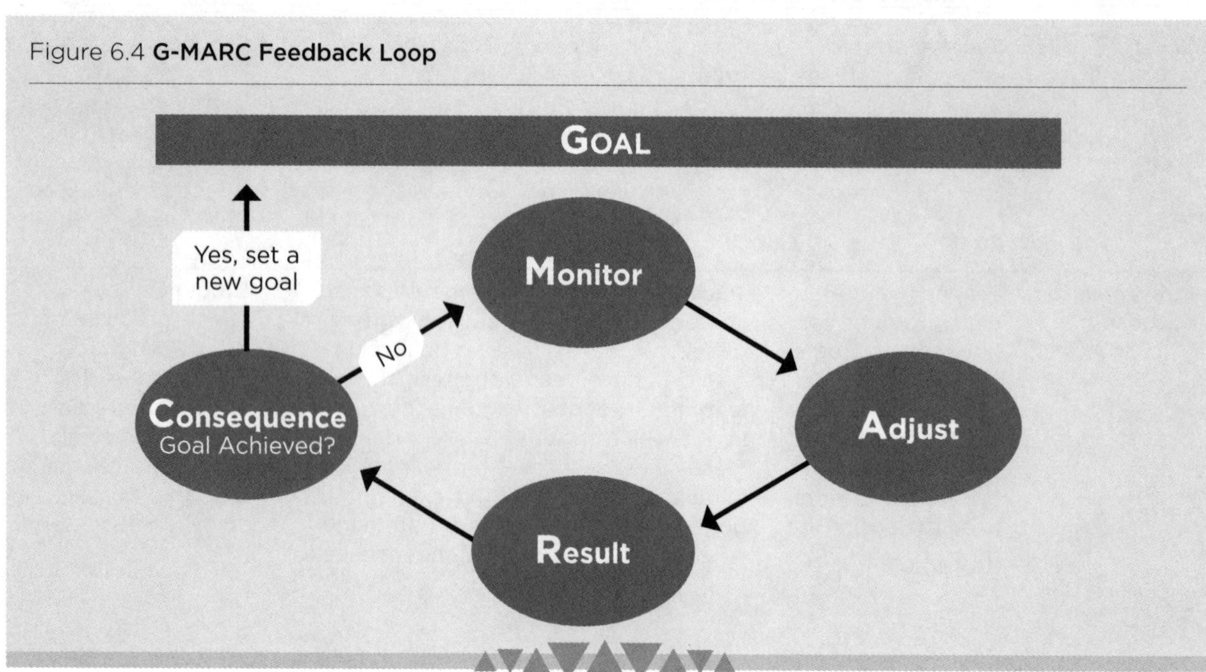

come from the teacher. Students can check in with other students, check actions against a list, or use an Internet program.

Ongoing: Students need feedback throughout the learning process (before, during, and after actions). The consistent use of feedback can help students monitor their own performance, assist others in monitoring their performance, and become less dependent on teacher direction.

Finally, to completely achieve a goal, students must know *how* to achieve the goal. Hence, their need for specific strategies to achieve the goal.

Chapter Summary

In this chapter, the goal process was defined beginning with a framework for structuring goals. In the goal hierarchy students must decide their ideal self; their affective, behavioral, and cognitive self-regulatory targets (ABC goals); and their learning/performance goals using the SMARTS/S design. Fundamental to achieving goals at all levels is using the feedback loop. Providing students with accurate, appropriate, and consistent feedback guides them toward greater achievement and learning autonomy.

Graphic Organizer for Creating Ideal Self Goals: Primary Grades

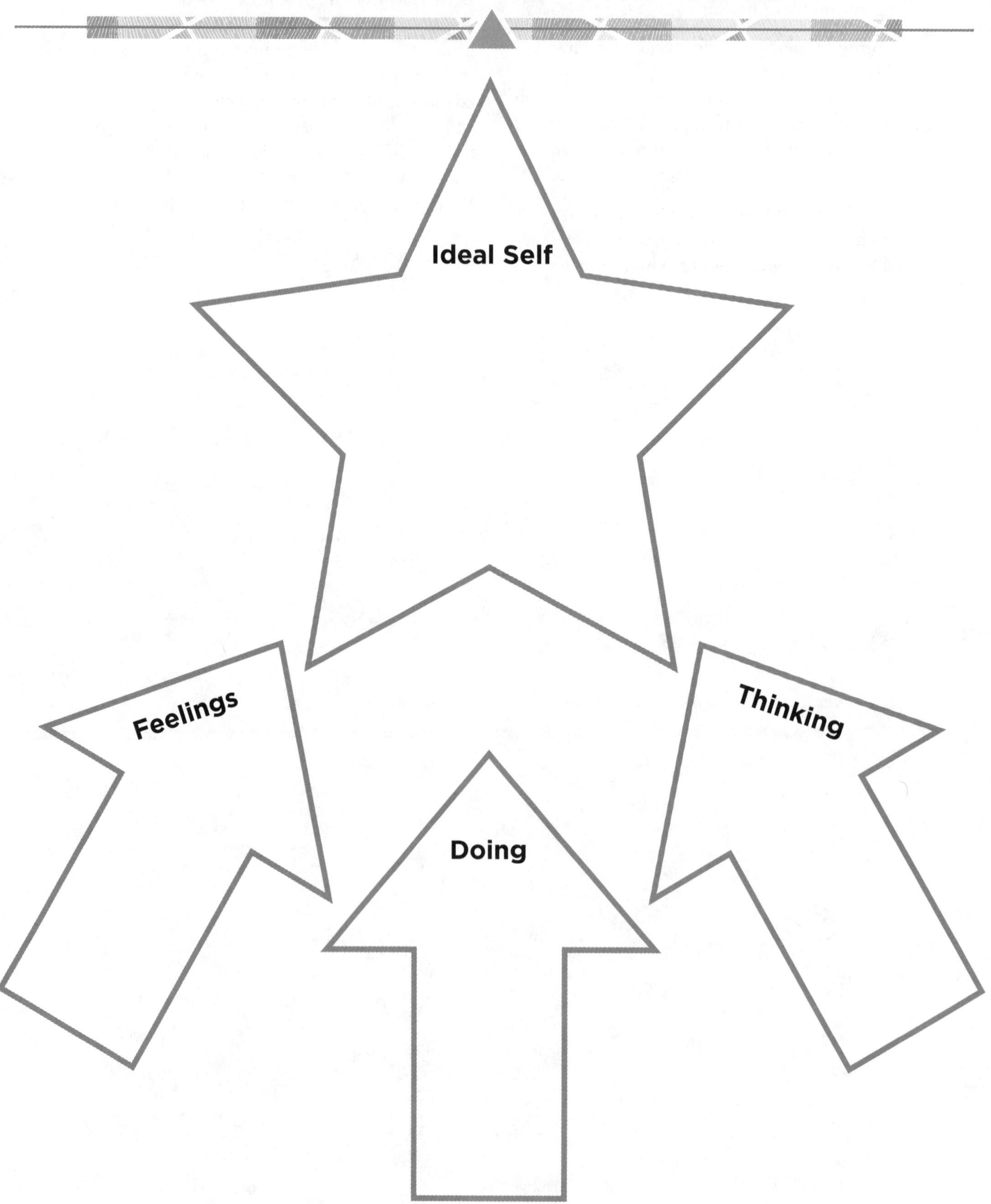

Graphic Organizer for Creating Ideal Self Goals: Intermediate Grades

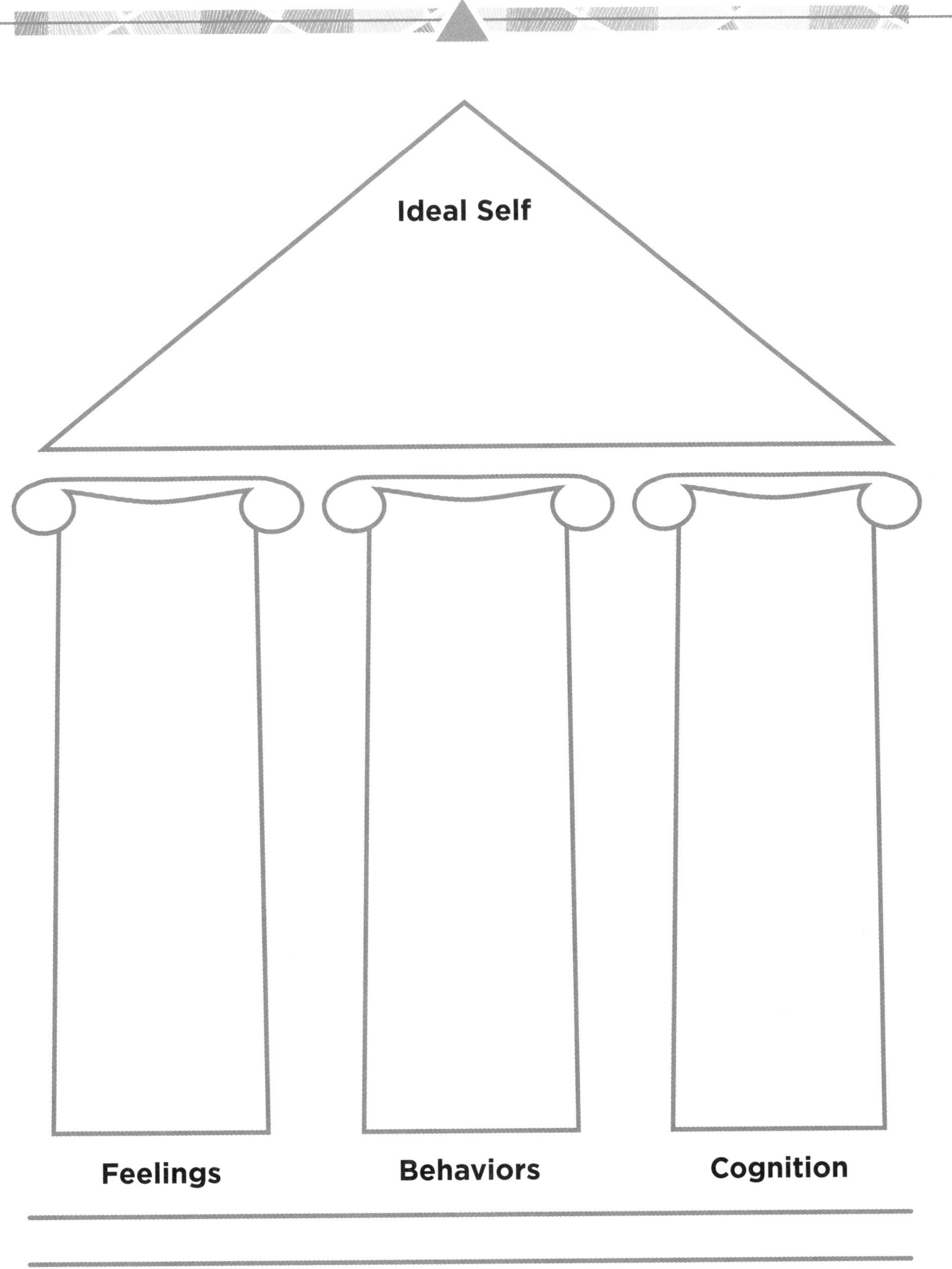

Graphic Organizer for Creating Ideal Self Goals: Secondary Grades

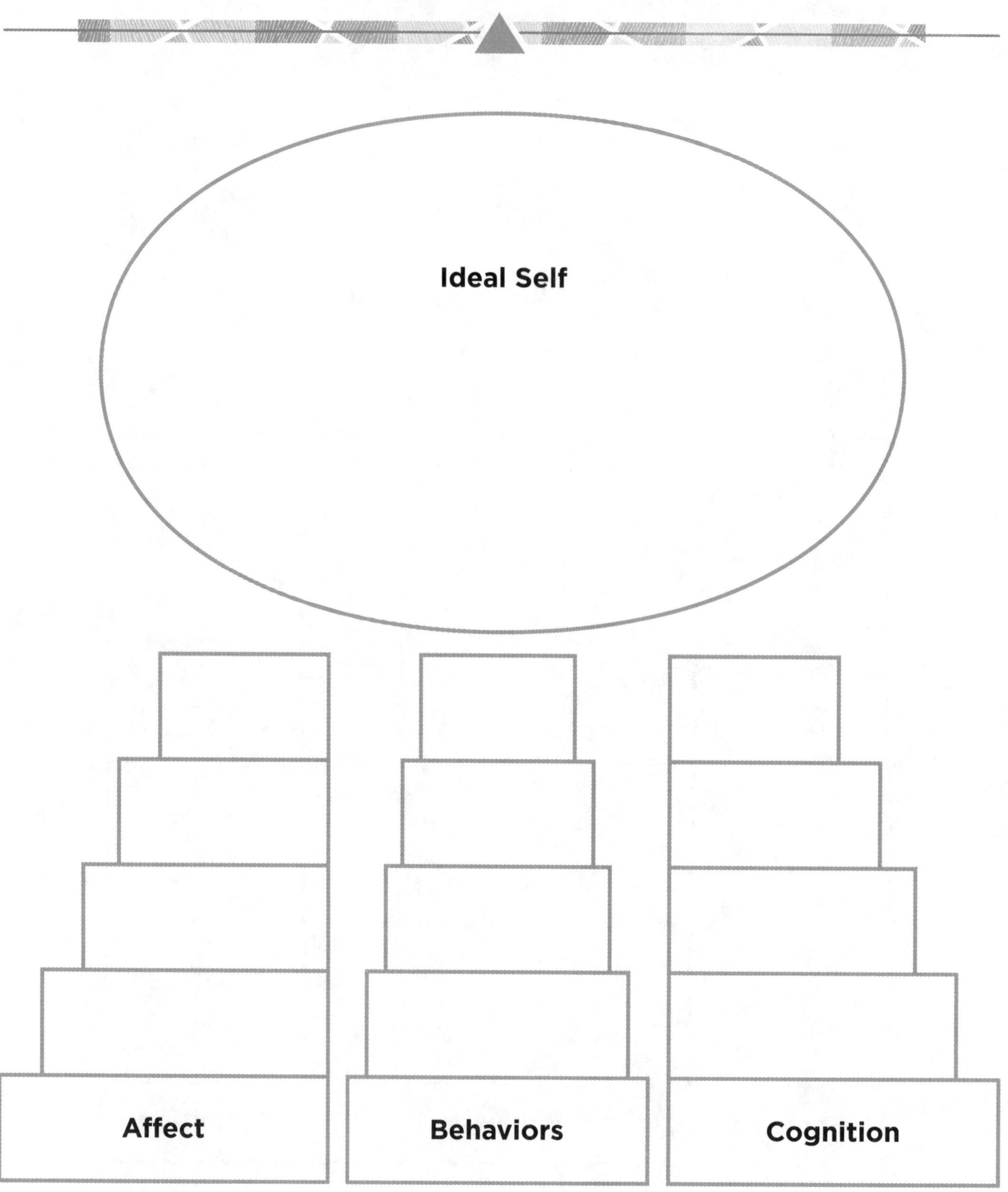

CHAPTER 7
Maintaining Focus

I learned the value of hard work by working hard.

—Margaret Mead

The amount and availability of information today has taught many of our students that learning should be quick and effortless. Many students have no working knowledge of persistence, perseverance, and patience. Therefore, it is essential for teachers and parents to guide students specifically in applying tools of self-regulation during the process of engaging in learning to help them pay attention, avoid distraction, manage time, and organize and achieve the goals they set. This chapter will provide numerous ideas, strategies, and techniques for assisting students in maintaining their focus both inside and outside the classroom.

To best utilize this chapter, consider which of the following issues your students struggle with and hone in on those strategies. When students have overlapping issues, combine strategies from the appropriate categories to address their needs. Also remember that a student's struggle may not be isolated to just one of the following issues. Again, using a combination of strategies will be most effective. This chapter provides support for procrastination, distractions, time management, organization, stress management, and boredom—that is, we will discover in this chapter how to develop students' sense of persistence toward managing and achieving learning goals.

Procrastination: What Stops Us from Starting?

Persistence is the ability to continuously engage in and put effort forward to accomplish a chore. One of the enemies of persistence is *procrastination*. Procrastination is the postponing or lack of initiating tasks that need to be accomplished to reach a goal. We all suffer from various degrees of procrastination from minor ("I'll do it later") to major ("I will do anything *except* that"). When procrastination becomes crippling or stress-producing, it is time to deal with it. Some of the many causes of procrastination are:

- A false sense of security in one's abilities to accomplish a task in a given amount of time
- The misperception of "working better under pressure" which can actually limit one's options to control the outcome
- Low self-belief in abilities
- Unrealistic expectations of self (set by self or others)
- Avoidance of challenging goals
- Over-scheduling (too many other things to do)
- Poor time management
- Lowered sense of value, worth, or ownership of the process
- Need to manipulate

- Need for extrinsic reward (I'll do this only if I get . . .)
- Stress or pressure
- Lack of awareness of a repeated pattern of procrastination as a reason for failure
- Need for excitement in doing things at the last minute
- Task difficulty
- Lacking skills to perform
- Fear of failure
- Perfectionism

Because there are so many roots to full-blown procrastination, there is no one best way to help students overcome the issue. But we can help them identify what is and is not procrastination. The following behaviors do *not* indicate procrastination.

- Waiting for the spark of inspiration
- Being caught in a rut
- Thinking about a topic before beginning
- Delaying gratification
- Taking time away from a project to recharge
- Spending time with an idea to connect it to other ideas
- Slowing down to "smell the roses" or see all the other options

When we have identified procrastinators and the students are self-aware, we can guide them through a process to alleviate or eliminate their procrastination to help them become better at developing a greater sense of self-regulation. Some options for helping students avoid procrastination:

- Do or think the opposite.
  - If you think about doing it "tomorrow," do it TODAY.
  - If you think it will be too hard, repeat to yourself: "Even though it may be tough, I can do this."
  - If you think you don't have the skills, say: "I DO have the skills, and may need help."
  - If you feel out of control, take control.
  - If you think you don't have time, make time.
- Know when it is "good enough."
- Praise yourself for getting started, for sticking to it, for getting it completed.
- Know that mistakes will be made—but a mistake is a learning opportunity.
- Seek out help—asking for help is NOT a sign of weakness—it's a sign of good character.
- Take short breaks to refresh, recharge, and revitalize.
- Give yourself compliments and accept them from others.
- See Figure 7.1 Procrastination—For/Against/Questions Example and the accompanying reproducible form on page 95.
- Use your ABCs.
  - Affective: How will it feel when the task is completed?
  - Behavioral: What do I need to do to get it done?
  - Cognition: Which thinking tools will be most useful?

More ideas for assisting students with procrastination:

- Breaking the task into smaller steps will make the overall project seem more manageable.
- Set manageable time limits *(I'll work for 20 minutes* or *I will work each day on the project for one hour).*
- Start small, but start somewhere.
- Tell others your plan—this will help you stay on top of the work, knowing others know.
- Get a study-buddy—someone who will encourage you, guide you, and help you.
- Modify your environment—frequently change where you do the work—this will give you a fresh perspective and may make the overall work seem new each time.
- Accept that there will be backsliding—be prepared for setbacks, obstacles, intrusions,

interruptions, and those unexpected occasions.

Avoiding Distractions: Staying Focused

Today's students must learn to avoid the almost constant level of distractions in their daily life. From smartphones, to text messages, to social media, our kids are bombarded with nonstop information—not all of it valuable in helping them reach their goals. Distraction and procrastination are intertwined—one can produce the other. Therefore, teaching students how to avoid or at least delay the distractions can be a useful tool in learning.

Strategies to assist learners in avoiding distractions are:

Know yourself as a learner. Identify the way you learn best. Whether through reading about information, listening to new ideas, or doing activities that help you make sense of a topic, knowing how you learn helps you when it comes to focusing on and completing a task with little distraction.

Get your distractions out of the way before you start a project. Spend time upfront getting the distractions out of your system.

Think *won't* instead of *can't*. Don't think about a tempting distraction as something you *can't* do. Think of it as something that you *won't* do. *Can't* thinking, such as *I can't text my friends while I'm studying*, is "out-of-control" thinking, which means that you take no responsibilities for your actions. Whereas, *won't* thinking *(I won't text my friends while I'm studying)* means you are in control of your actions and thoughts.

Set a time during the day where there will be NO distractions—shut down social media, eliminate texting, only use the Internet for research or idea generation.

Get a study-buddy who will help you stay on task. Choose this person wisely; you want to make sure this person can also avoid distractions.

Outline, make a schedule, or use a planner to decide what needs to be done. Put time limitations on the work you are doing.

From your outline, **schedule or create a prioritized list.** Do one thing at a time. Plus, decide whether everything needs to be done today or whether some things can wait until the next study period.

Make time to be distracted. For every hour of focus, give yourself five to ten minutes to engage in texting or social media (*if* this limit is realistic for you!).

Frequently change where you study to provide a fresh look on thinking and learning. Studies show that when we routinely change our positions, we actually remember more when we are in the new setting.

List and then eliminate those things that are potentially distracting. You may have to put your phone in another room, turn off the music, or tell your friends you are not available from 8 a.m. until noon. Clean up your space to make it free of the distractions.

Figure 7.1 **Procrastination—For/Against/Questions Example**

+ For Procrastination	- Against Procrastination	? Questions/Unknowns
I have better things to do.	If I get a start on it now, I can finish it in time to do what I want.	How long will it take me? What will be the consequences if I don't make the deadline?
I don't know where to start.	I should just start somewhere, at least I will get started.	Will I be on the right track? Can I ask someone to check if I have picked a good starting place?
I don't like this topic.	Maybe I will learn something from this topic.	Will my teacher allow me to switch topics? Can I figure out some connection to my interests?

Know how to get back on track after a distraction. Some things can't be ignored, such as a call from your mom, a fire drill, or announcement interruptions. Take a moment to breathe and then refocus.

When you do get distracted, **adjust your time frame to accommodate for the distraction.** If you spent five minutes texting your friend in the middle of a task, then expand your study time by five minutes. Don't look at it as a punishment but rather as an adjustment you can control.

Don't allow others to control your focus. Avoid sitting with or near those students who may not be as well-regulated as you would like to be or are. Don't let them bother you. If they do, seek assistance from the teacher in adjusting your situation.

Reward yourself when you have met your goal. If you plan for a 50-minute period of distraction-free work time and you make it, give yourself a reward of doing something fun or simply go on social media to tell others of your accomplishments.

Have students reflect on the ABCs as they think through avoiding distractions:

- Affect: What does it feel like to be/not to be distracted when I'm learning?
- Behaviors: What can I do to avoid the distractions?
- Cognition: What do I need to keep in mind so that I'm in control of the distractions?

Time Management

In today's hurry up, instantaneous, fast-paced world, students need to learn how to manage their time. For students who have activities or responsibilities outside of the classroom, this can be a critical "make it or break it" skill. In some cases, students will have little control over how they spend their time because it is managed or supervised by someone else (such as a teacher or parent). When students do have time in which they can control both the input and output, they will need strategies and practice making it work for them rather than against them. Being accomplished in managing time will lead students to greater self-regulation for learning (SRL). Those who manage time well tend to have lower levels of stress, are more productive, have higher levels of achievement, create more opportunities, have a greater level of satisfaction with life, complete work efficiently, meet deadlines, earn good reputations, are sought out by others when forming teams, and have more free time. The following ideas—some also discussed earlier in the book—are for helping students improve their time management.

Prioritize your day/tasks. Every day, make a "to do" list. Then, using the graphic organizer in the reproducible handout "Most to Least Important" (page 64), decide how much time to spend on individual tasks. See the reproducible handout, "Eisenhower Matrix for Managing and Prioritizing Tasks" (page 96) for deciding the most to least important tasks. As they say, "don't sweat the small stuff." Learn to let go of the little things so that you do not become a perfectionist—be OK with making mistakes.

Set a planned study time each day. Devote time each day to study, whether you need it or not. When you need it, it is there. When you don't, you've found time to enjoy yourself. Schedule no more than 90 minutes per day to study. Keep this time sacred and let others know that during this time you are not available, either in person or virtually. It is also wise to set a timer to let you know how much time you have remaining and when time is up. If you are still going strong, keep working until you hit a natural stopping point in the project or when you run out of steam. Celebrate your "flow" in learning. Think about what got you stimulated to continue to work and how that made you feel. Try to capture that feeling and behavior during your next study period.

Figure out when and where you like to learn. When and where do you have the greatest amount of focused energy? Morning people get a lot accomplished before noon. Night owls enjoy doing things after dark. Plan your study time for your most productive hours in the place you do your best work. If you like working in complete silence, the library may be your best bet. Or if you like a bit of background stimuli, then working in the school commons may be more your style. Avoid working in places where unplanned events, your friends, or media will interrupt you.

Create a clutter-free environment. Surrounding yourself with clutter can make it seem like there is too much to do. Organize your space by putting things in files, piles, or folders labeled by tasks or necessary outcomes. Having a tidy space may increase your creative thinking and critical reasoning skills.

Set realistic goals that can be accomplished. As Chapter 6 stated, setting goals that are doable within your time constraints can be useful in getting projects or tasks completed. Be willing to adjust your goals based on how much you get completed each time.

Store your work electronically so it is easily transportable. Using the cloud or a jump drive allows you to access and continue your work whenever you have spare time.

Learn to say NO! Sometimes we run out of time because we commit ourselves to too many things. Learn to say no to your friends when they ask you to join them for a movie, play a video game, or text-chat with them. Make those pleasures rewards for getting your work completed on time.

Get a good night's sleep. Studies show that it's not about how much you sleep, but the quality of that sleep that matters most in learning. Some people function best with eight hours of sleep, while some function best with less than eight hours. Chart your sleep patterns for a week to find out what is the optimal amount of sleep you need to feel rested and ready for the day. Plan to get that amount of sleep on average throughout the week. Sleep gives the brain time to process information, eliminate stress, calm emotions, and build a healthy body. Don't shortchange yourself on sleep; it is vital to your success.

Know your deadlines. Using a large wall calendar or a smartphone calendar, note when assignments are due and then plan backward. Starting with the due date, back up at least two days and set that date as the due date—this will allow you a buffer zone of time so that when unexpected intrusions happen (the passing of a family member, a surprise party you just can't miss, the opportunity to meet your local representative) you have budgeted time.

Take scheduled breaks. Taking breaks allows the brain time to digest and process information, reduce stress, and support concentration. Taking breaks allows the brain to shift from one topic to the next. Use your break time (no more than five to ten minutes) to catch up with friends to alleviate the feeling of isolation when studying.

Celebrate your time management. When you meet your deadlines and have checked off all the items on your daily to-do list, take some time to celebrate your accomplishment. Give yourself a reward that fits the accomplishment—a small reward for meeting the daily schedule, a big reward for meeting a project deadline. Your reward should be realistic, within your budget, healthy, and meaningful. Avoid punishing yourself when you don't meet your goal. Use your ABCs to plan for next time:

- Affective: How do I feel when I don't meet my goal?
- Behavioral: What can I do next time to meet my goal?
- Cognitive: How will meeting my goal help me be a better learner?

Organization

For many students, especially adolescents, getting and staying organized is a difficult task. When students lack organizational skills, their performance suffers, which causes them to doubt their capabilities. The act of organization is critical to self-regulation both in and outside of school. Organization is the ability to manage materials, information, and time to efficiently and effectively complete tasks. For students, management includes the capacity to prioritize, arrange, structure, and fine-tune the many papers, texts, project materials, and ideas they gather each day. This section provides numerous techniques to improve students' organizing. Introducing and practicing various strategies will help children find one that best fits their needs. Many of the ideas shared in the earlier part of this chapter can be helpful in getting and staying organized. The best way to help students get and stay organized is for the teacher and classroom environment to be organized. Consider modeling the strategies and presenting examples such as those that follow.

Master Notebook System

This method helps students manage the materials they will need on a daily basis. The notebook is a three-ring binder where papers and materials are filed and stored. Either files within the binder or section dividers arrange the work by due dates, completion, and reference. The sections within the system are categorized to make materials easy to find when needed, and they consist of the following parts: in-progress work, completed work, and reference file.

IN-PROGRESS WORK SECTION

This section holds papers currently being used, such as homework assignments, readings for class, or practice sheets. Divide this section into classes. Make a section for each subject that is then organized by due date, with the nearest date first and later dates toward the back. Have students label each page with the due date at the top of the page in a bright color for finding the date quickly. Colored sticky notes or flags are also helpful, but consider that sticky notes can fall off—so having the date written on the page can be more effective. More tech-savvy students can collect and organize materials in an Internet file, and then section off each class or course into separate folders. This reduces the amount of paper that can be lost, left behind, or misplaced. Plus, students can then quickly email or transfer assignments within an intranet system to the teacher.

COMPLETED WORK SECTION

This section can be within the same binder or another binder that is kept at home or in the classroom. Students can reflect on completed work, use the materials for other assignments, or construct a portfolio of work for conference purposes. Keep assignments that show improvement or are high-quality works. A great way to reduce the amount of paper materials kept post-instruction is to scan the materials into a PDF file and then upload them into an electronic "completed work" file. Within the file the students can create folders for each of the courses or classes they are taking. Uploading the materials makes them accessible no matter where the student is as long as there is access to the Internet. Another way to store completed work is on a jump or thumb drive. Students can purchase inexpensive small data drives for each course or subject. The classroom teacher holds the individual drives to ensure the drive doesn't get lost or left somewhere.

REFERENCE FILE

This folder, notebook, jump drive, or Internet file is a collection of often-referred-to information. This would include vocabulary lists, tips for writing a good paper, formulas, and often-needed equations, schedules, and other necessary reminders. Another file that should be included is a "musing" list. In ancient Greece, goddesses were said to be inspiration for and sources of knowledge. The Muses were referred to when people tried to solve problems or come up with new ideas. Using this idea, have students create a "musing" list of their ideas, passions, thoughts, and dreams. Keeping this collection can help them when they are in need of topics to write about or study.

Ideas for Staying Organized

Label all your folders, files, notebooks, and papers. The label should include your name, date due, subject, and other important information. Make sure the label is a bright color and easy to recognize; use one color per class or subject.

Delete materials to avoid clutter. If you are not sure whether the materials will be needed again, rather than throw away the paper, scan it into a PDF file and keep it on a jump-drive or in the cloud.

Make space for all the things you will need, whether at school or at home. At school, organize your locker or storage space so that everything is easily retrieved. At home, get a bookshelf, boxes, or a storage container to keep all your materials (pens, pencils, paper, tape, thumb-drives, etc.) in one space. This will ensure that you won't spend valuable study time looking for and collecting the necessary tools.

Figure 7.2 **Example of Visual Representations of Homework Assignments**

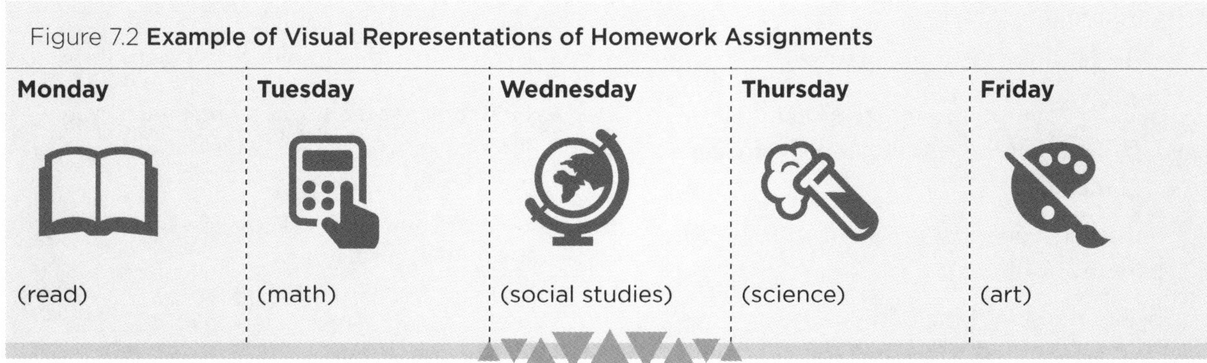

Use a calendar or planner to stay on top of due dates. Many students use planners for school—these can be very helpful in getting organized as well as managing your time efficiently. For those who are more visual: sketch little pictures on each of the dates that reminds you what needs to be done each day (see Figure 7.2).

Use apps to remind you of due dates and other commitments. Download an app to your smartphone that is easy to use and will automatically remind you when projects are due or what you will need for the next day. A key to the apps success is that you will have to stay on top of inputting the information—because the app can't read your mind or know what to do unless you tell it.

Schedule 30 minutes each day to get organized. Sometimes we get so busy with life that order goes by the wayside. Schedule yourself at least 30 minutes each day to plan out the next day, get your materials organized for tomorrow, and review homework to ensure it is complete. Vital to staying self-regulated and reducing your stress is to give yourself time to get organized each day.

Remember your ABCs when trying to get and stay organized:

- Affective: How do I feel when I'm organized (or not organized)?
- Behavioral: What did I do to get and stay organized (or what didn't I do that kept me from getting and staying organized)?
- Cognitive: How will getting and staying organized help me in my future endeavors?

Managing Stress

Sometimes students can get caught up in the stress of a learning situation, when they can't continue or they lose sight of the desired outcome. Stress is the body's natural response to intense physical, emotional, or mental demands. Body responses to stress are increasing heart rate, tightening muscles, and increasing blood pressure. These are all normal physiological "fight or flight" mechanisms that keep us alive.

Students can experience stress in positive ways, such as playing a competitive game or involving themselves in a lively debate. Positive effects of stress include:

- maintaining focus and sharpening concentration
- providing additional or needed strength
- motivating us to meet challenges
- increasing speed
- energizing us
- increasing alertness

Stress can also be the reaction to negative situations such as rushing to class, dealing with an unlikeable teacher or student, or taking a test or quiz. Prolonged periods of stress can lead to distress, which is the negative effect of stress on our affect, behavior, and cognition. Physical manifestations of stress include:

- headaches
- body pains
- digestive ailments
- sleep problems
- depression
- weight gain/loss

- autoimmune issues
- skin condition changes

See the "Symptoms of Stress" handout on page 97. Some of the reasons students may be stressed include:

- unrealistic expectations (set by the student, parents, or others)
- fixed mindset ("I can't do this")
- impostor syndrome (the feeling that you are fooling people by your performance)
- self-esteem issues (whether too high or too low)
- ego (having too much or not enough)
- lack of challenge or being overly challenged
- heightened sensitivities (environmental, physical, or emotional)
- lack of ability to adapt to new situations
- inability to accept being wrong
- asynchronous development (one aspect of the child is developing at a greater or lesser rate than other aspects)

Critical to developing good SRL is identifying "good" stress from "bad" stress. Good stress pushes us to be better, run faster, and meet challenges. Bad stress undermines our potential. A great way to deal with stress is to keep in mind the Four A's of Dealing with Stress (see Figure 7.3).

One of the most important factors in dealing with stress is having a quality night's sleep. Based on research by the Mayo Clinic, get quality sleep (between six to nine hours is preferred) by:

- Sticking to a sleep schedule: go to bed and get up every day at the same time.
- Create a bedtime ritual: do something each night to help you unwind from the day, such as reading a book, listening to calming music, or writing in a journal.
- Avoid using your computer, smartphone, or tablet 30 minutes before bedtime. The screens on these devices are very bright and can trick the brain into thinking it is daytime.
- Avoid caffeine and sugar two hours before your bedtime
- Create a comfortable room and bed environment. A cool, dark, and quiet space makes for the best sleeping. If necessary, use earplugs or a sleep mask to block out other noises and light.
- Limit nap times during the day. Keep your naps to between 10 and 30 minutes and take them during the middle of the afternoon (no later than 4 p.m.).
- Make sure you get physical activity each day. You are more likely to have a restful sleep if you exercise daily.

Figure 7.3 **The Four A's of Dealing with Stress**

Avoid unnecessary stress by managing your time:

- Learn to say "no."
- Analyze your schedule to allow for downtime.
- Set plans and know your deadlines.

Alter the situation:

- Advocate for what you need.
- Take your power back (using "I" language to stay in control: "I don't like the way I'm being spoken to").
- Learn to compromise (whether it be with others or with yourself).

Adapt to the stressors:

- Think positively. It can have a great effect on how you deal with stress.
- Use affirmative language ("I feel best when I can use my computer to compose my thoughts." Rather than: "I don't like writing down my thoughts.")
- Look at the big picture, or "Don't sweat the small stuff" (learn to see the forest rather than each tree).

Accept what you can't change:

- Be accountable for your actions, not expecting others to react to your lack of planning.
- Find the silver lining or learn from the situation ("Oh well, I won't do that again.")
- Remember: NO ONE is perfect.

- Eat a healthy diet. Avoid overly processed food, fast food, and food high in sugar and fat. A healthy diet will lead to a healthy sleep.

Here are additional strategies to help students when they encounter negative stress situations:

- Manage your time wisely.
- Learn to breathe effectively. Take deep breaths often throughout the day: draw in air through your nose, hold for three seconds, and exhale out your mouth.
- Listen to music that can calm you. This type of music can be found under "relaxation" or "meditation."
- Relax using visualization.
  - Find a quiet space.
  - Sit comfortably.
  - Close your eyes.
  - Picture in your mind what it looks like to be stress-free.
  - Keep this image in your mind for at least two minutes.
  - When you feel stressed, think about this image.
- Talk to a friend, parent, or someone you trust.
- Limit the amount of time you spend using technology and instead interact with people in person.
- Play games, go for a walk or run, do something fun.
- Carry a lucky charm (such as a rabbit's foot or special gem).
- Connect with your friends on a daily basis (face-to-face NOT through texting).
- Find humor in tough situations.
- Say a prayer, repeat a mantra, or sing a song to help reduce your stress.
- Avoid raging: count to 10 before you say something you might regret.
- Learn to "reframe" situations
  - Look at the situation from another's point of view.
  - Consider what you might do differently or better next time.
- Believe in yourself:
  - Know your strengths and limitations.
  - Be comfortable with not being good at everything.
- Know:
  - Your likes and dislikes.
  - Your interests.
  - What challenges you.
  - What comes easily or hard to you.
  - What makes you comfortable/ uncomfortable.

Have students use their ABCs when dealing with stress management:

- Affective: How do I feel when I'm stressed? What feelings can alert me to when I'm stressing out?
- Behavioral: What can I do next time I'm feeling stressed to reduce its effects? What effect did my behaviors have on my levels of stress?
- Cognitive: How will reducing my bad stress help me in the future? How can I use my good stress to my advantage next time?

Owning Boredom: Taking Charge

Boredom is the opposite of engagement. Like engagement, boredom is a self-induced state. Boredom is a feeling—the internal cognitive readout of the biological-neurological reaction to the external stimuli (or lack of a stimulus). Boredom can be caused by:

- Too much challenge.
- Too little challenge.
- Lack of interest.

Students with a prevention focus will deflect responsibility of boredom onto others, making it someone else's responsibility to alleviate or change the situation. These students shame and blame others for their boredom ("She's a boring teacher." "He doesn't make the topic interesting."). While students with a promotional focus will take charge of the situation and try to consider ways to eliminate their boredom. They take responsibility and control of their own feelings (affect), behaviors, and cognition ("Though this topic is not my favorite, I'm going to find something interesting that connects with this study.").

The following are ways we can help students shift from deflecting control of their boredom to taking responsibility for it and eliminating it.

Know the signs of boredom. This includes lack of attention, fidgeting, and daydreaming. When you recognize you are heading into boredom or are bored, think about what will help you avoid or get out of that state.

Link your interests to the topic of study.

Surround yourself with active people. Boredom can be contagious. Therefore, if you are with those who don't get bored easily, you will have a tougher time getting bored.

Change the way you do things. By changing the ways you work or adjusting the situation, you can reduce the chances for boredom. If you usually take notes through outlining, try sketching pictures of what the teacher is saying or what you are reading. Moving from the textual to the visual can be a powerful tool for learning.

Don't escape through hiding. If you are feeling bored, don't hide yourself in a book or in media. Break the pattern by getting active—get up, take a short walk, go for a run, take a few deep breaths. Getting physical can help shift the way you perceive the situation.

Get excited about something. Boredom can be caused by our lack of excitement over what is going on around us. Your job is to find something/anything to get excited about, whether it be a character in a novel that is a lot like you or the fascination with prime numbers. Find something to engage you.

Turn the situation into a game. If doing your math homework is boring, pretend you are a spy trying to decode messages sent by the enemy (each number corresponds to a letter). If you find reading a book tedious, read it out-loud using various voices for each of the different characters and narrator. Create a song for the dates or issues you need to organize for the world history exam. Get creative with the way you manage this type of work.

Help students process their boredom through the ABCs:

- Affective: What feelings do I associate with being bored?
- Behavioral: What can I do when I'm feeling bored?
- Cognitive: How will managing my boredom help me in my future?

Chapter Summary

Once students have set their learning goal, it is important for them to know ways to maintain focus and manage the commitment toward the goal. Several things can derail students from achieving the goal such as procrastination, the ability to avoid distraction, inefficient time management, poor organization, stress, and boredom. This chapter lays out numerous ideas for you to model and share with your students to decrease these issues and increase their focus toward achievement.

Procrastination—For/Against/Questions

+ For Procrastination	- Against Procrastination	? Questions/Unknowns

Eisenhower Matrix for Managing and Prioritizing Tasks

	Urgent	Not Urgent
Important	*For example, assignment is due tomorrow*	*For example, assignment is due at the end of the week*
Not Important	*For example, interruptions from a friend seeking help or advice on a noncritical matter*	*For example, interruptions from a friend sharing a fun video or asking what you are doing this weekend*

The exact origin of this matrix has not been identified but is attributed to the leadership lessons from the life of Dwight D. Eisenhower.

Symptoms of Stress

Watch for these signs of stress. If they appear for prolonged periods of time, seek help from a parent, teacher, counselor, or other trusted adult.

Affective: If you . . .

- lack a sense of joy or happiness
- have a negative attitude or behaviors
- approach schoolwork with resentment or resignation
- express boredom
- become easily agitated, frustrated, or moody
- feel overwhelmed or out of control
- have low self-esteem
- feel worthless
- feel depressed

Behavioral: If you . . .

- have sleep issues
- procrastinate or avoid responsibilities
- overreact to normal or simple situations
- suffer fatigue, low energy, chronic tiredness
- have nervous habits (bite nails, chew on lips/clothes, pick at self)
- suffer frequent physical ailments such as headaches, stomachaches
- experience colds or other sicknesses often
- exhibit increasing neediness or clinging behaviors
- avoid being with others
- experience muscle tension or tightness

Cognition: If you . . .

- are unable to get or stay focused
- have disorganized thinking
- lost perspective on normal or simple situations
- are unable to "quiet your mind"
- worry continually
- have racing thoughts
- make poor decisions
- have constant negative thoughts

CHAPTER 8
Building Study Habits

Studying whether there's life on Mars or studying how the universe began, there's something magical about pushing back the frontiers of knowledge. That's something that is almost part of being human, and I'm certain that will continue.

—Sally Ride

A critical component of students' developing self-regulation for learning (SRL) is the building of habits and strategies for study and research. They will apply these in both their academic and nonacademic lives. Every critical life decision they will make from parenting to voting to planning their household budget requires such skills. For students to reach Reflecting, the fourth phase of the engaging in learning (EiL) process, and the Release stage of SRL, they need explicit directions about how to study and guidance and support as they endeavor to learn good habits and skills. In this chapter we will investigate the various ways to develop a productive study environment, explain strategies for home study, and identify ways for students to ask for help.

Maintaining a Productive Learning Environment

To assist students in developing greater SRL, teachers and other significant adults must create a climate that ensures students' affect is focused on being safe, secure, and at liberty to take intellectual risks. Students must be clearly aware of behavioral norms and expectations. Adults must encourage students to stretch themselves and to discover that making mistakes opens up opportunities to learn new things.

Affect: Strategies to Support Positive Affect

These are strategies for ensuring students feel welcome and safe in the classroom:

- Address all students by their names. For some students it may be the only thing that they can call their own.
- Provide space for each student to "own" in the room. For elementary teachers this may be a cubby or a desk. For secondary students this might be a preferred seat in the room, a file folder, mailbox, or basket. Having a space to call your own can help students take ownership of the learning space.
- Develop a classroom community in which learning is the expectation not the exception. Provide students with opportunities to get to know each other by having them share their unique qualities, interests, family backgrounds, accomplishments, and even struggles. Make the norm of the community respect, appreciation, and support.
- Use the "study-buddy" method. Each member of the class has a study-buddy, another student in the class he or she can go to for assistance—or just someone to talk to while in class. Study-buddies should be self-selected and be groups of two (or three students when you have an odd number). In some cases you may need to assign students a study-buddy, but make sure the students can

get along. This is discussed in detail later in the chapter.

- Use affirmative rather than punitive language. Students will feel welcomed and safe when they are directed with positive remarks such as "I really like how Jana's group is working together." Negative remarks potentially create a negative environment.

These strategies increase motivation:

- Post essential questions and objectives for each lesson or day and direct students'

Figure 8.1 **Anchor Activities for Self-Directed Learning**

Anchor Activities are ongoing assignments that encourage students to work at their own pace and with self-direction throughout the course of a unit, semester, or school year.

Anchor Activities should:
- Offer meaningful experiences that extend learning.
- Connect in some way to the classroom content.
- Allow for starting and stopping easily.
- Be expectation- and outcome-driven.
- Encourage student and teacher to collaborate on assessment criteria.
- Nurture students' independence and development of self-regulation.
- Be timely, interesting, and fun!

Anchor Activities can be:
- Used in any subject at any grade level.
- Done by all students.
- Worked on in whole or small groups.
- Independently completed.

Anchor Activities offer students:
- choices
- engagement and motivation
- strategy development for overcoming barriers
- a sense of accomplishment

Anchor Activities offer teachers:
- time to work with individual and small groups
- ideas of student interests
- sponge time activities
- options not offered in the core curriculum

Anchor Activities can be used:
- As students enter the classroom.
- When a student completes assigned work.
- When students are compacted out of a unit or lesson.
- When waiting for assistance from the teacher.
- During days that are rainy/snowy/too cold or hot to go outside.
- On days classes have substitute teachers.
- To enrich, enhance, or extend the core content.

Anchor Activity options:
- individual interest project
- passion projects
- author study
- journal writing
- vocabulary log
- logic problem solving
- learning centers, stations
- early assessment options
- book writing
- Web quests
- wiki creations
- daily brain teasers
- independent investigations
- magazine/book reviews
- silent reading
- experiments
- listening stations
- webinars
- creating a movie about topic
- garage band/music creation
- case study
- games or puzzles
- brain builders
- portfolio construction

Anchor Activity assessment:
- rubrics
- performance
- portfolio
- check lists
- tests
- reports
- peer assessments or reviews

attention toward them throughout the lesson or day. Keeping students focused on the intent of the instruction helps them build intrinsic motivation to learn.

- Allow for interest-based study. Give students a chance to work on a topic of interest, such as through an anchor activity (see Figure 8.1).
- Use descriptive feedback as an ongoing assessment format. Students will feel better about learning when they know precisely what they are doing well and where they need to apply effort to improve. For more information on descriptive feedback, see Figure 8.2.

Behavior: Strategies for Maintaining Learning Behaviors

Strategies for setting classroom behavioral expectations:

- Have students discuss their ideas for classroom behavioral expectations. Not only does this give them ownership of the classroom community, it also motivates them to adhere to the norms.
- Use the terms *expectations* or *norms* rather than *rules*. While the word *rules* has a punitive connotation, *expectations* and *norms* convey a sense of duty and common behaviors, and they have a more positive ring.

Figure 8.2 **Using Descriptive Feedback to Increase Intrinsic Motivation**

1. Give ongoing, timely descriptive feedback during instruction to inform students about what they are doing well and on what they need to focus their attention. If the feedback comes too long after the work has been completed, the students may not remember what they had done, and their potential for learning is lessened.
2. Direct descriptive feedback toward the learning objectives, strategy development, or standards. When giving the feedback, keep the criteria limited so both the comments and students' awareness is focused.
3. Use the "sandwich" model for providing feedback: the first comment is positive, the second comment tells where the student needs to apply effort, and the third comment tells what the student is doing well overall. For example: *You are using the correct method to solve this problem. You may want to consider using your graphing calculator to check your answer. I am impressed by how much you have progressed this semester.*
4. Make sure your comments are specific and focused on what students are currently working on. Avoid comingling too many different ideas into one set of comments.
5. Give an example of how to correct the work.
6. Make brief comments. Too much information is just as confusing as too little information. Focus on the quality of the remarks, not the quantity.
7. Use affirmative language when constructing your remarks. Positive remarks are more helpful to students, even when you point out mistakes. For example: *I can see how you may have gotten confused reading the story. It will be best for you to reread the passage to find the author's point of view.*
8. Do not compare one student's work to another's. This only sets up an adversarial learning environment.
9. Give students examples of quality work (with the student names blocked out). Consider keeping student work from year to year as examples. Make a PDF of the original, make an iMovie of the performance, or take electronic pictures of the project. Make the exemplars anonymous so you are not inadvertently sending the message of comparison.
10. Eliminate the fear that some students have of assessments and evaluations by making your comments to students as conversational as possible. Keep the focus on the work rather than the person.
11. Make comments referring to a growth mindset. The focus of your comments should be on the application of effort versus the student's abilities or capacity. For example, *I was impressed by how hard you worked on this essay.*

- Use affirmative community-building language in stating the expectations or norms. Set the tone by using positive words such as *will*, *are*, and *do* rather than *don't*. Also, use the terms *we* and *us* rather than *you*. Collective terms are more community focused. Examples:

Affirmative Community-Based	Punitive
As a community of learners, we will be on time and prepared for class.	No late arrivals
In classroom discussions, we will use listening skills and allow others to share opinions and ideas.	Don't interrupt others.

- Keep expectations/norms short. Too many will be hard to remember and adhere to. Consider using an acronym or symbols for memory purposes.
  - Acronym: SMART Expectations: **S**peak politely to others. **M**ake sure others are heard. **A**ttend to the task at hand. **R**espect ourselves and others. **T**ry our best.
  - Symbolic: These norms could be pictured: Hands to ourselves. Eyes on the speaker. Lips sealed. Walk.

Strategies for study behavior:

- Directly teach students specific study habits. Study habits are different from learning tools or study strategies. Study habits are the techniques we use to prepare ourselves to learn. In the classroom, practice the study habits in "10 Important Study Habits" on page 112.

Cognition: Strategies That Encourage a Thinking Environment

Embed the following traits in your classroom.

- Students are encouraged and expected to think independently.
- The classroom environment nurtures healthy brain development.
- Students are supported in taking intellectual risks.
- Students feel safe to think aloud, alone, or in a group.
- Questioning and its responses support more than one right answer.
- Social relationships and a sense of community are cultivated.
- Students feel a sense of control and choices.
- Teacher releases control so students can build responsibility.
- Students and teachers are having fun!
- Help your students identify their own efficacy toward the learning activity with the "Student Perception Questionnaire" on page 113.
- Cultivate broad study skills. Study skills are the direct application of strategies to improve understanding, retention, and achievement, and each content area has its own specific types of learning strategies. Broad study skills that apply across the curriculum include note-taking systems such as Cornell note taking, outlining, and idea maps.

Important Study Strategies

Study strategies that will help students improve self-regulation and reach their goals include note taking systems, memory strategies, listening strategies, and study partner strategies.

Note Taking Systems

Demonstrate the various systems and help students find the one(s) that best suit their needs. Cornell note taking, outlining, and idea mapping are shown in Figures 8.3. 8.4, and 8.5.

General Note Taking Strategies

Strategies that students can use to make note taking more effective include:

- Use different color highlighters (maximum of three) to color-code specific information. Keep the highlights to a minimum, highlighting key words or phrases.
- Use different color sticky notes to jot down ideas, questions, reflections, reviews, key words or phrases, and evidence to support arguments.

- Self-assess by covering the main part of your notes with only the key words or phrases visible. Write the full idea by referring to the key words.
- Make connections between ideas or connect the learning in one class to that in another class.
- Use your notes to create metaphors (one thing is another; for example, math is the language of problem solving).
- Use your notes to create similes (use *like* or *as;* for example, numbers are as beautiful as a garden of flowers).
- Record lectures using your smartphone or computer. Then, review the recording and jot down the main points.
- Take pictures using your smartphone during observations or presentations. Afterward, write comments on each of the pictures.
- Highlight, underline, color-code, or write additional details on notes the teacher provides.
- Sketch or doodle notes (a tool for visual-spatial learners); see sunnibrown.com.
- Use abbreviations or text language to speed up your note taking.
  - w/ = with
  - w/out = without
  - @ = at
  - Btw = by the way

Figure 8.4 **Outline**

1. Main idea/general topic
   a. Point that supports main idea
   b. Point that supports main idea
   c. Point that supports main idea
      i. Specific note to support point c
2. Main idea/general topic
   a. Point that supports main idea
   b. Point that support main idea

EXAMPLE: Italian Renaissance
1. Period of time
   a. From the 14th to the 16th century
   b. The transition between Medieval and Early Modern Europe
   c. Great cultural change
      i. architecture
      ii. dance
      iii. fine arts
      iv. literature
      v. music
      vi. philosophy
      vii. science
      viii. technology
      ix. warfare
2. Early leaders 14th–15th centuries
   a. Petrarch
      i. sonnets
      ii. book collecting
   b. Pulci
   c. Boiardo
   d. Machiavelli
   e. da Vinci
      i. scientist
      ii. inventor
      iii. engineer
      iv. sculptor
      v. painter

Figure 8.3 **Cornell Note Taking**

Name:____________________ Subject:____________________

Period:________________ Lesson:____________________

Key Words	Notes:
Summary:	

- Be prepared to take notes in every class and make them as clear as possible to aid you when you come back to them.
- Review your notes during class to ensure accuracy.
- Share your notes with a study partner—have your partner check them for accuracy and clarity.
- Keep your notes organized. Use a notebook, a three-ring binder, a jump drive, or clearly labeled files.

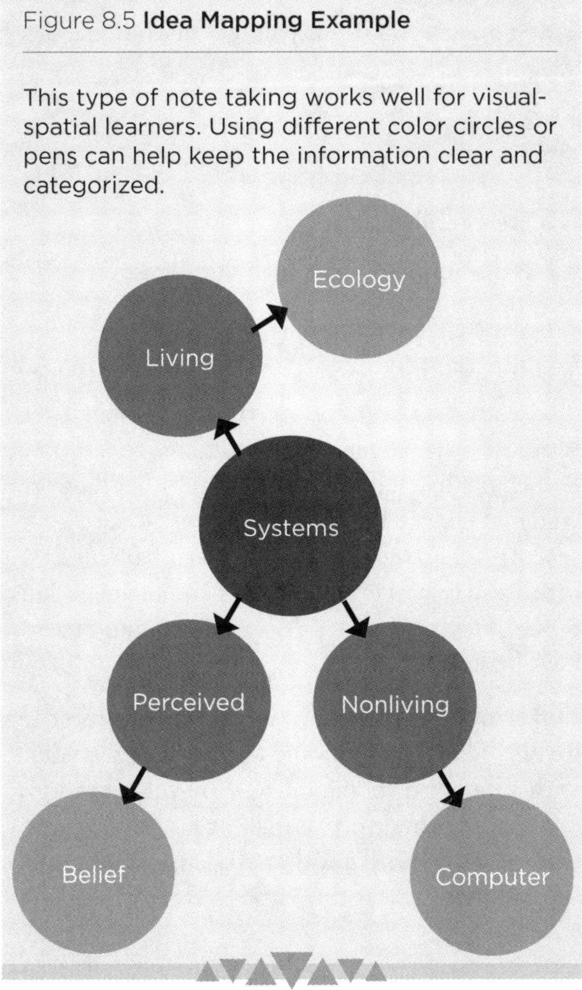

Figure 8.5 **Idea Mapping Example**

This type of note taking works well for visual-spatial learners. Using different color circles or pens can help keep the information clear and categorized.

Memory Strategies

Memory strategies are ways to remember information for a long period of time. The ability to retain and recall information can have a positive effect on achievement. Demonstrate and help students determine which strategies work best for them. Some examples to model are:

- Sketch pictures of ideas you are learning in class. Nonlinguistic representations of information provide a greater understanding of the topic. As the old saying goes "A picture paints a thousand words."
- Create diagrams, flow charts, cause-and-effect chains, graphs, or charts.
- Use mnemonics to remember facts, processes, or details.
  - My very energetic mother just served us nachos = Mercury, Venus, Earth, Mars, Jupiter, Saturn, Uranus, Neptune
  - Oil Rig = Oxidation is losing, Reduction is gaining
  - PEMDAS = Order of operations: parenthesis, exponent, multiply, divide, addition, subtraction
  - PMAT = Phases of mitosis: prophase, metaphase, anaphase, telophase
- Use rhymes or alliterations: Thirty days hath September, April, June, and November (to remember how many days in a month)
- Use physical memory techniques, such as
  - Doing multiplication using the parts of your fingers
  - Physically act out processes, such as the phases of mitosis, with a partner.
    - Prophase: stand close facing a partner.
    - Metaphase: act out pulling apart from your partner.
    - Anaphase: stretch out your arms pulling away from your partner.
    - Telophase: stand away from your partner on your own.
- Use visualization when reading text.
  - Create a three-panel "cartoon" or storyboard (few or no words) to explain the beginning, middle, and end of the text (see Figure 8.6).

Listening Strategies

Being a good listener is an important quality for learning and success. Active listening strategies are also helpful in gaining a greater understanding of what is said and read. Following are five listening strategies.

Look at the person speaking. Giving the speaker eye contact will provide you more than just auditory information, it will offer you an amazing amount of visual information as well. Such as, when the speaker may be trying to be funny, sarcastic, or forceful in his or her point of view. Over 80 percent of human communication is nonverbal—so look at the speaker to get a complete understanding of the message.

Restate what the speaker has said in your own words. If you can restate the message then you are most likely in full understanding of the information. Be careful not to repeat exactly what the speaker says—repeating the message may not convey understanding. Using your own words is more powerful.

Ask questions of the speaker. When you ask well-formed questions you demonstrate thoughtfulness and a scholarly disposition. Well-formed questions first restate the key point made by the speaker, are nonthreatening (meaning you are not angry or upset), and invite a response from the speaker.

Use positive nonverbal responses to the speaker. Such as head nodding, smiling, eyes on the speaker, note taking, and upright body posture. Nonverbal responses that are encouraging can put the speaker at ease, making the message clearer to the audience. Also, your positive attitude will help you maintain focus on what is being said (remember: "how you feel about a situation determines the focus of your attention").

Check for your own understanding. At the end of the message, either rephrase or summarize what the speaker has said. You can pose this as a question (such as: "So, you are saying that . . . ?) or as a statement that can elicit a response (such as: "What I hear you saying is . . . ").

Study Partner Strategies

Having a study partner can be useful in the learning process. Your partner can be someone who

- Helps answer your questions
- Is your "go-to" person when you get stuck
- Helps you avoid distraction
- Keeps you motivated
- Supports you when you feel discouraged
- Cheers you on
- Assists in getting projects completed
- Is a source of information
- Helps collect materials
- Is a sounding board for your ideas

STUDY PARTNERS OR STUDY-BUDDIES

These are two or three individuals with an interest in working together for a set amount of time. Either the teacher assigns the study-buddies or students choose them. Be sure that all partner sets are able to cooperate and learn from each other and that everyone knows about the various types of learning styles. Ways of grouping partners include:

Differing ability, learning type, or interest levels: This is a technique of grouping a student with a higher level of ability, differing learning type (such as auditory, visual, or kinesthetic), or interest levels with another student of lower ability, or different learning type or interests. Using

Figure 8.6 **Three-Panel Cartoon or Storyboard Example**

this technique requires care not to group learners of types and levels that are too disparate, which allows one partner to easily take over, not be able to communicate effectively, avoid doing the fair share of the work, feel neglected/disrespected, or feel burdened with someone who may not be able to proceed as quickly. Keep the partners' levels within a zone of proximal development—not too far apart. However, if both partners agree to the grouping—let it take shape. Sometimes differing level students enjoy teaching what they know and both partners have something valuable to share.

Like ability, learning type, or interest levels: This can be a useful technique for building confidence in both students. The partners can push each other and will have a greater grasp on how to support their partner.

When students select their own study partners, have them keep these five tips in mind: Your study partner should be someone who

- Takes notes or records information from class and outside of school.
- Participates in class discussions, whether verbally or physically.
- Works hard at doing his or her best.
- Has a learning, working, studying, or performance style that complements your own.
- Is easy to get along with.

"Home Study" Not Homework

Few topics in education stir more conversation and controversy than that of homework. Typically, we consider homework any practice that is done outside of the school day or classroom. Most often, homework is practice of what was taught during the day, completion of work assigned during class, or work toward a product for presentation in school.

There is little to no evidence that would support the use of homework as a practice that increases student achievement, test performance, or engagement in future learning. In fact, studies show that too much homework can actually have an adverse effect on learning and school engagement.[1] Study after study and conversation after conversation with teachers, parents, and students continues to cite homework as a huge matter of discontent. Teachers dislike it because they don't have the time to evaluate the materials or provide feedback to the student in a timely manner to have an effect on the learning process. Students are frustrated by it because there is little connection or memory about what they did during the day and what is expected in the practice. Parents hate it because they don't understand the new methods employed in the subject (especially mathematics), can't help their child, or don't know how to support their child during the practice process. So, why do we continue to give, do, and support homework when there is so much evidence that it is not a worthy use of our time (teacher, student, and parent)?

We may continue to assign and reinforce homework because we are still influenced by the educational mythology that repeated practice will improve ability. This idea was created during the industrial period (19th century) when information was less accessible. Today's children live in an increasingly differentiated world where new ideas and discoveries are far more important than the repetitions of the past. What matters more than practice is the students' determination, application of effort, and motivation to succeed: self-regulation for learning!

Based on the research evidence and overwhelming opinions on homework, changing the terminology to home *study* will have a far greater result in effective learning. Reframing homework as home study focuses on aspects of studying rather than working (an often foreign concept to our 21st century learners). Home study is any task that is assigned to students by teachers to be done outside school hours. These tasks can reinforce classroom learning and help students discover and build their own personal learning strategies by engaging them in independent work (aka: self-regulation).

As educators, we strive to interest students in the curriculum and help them see how what we teach them prepares them for the world beyond school. We also want to teach our students to be curious, resourceful, and self-motivated so they continue to learn well beyond their school years.

1. Cooper et al., 2006.

Strategies to assist in reaching these goals include the use of home study assignments that are age-appropriate as well as challenging. Elements of efficacious home study can vary at the elementary and secondary level. Home study at the elementary level should foster positive attitudes toward school and begin the journey toward self-regulation by:

- Making home/school connections with the curriculum.
- Supporting parent involvement in school activities.
- Reinforcing skills developed during the school day.
- Encouraging students to develop their own strategies of time management and work completion.

Home study at the secondary level should:

- Work toward improving classroom and test performance.
- Relate curriculum content to students' lives.
- Reinforce and practice self-regulation skills developed during the school day.

When students are engaged in quality home study practices they are more likely to become self-motivated and put forth more effort, thus achieving higher grades. They build academic success skills by increasing personalized approaches to thinking and learning, problem-solving skills, and other learning strategies. Students also build self-efficacy when they persevere through tasks without immediate rewards (delayed gratification).

In general, teachers can design and assign three types of home study exercises that provide opportunities for students to work toward self-efficacy at the same time they are broadening their knowledge base.

1. Practice. Home study is a way for students to practice, review, and reinforce the objectives taught during the school day. The main focus of practice home study is to provide immediate reward for effort by allowing students to make and correct mistakes, which encourages students to develop independent learning skills. Students can make (on-the-spot) corrections during the practice phase by referring to an answer key or online resource.

2. Preparation. Home study assists students in developing a knowledge base for upcoming lessons and connecting new information with familiar information. This can include reading chapters before the next day's class discussion, collecting information and resources related to a unit topic from outside sources, or preparing to participate in classroom discussion and activities. Preparation home study is not graded and doesn't contribute to a final achievement grade. Home study products do aid in assessing student effort and development of responsibility, a foundation of self-regulation.

3. Integration. Integration home study is long-term continuing projects based on unit objectives. These projects do inform achievement toward academic goals. Students are required to apply skills learned during class work and develop authentic products that have value to an authentic audience. These assignments encourage opportunities for integrating problem solving, critical thinking, and creativity into the products. Integration assignments can be used to enrich units by having students investigate topics not covered during the classroom sessions. The grading of integration assignments is used to provide evidence of academic goal attainment, in other words, summative assessment.

Teachers can encourage self-regulation growth through designing engaging interactive home study activities that boost student self-efficacy and ensure success—activities that are neither too hard nor too easy. These home study assignments should require students to set a goal for completion, be of high interest, and provide a certain level of fun as well. Other practices teachers can implement that build students' self-regulation are:

- Setting clear goals and expectations for each home study exercise.
- Discussing the home study exercise with students before and after completion.
- Focusing on students' strengths over weaknesses.

- Using a home study checklist/log that charts (see the "Home Study Checklist" on pages 114–115):
  - time started and completed
  - level of self-motivation
  - behaviors that are productive or unproductive
  - distractions and how they were/were not avoided
  - rewards for work completion

The most effective strategy teachers can use for ensuring that home study is productive, builds self-regulation skills, and improves achievement is by consistently providing immediate meaningful feedback to students on their study practices. This can be difficult for teachers with numerous classes or when multiple assignments are due. In these cases, limit the amount of out-of-class assignments that require extensive review beyond checking for the correct answer. Keep in mind that home study that cannot be reviewed relatively quickly should not be assigned. This does not include long-term projects or extensions of work from the classroom. Long-term projects and extensions should be viewed as culmination or presentation events where students are receiving feedback at that time.

Amount of Home Study Time

The general rule for home study time is 10 minutes multiplied by the student's grade level. For instance, second graders should spend 20 minutes per night studying, while sixth graders should spend 60 minutes per night studying. For secondary students, the time should be limited to no more than 90 minutes per night. As stated above, research suggests that more than 90 minutes per night can diminish the effectiveness of the study time and become counterproductive to learning.[2]

When assigning home study, be aware of the study time rule and what students can most effectively accomplish within the timeframe. Carefully calculate the amount of time students should spend on your assignments, considering assignments given by other teachers in the same grade level. Respecting this time rule will ensure students have quality time to do other things. Parents will appreciate your understanding of family time and the needs of their child.

Also consider how much time a student should spend on individual tasks during the total study time. Give students an idea of the average time they should spend on each of the components of the home study, so they can plan their total time accordingly. Let students know this is an average; some may take more time, while others may take less.

Teach your students to know when to stop an activity, such as when they are frustrated to the point of inaction or failure, unsure about how to proceed, unable to "get" the problem, and so forth. When this happens, have students document:

- how much time they spent on the task
- what was not making sense, was too difficult, or caused frustration
- what they might need to complete the task

When a student makes an attempt but isn't able to complete the task and documents his or her actions, do *not* count this against the student, even if a parent completes the task for the child. Documenting when you don't understand something is a valuable learning tool and a sign the child is becoming self-regulated.

For additional ideas on home study time, see Figure 8.7.

Home Study Strategies for Parents

Consider incorporating parent interaction within home study exercises when appropriate. Providing parents with tips for helping their child with home study issues can be a valuable way to empower parents to address their child's questions or struggles without interfering with the process of developing self-regulation skills independently. Suggestions for parents on how to help their child study at home include:

- Have a regular time and place to do home study.
- Set time parameters for doing home study.

2. Cooper et al., 2006.

- Provide proper lighting.
- Be prepared for questions—know where to find the answers or support.
- Support/coach when frustrated, but don't do the work for your child.
- Celebrate successful completion of study time by praising effort and efficient use of study habits.
- Limit extrinsic rewards/punishments; instead, develop intrinsic motivation.

Research on Effective Studying

There are many myths in the field of education—such as repetitious practice leads to success—that are actually contrary to effective learning techniques. However, the following ideas are all based on numerous research studies about how to store and retrieve information more efficiently.

- Re-create class notes without looking at the original notes. After re-creating them, identify what you remembered and what you forgot. Add the items you forgot to the re-created notes in a different color pen or marker to highlight what you didn't remember from class.
- Write questions you have after the day's lessons. Include questions about what you didn't understand, what was confusing, or why you made mistakes during the class session. Use the previous strategy to create questions about what you forgot from your original class notes.
- Change your study environment. Studies show that when you change the context or environment in which you are studying, you

Figure 8.7 **Five Ideas for Enhancing Home Study**

1. Have your students select a topic of interest outside of the classroom or school content. Ask them to create a list of websites, texts, or expert resources that can enhance or enrich their understanding of this topic. Studying topics of interest can shift your students' mindsets toward thinking positively about learning new skills and abilities.
2. Ask your students to survey their home or usual study environment. They should look at the surroundings for organization, proper lighting, low distracting sound volume, necessary space to spread out materials, and access to the proper technologies. Ask students to report how conducive to studying their environment is and what they can do to enhance or change it.
3. Assign students the task of re-crafting the notes they took during a class session. If they took linear notes (bullet points) then have them craft their notes into a "nonlinguistic" format—such as drawing a picture of the main ideas or concepts or using a Frayer model (see Figure 8.8). You could also have them re-craft their notes into a Cornell-style graphic or write a script to explain the ideas or concepts within two to three minutes.
4. Set time limits for your students and enforce them. Most research on amount and time required to do homework suggests that the effectiveness of homework recedes after two hours. Therefore, require your students to stick to the 10-minute rule (10 minutes for first grade, 30 minutes for third grade, up to a maximum of 60 minutes for middle school, and 90 minutes for high school). This is a total amount of time, NOT time per class or course. Have your students set a timer or ask a parent to tell them when time is up. No matter where they are in the completion of the work, they should stop! This will help them learn to manage their time efficiently and effectively. They can report in class how much they accomplished and what caused them to stumble or succeed. DO NOT GRADE THIS TYPE OF AT-HOME WORK! The goal is for students to reflect on the regulation process of studying outside of the class or school.
5. Have students monitor their work time at home by listing things that were disruptive, pleasurable, necessary to avoid in the future, and how well prepared they were for the study time (did they have all the materials they needed; did they have help when needed). Again, don't grade the work, but assist students in reflecting on the productivity of their time outside of the classroom.

are more likely to remember the material you are studying. Changing the environment will also help you be flexible in recalling information in different places. You can't always predict when and where you will be required to perform—so changing the study environment can sharpen your ability to access information quickly. Dr. Robert A. Bjork, a psychologist at the University of California, Los Angeles, states that altering the learning environment, even simply moving from one seat to another, helps us in improving retention of information. When the context of learning is varied, the new surrounding enriches information and forgetting is slowed down. Learning becomes independent of the surroundings.[3]

- Spread out the times when you study a particular topic. Research calls this "distributed learning," learning specific information over a longer period of time. Rather than cramming all the information into one night, consider a continual review of information or "rolling" learning. An example of rolling learning: if you have 20 vocabulary words to learn, on Monday study five terms, on Tuesday study five new terms but review three of the five from Monday, on Wednesday study five new terms and add five terms from Monday and Tuesday's list, on Thursday study the last five terms and add 10 from the Monday, Tuesday, and Wednesday lists. On Friday, randomly select 10 terms to test your memory in the morning and the remaining 10 in the afternoon.
- Continuously assess your knowledge. Researchers have found that self-assessment or what is called "retrieval practice" is an excellent way to study. "When the brain is retrieving studied text, names, formulas, skills, or anything else, it's doing something different, and *harder*, than when it sees the information again, or restudies."[4] Continual self-assessment deepens the storage and strengthens the retrieval process. Forms of self-assessment can be:
  - answering a set of questions at the end of a chapter.

Figure 8.8 **Frayer Model**

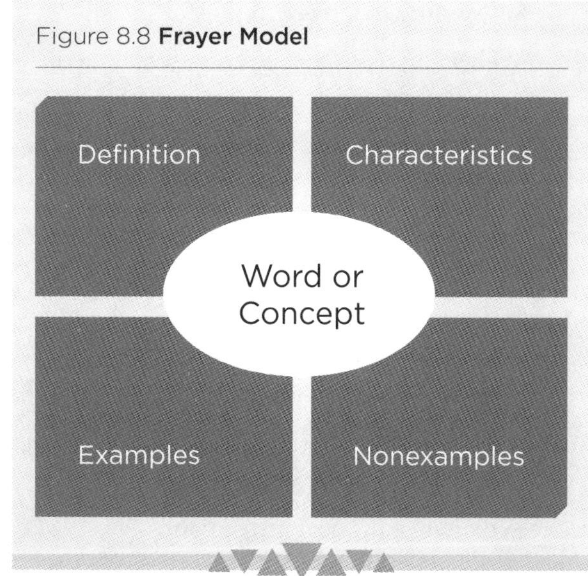

  - solving practice equations.
  - working with flash cards.
  - creating your own test questions and then answering those questions.
  - having a friend test you on your knowledge either through a test or by asking you questions.
  - reciting or restating what you just read or learned.
  - writing a three-sentence summary to capsulize what you just studied.
  - writing a commentary on information just learned.
- Use "productive distractions" as a way to regain your focus and refresh your brain during studying. These interruptions should be kept to a minimum throughout the study period and should be no longer than three to five minutes. Also, be careful that the interruption doesn't turn into an unproductive distraction. Try switching up the modality when you use productive distraction. For example, if you are reading a long, complex text, after 30 minutes you stop reading and go for a walk (moving from a visual activity to a kinesthetic activity). Productive distractions can be:
  - playing a quick game on the computer or with a friend.
  - going for a walk or exercising.

3. Carey, 2014.
4. Ibid.

  - listening to a piece of music.
  - checking your email, using social media, or texting a friend.
  - reading a news article or short chapter in a book.
  - getting a drink of water or going to the bathroom.
  - daydreaming about what you will do next or what you like to do.
  - having a quick conversation with a friend, sibling, or parent.
  - watching a short video clip.
  - playing a musical instrument.
  - shooting a few baskets or throwing around a football or baseball.
  - stopping to check your self-regulation (ABCs).
- At the end of study time, write about the learning experience. We learn more from our reflection on the experience than we do from the experience alone. Ways to reflect on your learning can be:
  - Jot down thoughts about what you learned, how you felt about it, and what you did to stay focused (ABCs).
  - Sketch a picture of what you learned.
  - Draw a billboard or "pop-up" for a website that advertises what you have learned.
  - Create a 90-second movie about what you studied.
  - Create a Tweet on what you learned (using only 140 characters including spaces).
- Give yourself time to "percolate" new information. Percolation is thinking time necessary to process new ideas, make connections between topics, and consider different ways to do something. During percolation, keep your focus on the information and avoid letting your mind wander to other things.
- Vary your study by interleaving new information with something you already know how to do. Example: after practicing a new mathematical equation, switch over to an equation process that you know well, then go back to try the new equation again. Mixing up your practice builds overall mental dexterity and helps your brain identify when things have gone wrong.
- Get quality sleep. Science tells us that learning is most efficient when we have six to eight hours of quality sleep. A good night's sleep is when the brain has time to store information learned during the day, process emotions to make sense of them, and refresh the neural connections. A healthy diet, exercise, and avoiding harmful drugs and alcohol all have a strong effect on getting a good night's sleep.

Ask for Help

Some students may struggle in school because they don't know how to ask for help or seek assistance. Gifted and advanced students can also be afraid to seek assistance because they believe they may appear weak or ungifted. Asking for help when it is needed is an essential quality of a scholar and is not the same as being helpless.

It is important in the SRL process that students identify when, how, and whom to ask for help. Also ensure students understand that asking for help doesn't mean they will lose control of the process they are managing and it may save time in the long run. Encourage them to ask for help by noting that rather than bothering the person who helps them, they will be allowing someone else to shine and they will be creating a positive collaborative learning environment. Above all, it is a positive self-regulatory action because no one is good at everything and learning to ask for help is essential for success. Ask for help:

- When you have "hit the wall" during practice. This means that you have gotten to a frustration point and can't find your way.
- When you are unclear about directions, expectations, and goals.
- Anytime during the learning process when you don't feel secure (affectively), are unsure of how to do something (behaviorally), or can't clarify your thinking (cognition).

How to ask for help:

- Think through your question before approaching a person for help.
- Use affirmative language when initiating the help seeking. Start the conversation with *I know you are really strong with this process. I would find it extremely helpful if you could share with me how to do it.*
- Don't assume someone doesn't want to help you. Using the language above can be a safe and nonconfrontational way to approach seeking help.
- Really listen and observe closely when someone is offering you help. Pay attention to what the person is saying, rephrase often. Ask the helper to watch you do it to ensure you have it correct.
- Stay with the person helping you until you are clear about how to do something or your question has been answered.
- Thank your helper for his or her time and talent. It is always courteous to simply say, "Thank you for your time and expertise."

Know whom to ask for help. Teachers are always a best bet for seeking help. Don't forget to seek out assistance from classmates, other students, your parents, or community members who you are in close contact with on a routine basis.

Chapter Summary

A critical aspect of college and career readiness is the ability to self-regulate the learning process. To do that, students must have strategies and techniques for learning how to study. This chapter highlighted three factors that influence how well students monitor goals. Students should learn to create and maintain a productive learning environment where they feel safe to take intellectual risks, know the expectations, and have the tools for thinking. Students need to learn that seeking and asking for help is not a sign of weakness but rather an indication of scholarly strength. Finally, refocusing the concept of homework to that of home study can have a highly productive effect on students' preparedness for post-secondary learning.

10 Important Study Habits

1. **Set a regular study time each day.** To get the most out of your time after school, set a specific minimum amount of time (at least 20 minutes) and part of the day when you will study. Even if you are not assigned homework, use your set study time to read a book, magazine, newspaper, or website related to what you are learning in school. It's also wise to set your study time for later afternoon or early evening. It's not a good idea to study right before bedtime; you will most likely be tired or the study could cause you to become too stimulated to sleep.
2. **Create a space** where there are few distractions, such as noise, clutter, other people, or visuals.
3. **Manage time** during your study period. During your set amount of study time, parcel out how much time you will spend on the homework for each class. Work on the hardest materials first and finish up with the easiest materials. Don't spend too much time on any one piece of work.
4. **Organize yourself and materials.** Use a method that works for you. File folders, boxes, computer files, and jump drives are all examples of ways to organize materials.
5. **Know your preferred style of learning.** Whether you are an auditory, a visual, or a kinesthetic type of learner, consider applying the style while you study.
6. During study time, **take a two- to three-minute break** every 20 minutes. The break can include a stretch, a quick look at email or social media, or getting a glass of water.
7. **Be responsive to your regulation.** Recognize when you are wasting time or procrastinating. Always do a check on your self-regulation. When wasting time or procrastinating, take a moment to adjust your ABCs. Ask, answer, and act upon these questions:

   (A) What am I feeling right now? Why am I feeling this way? What can I do to feel better about what needs to be done?

   (B) What am I doing now? What should I be doing now? What will I do to get the work completed?

   (C) What thoughts are going through my mind now? How can I adjust the way I am thinking about the work that needs to be done? What thinking tools will I need to apply during the work ahead?
8. **Plan to ask for help.** Identify a person, a website, or materials that you can rely upon when you run into difficulties.
9. **Assess yourself after you complete your study.** Write five questions about the materials you covered (no need to answer them—as a well-worded question can tell you a lot about how much you know about a topic), or use questions at the end of the chapter to check your understanding.
10. **Reflect on your study time** each day. Ask yourself ABC questions:

    (A) How do I feel now that study time is over? What motivated/didn't motivate me during my study time? How can I ensure I feel good about studying next time?

    (B) What distracted me during study time? How did I manage my time and stay organized? What will I do better next time?

    (C) How did today's study time help me become a better learner? What thinking tools did I practice during my study time? What tools will I use next time?

Student Perception Questionnaire

ATTITUDE/Efficacy

How do I feel about this learning activity?____________________

What issues am I dealing with that may be distracting my attention?__________

What can I do to adjust my attitude toward this learning activity?__________

What do I need in order to make this a more successful experience?__________

SKILL/Regulation

Do I completely understand the tasks involved in this activity?__________

Do I have the skills required to complete the tasks?__________

Do I have all the resources I need?__________

Do I have the time to complete the tasks?__________

Do I have the support to complete the tasks?__________

CONFIDENCE/Self-Esteem

Who can I ask for help if I need it?__________

Who can I ask for support if I need it?__________

What skills do I possess that will help me do well on these tasks?__________

What will I do to celebrate my accomplishment?__________

REFLECTION/Metacognition

This was my best work because:__________

I could have worked harder on:__________

Next time I will:__________

Adapted from *Advancing Differentiation* by Richard M. Cash, Ed.D., Free Spirit Publishing Inc., 2011. Used with permission.

Home Study Checklist

Name: ______________________ Date: ______________

Class: ______________________ Period: ______________

Assignment: ______________________________

In your own words, state the goal of the assignment or exercise: ______________

____

____

The assignment is due: ______________

Steps to completing the assignment:

1. ______________________________
2. ______________________________
3. ______________________________
4. ______________________________
5. ______________________________

Materials needed:

1. ______________________________
2. ______________________________
3. ______________________________
4. ______________________________
5. ______________________________

Reward for completing the assignment and turning it in on time: ______________

____

continued ➡

Home Study Checklist (continued)

WHILE WORKING AT HOME ON THE ASSIGNMENT

Time started: ________ Time stopped: ________

Amount of minutes devoted to assignment: ________

Motivation level (My interest level while doing the assignment)

(Low) 1 2 3 4 5 (High)

During my work time, I was thinking about: ____________________

____

____

____

____

Distractions I encountered during my work time: ____________________

____

____

____

Productivity level

(Low) 1 2 3 4 5 (High)

What I will do differently next time: ____________________

____

____

____

____

What I will do the same next time: ____________________

____

____

____

____

CHAPTER 9

Reflecting and Relaxing

Reflection—true reflection—leads to action.

—Paulo Freire

This chapter provides support for the final phase of the engaging in learning (EiL) loop. Reflection is the method through which we think about our affect, behaviors, and cognition while processing what we have achieved. Think of reflection as the solidifying action of the four phases of EiL. Included in this chapter are strategies and techniques for students to use to help them analyze their ABCs (affect, behavior, and cognition) for creating and maintaining success.

Additionally, I've included ideas for assisting your students in developing their relaxation abilities. In this case, relaxation will go beyond entering a contemplative state to also include finding time for enjoyment both in and out of school. "Students with a leisure time engagement of one to four hours a week had a significantly more positive attitude toward schooling compared to students spending no time in leisure activities."[1] Research about the amount of time students devote to studying and leisure (or competing) activities suggests that there must be a balance between these activities. The challenge is to find that "just right" balance between the act of studying and relaxation or leisure activities to create an integrated continuum of equilibrium.

Reflection on Learning

From classic Greek philosopher Plato ("Know thy self") to progressive education expert John Dewey ("We do not learn from experience . . . we learn from reflecting on the experience"), to Brazilian educator and critical pedagogy philosopher Paulo Freire ("Reflection—true reflection—leads to action"), the act of reflection has long been an important part of the learning process. Reflection is the act of analyzing, interpreting, and making judgments upon experiences. The impact of reflection happens when students are able to reflect and make positive adjustments to their affect, behaviors, and cognition. Many students don't know how or are not provided the time and opportunity to do effective reflection. For gifted and struggling learners, directly modeling and including practices of reflection can significantly improve students' self-regulation for learning (SRL) and thus, their achievement.

The act of reflection prior to, during, and post-instruction is a process that has been recommended for decades but has not been implemented often in the classroom. For students to be fully self-regulated, we must assist them in developing an effective way to reflect not only on what they have learned (the cognitive dimension) but also on the feelings and motivations associated with learning (the affective dimension) and what they did to achieve (behavioral dimension).

Characteristics of a Reflective Classroom

Reflective practices in the classroom result in these student behaviors:

1. Schunk and Zimmerman, 2008, p. 150.

Students process information during "wait time." Before accepting an answer to a question, wait at least 10 seconds. Given time to process, students can think through their answers, and even more reluctant or introverted students may offer input.

Students take risks and make mistakes. An emotionally secure and supportive environment encourages students to come up with new ideas, feel free to share information, and even be wrong. Everyone in the classroom accepts mistakes as a critical component of learning.

Students use what they know and what they have experienced to connect to new learning. The classroom environment has materials, diagrams, photos, and other visuals that help students recall past information and experiences.

Students engage in authentic problems and tasks that are worth accomplishing. Teachers construct lessons and projects that include working on problems that are worth solving and make sense to a 21st century learner.

Students engage deeply in the content as they answer questions that stimulate thinking. By processing open-ended questions (versus dead-end questions that have one-word answers), students must take time to reason and provide evidence for their thinking.

Students work in groups to come up with new ideas. Flexible grouping of students based on readiness, interests, and learning preferences gives students the opportunity to bounce around ideas and even refine their own thinking.

Students reflect daily. Students take the time daily to reflect in a manner that is most effective for them. Options are available for the different types of learners—there is no one right way to reflect.

Questions to Stimulate Reflection

Here are some affect, behavioral, and cognition questions that will stimulate your students' reflective thinking:

Affect

- How do you feel when doing this activity?
- How do you feel when you make a mistake?
- How do you feel when you succeed?
- What drives you to do well?
- How often do you seek approval from others for your accomplishments?
- In what ways do you adjust how you feel about school?
- How can you view the work you do as emotionally fulfilling?
- What strategies can you use to keep your focus on doing well?
- Why is it important for you to succeed?
- In your learning and study, what makes you feel the best?

Behavior

- In what ways does your behavior change in and out of school?
- What study habits do you use successfully?
- What study habits do you have difficulty implementing?
- Why are study habits important?
- What do you do in school that keeps you focused on the learning?
- What strategies are the most helpful for you when you meet a challenge?
- How do you ask for help?
- From whom do you ask for help?
- Why is it important for you to adjust your behaviors and study habits in and out of school?
- How have your behaviors impacted your learning?

Cognition

- What specific thinking tools do you use routinely?
- How often do you seek out new learning tools?
- What do you think about when you encounter a difficult situation?
- Why is thinking so important to your success in school and beyond?

- How often do you reflect on what you have learned?
- When you reflect on what you have learned, what comes to mind most often?
- How do you transfer what you have learned at school to other places?
- What types of questions do you ask teachers and others?
- Why should you be able to apply different thinking processes?
- How flexible are you when it comes to changing the way you think?

When to Reflect

Students benefit from reflection throughout the learning process. The following are example questions for affect, behavior, and cognition dimensions for each stage of the learning process.

Prior to learning a new topic:

A) How do I feel about the new topic we are about to begin?

B) What do I need to do to be ready to learn?

C) What do I already know about this topic or content?

When setting the plan:

A) What do I need to plan for in case I encounter distractions?

B) What study tips can I practice during this topic?

C) How will I apply the new learning to what I already know?

During instruction:

A) What is my level of motivation during each of the different activities?

B) What can I do to adjust my behaviors to be more productive?

C) How does this new information help me in my daily life or in future endeavors?

Post-instruction:

A) How do I feel now that I've reached this point in the content?

B) What did I do well or what should I change to get a better effect?

C) What have I learned about this topic that I didn't know before?

Kolb's Model of Reflection

In 1975, David A. Kolb, a learning theorist, fused the works of Dewey and Piaget to create a model of reflection that moves from experience to knowledge application. His design (see Figure 9.1) highlights his theory that "learning is the process whereby knowledge is created through transformation of experience."[2] In the reflective cycle, the learner (1) has an experience, (2) directly reflects on the experience and connects it to past experiences, (3) makes a generalization of the concepts that are included in the experience (by coming up with new ideas or modifying past experiences to fit with the new experience), and (4) applies the new idea or modification to another experience and then analyzes the results for further learning. The cycle then continues.

Kolb's reflective cycle gave rise to development of learning preferences that correspond to the differing types of processing and perceptions we all possess (see Figure 9.2). Kolb states learners tend to prefer one type of learning over others, which then makes different phases of the learning process more or less effective. Kolb's model can be helpful in understanding learners as they develop their senses of self-regulation. He aptly defines in his model how affect and cognition interact with behaviors (observation and/or practice) to create a process through which learners acquire new knowledge in the reflective practice. Figure 9.3 describes the different thinking styles and gives suggestions for supporting each in the classroom. See Figure 9.4 for ideas of various graphic organizers helpful for each preferred way of learning. Examples of many of these are included on pages 132–136.

Gibbs's Cycle of Reflection

Education researcher Graham Gibbs added to Kolb's model of reflection by structuring five key types of questions to assist learners in reflecting and frame their thinking for future actions.[3]

2. Kolb, 1984, p. 38.
3. Gibbs, 1988

Figure 9.1 **Kolb's Reflection Model**

Experience
Reflection on the experience
Generalization of concepts in the experience
Application of concept understanding to a new situation

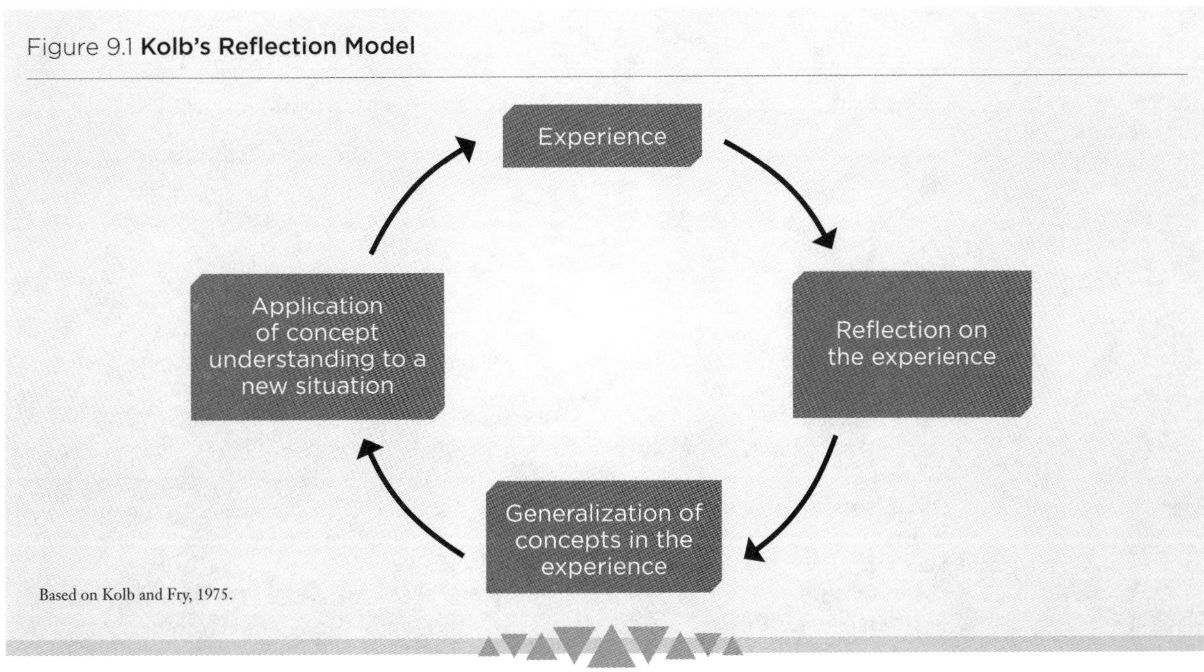

Based on Kolb and Fry, 1975.

Figure 9.2 **Kolb's Learning Preferences**

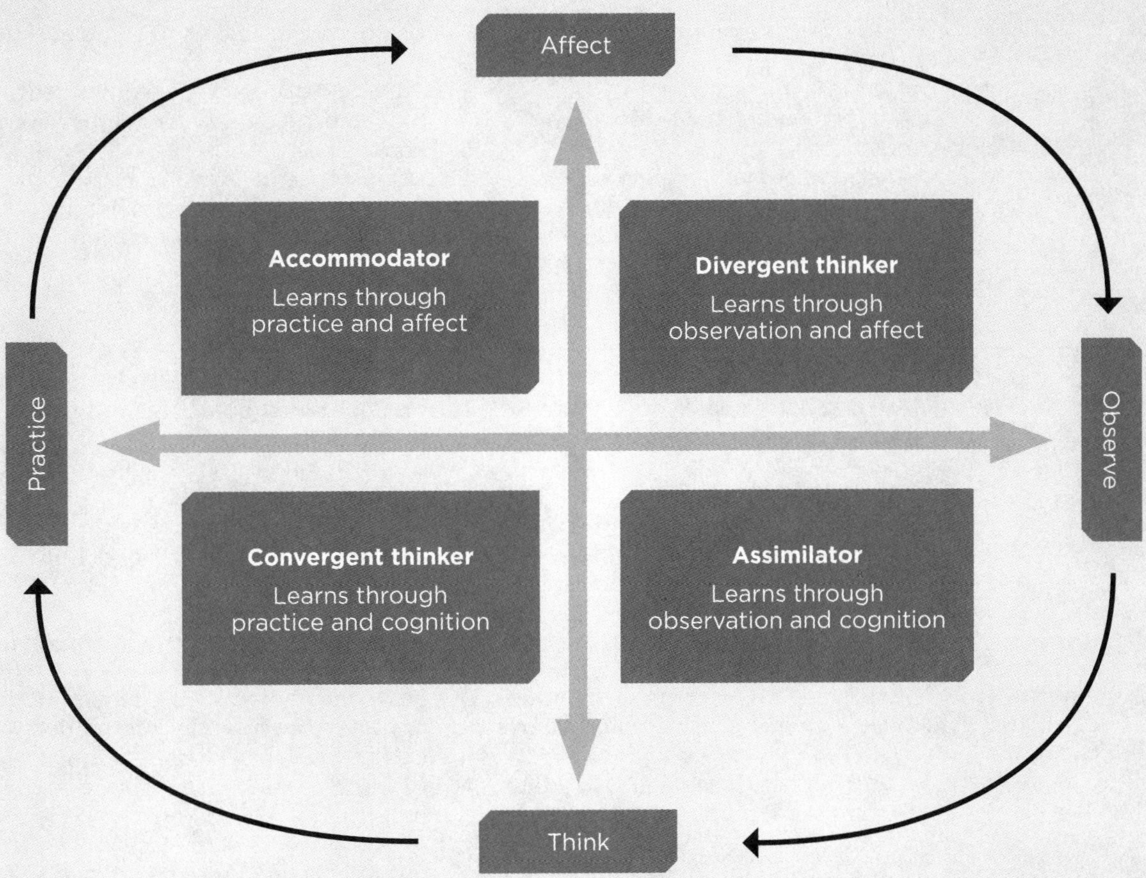

Affect
Accommodator
Learns through practice and affect
Divergent thinker
Learns through observation and affect
Practice
Observe
Convergent thinker
Learns through practice and cognition
Assimilator
Learns through observation and cognition
Think

Figure 9.3 **Support for Learning Preferences**

Learning Preference	**Description**	**Provide support by . . .**
Divergent thinkers learn through observation and affect.	› See things from varied perspectives › Have high level of emotional sensitivity and empathy › Prefer to learn by observing › Like to generate a lot of ideas such as through brainstorming › Have broad interests › Can connect different ideas and topics together › Understand the human side of information › Are creative and imaginative › Enjoy group work › Have good listening skills › Are receptive to feedback › Are open-minded	› Creating opportunities where ambiguous situations can be discussed and studied › Including the human interactions in learning, such as seeing images, videos, or interviews › Providing opportunities for students to work in groups to generate ideas and outcomes › Assisting learners in connecting topics or content areas not often considered (such as math to literature; science to music or theater; physical education to history) › Giving learners an opportunity to sketch out ideas or come up with "off the wall" thoughts › Using group reflection time
Assimilators learn through observing and cognition.	› Are logical and sequential in approaching information › Are indifferent to emotion in acquiring information › Prefer concise information without extras › Are big-picture thinkers › Are more interested in logic over practicality › Are good at mathematics and scientific thinking › Have a propensity toward direct instruction, readings, and models › Need time to digest and think through information	› Providing information in a sequential way › Helping students find the logic in different solutions › Using logic problems to stimulate thinking › Providing opportunities for students to watch logical/sequential thinkers in action › Using sequential graphic organizers › Allowing for individual think time
Convergent thinkers learn through practice and cognition.	› Enjoy solving problems › Are practical in application of information and solution finding › Prefer technical tasks › Are indifferent to the emotional (personal and interpersonal) implications of solutions › Like to experiment, perform simulations, and come to practical solutions	› Offering opportunities for students to practice solving practical and authentic problems › Using situations that require "putting things together" › Avoiding situations that may have high levels of emotional language or implications › Allowing students to try out different solutions and reflect on the outcome
Accommodators learn through practice and affect.	› Prefer to learn by doing or "hands-on" › Have a greater sense of intuition over logic › Rely on others when analyzing data › Prefer practical approaches and solutions › May succumb to "group think"	› Providing students with authentic opportunities to apply information › Letting students infuse "gut" thinking (using phrases such as "How does that solution feel to you?") › Allowing students to discuss in small groups the outcomes and "ah-ha" moments

Figure 9.4 **Graphic Organizers for Kolb's Learning Preferences**

Divergent Reflection Graphic Organizers
(observation and affect)

- Concept mapping
- Frayer model
- Group discussions
- Nonlinguistic representations
- Portfolios or logs

Convergent Reflection Graphic Organizers
(practice and cognition)

- If-then chart
- Cause and effect chain
- What, so what, now what
- Thinking journal
- 5 whys to therefore

Assimilator Reflection Graphic Organizers
(observation and cognition)

- Outlines
- What would happen if . . .
- If-then chart
- Individual journal or diary
- Sequencing and prioritizing/rank order

Accommodator Reflection Graphic Organizers
(practice and affect)

- Cornell notes
- What would happen if . . .
- Positive, negative, interesting
- Small-group discussion
- Thumbs up/thumbs down

Figure 9.5 is Gibbs's design adjusted to incorporate the ABCs of SRL.

Step 1: Describing behaviors: After something has taken place, it is important for the learner to state in a simple way what happened. This can be challenging for some students because they are tempted to draw conclusions or define the next actions, both of which muddy the description. Note that the learner may not be clear about what really happened or what outcome was produced. Ask questions such as:

- Specifically, what happened/what was the outcome? Be as descriptive as possible without using "feeling" words or "I think" statements.
- What did you do or not do to reach the outcome?
- Who helped you reach this point?

Step 2: Discussing thoughts and feelings: After clarifying the specific behaviors to reach the outcome, ask the student to discuss his or her feelings and thoughts about the outcome. Ask questions such as:

- How did you feel at the outset of this project?
- How were you feeling during the project?
- How do you feel now that the project has ended?
- How did others you worked with feel about the project?
- What do you think you learned from the situation?
- What do you think others you worked with think about the outcome?

Step 3: Evaluating self-regulation: Using the ABCs of SRL, the learner justifies or evaluates how well he or she performed. Ask questions such as:

- What went well?
- What didn't go well?
- What was your contribution to the final outcome?
- What needs to be adjusted or improved?

At this point, use the "5 Whys to Therefore" graphic organizer on page 135.

Step 4: Drawing conclusions: Now that the students have unpacked what affect, behavior, and cognition has occurred, they are ready to draw conclusions on what can be done to ensure success or what should be avoided next time. Ask questions such as:

- In what ways could this experience have been more positive?
- What behaviors should be used next time to achieve greater results? Or what behaviors should be avoided to achieve greater success?
- What skills and strategies do you need to develop or improve upon to get better results?

Step 5: Planning for action: After all the information has been unpacked and conclusions have been drawn, it is time to set a plan of action for future experiences. Have the students focus on the prior steps to create a positive plan of action. Ask questions such as:

- Now that you know how your feelings affected the outcome (whether positively or negatively), how will you focus your feelings next time?
- Looking back at the behaviors that were productive, what will you do next time to continue this success?
- Looking back at the behaviors that were unproductive, what will you avoid in your next endeavor?
- What skills and strategies will you need to learn, develop, or refine before you attempt your next project?
- What skills and strategies do you have that will make you successful next time?

Additional Reflection Practices

Graphic organizers for some of the following examples are included on pages 132–136.

Log/portfolio of learning: Portfolio assessment can be a valuable tool in developing students' self-regulatory practices. There are two types of portfolios: process and product. A process portfolio is a collection of a student's "works in process." Students reflect on each piece of work and communicate their feelings about the

Figure 9.5 **Gibbs's Cycle of Reflection Form**

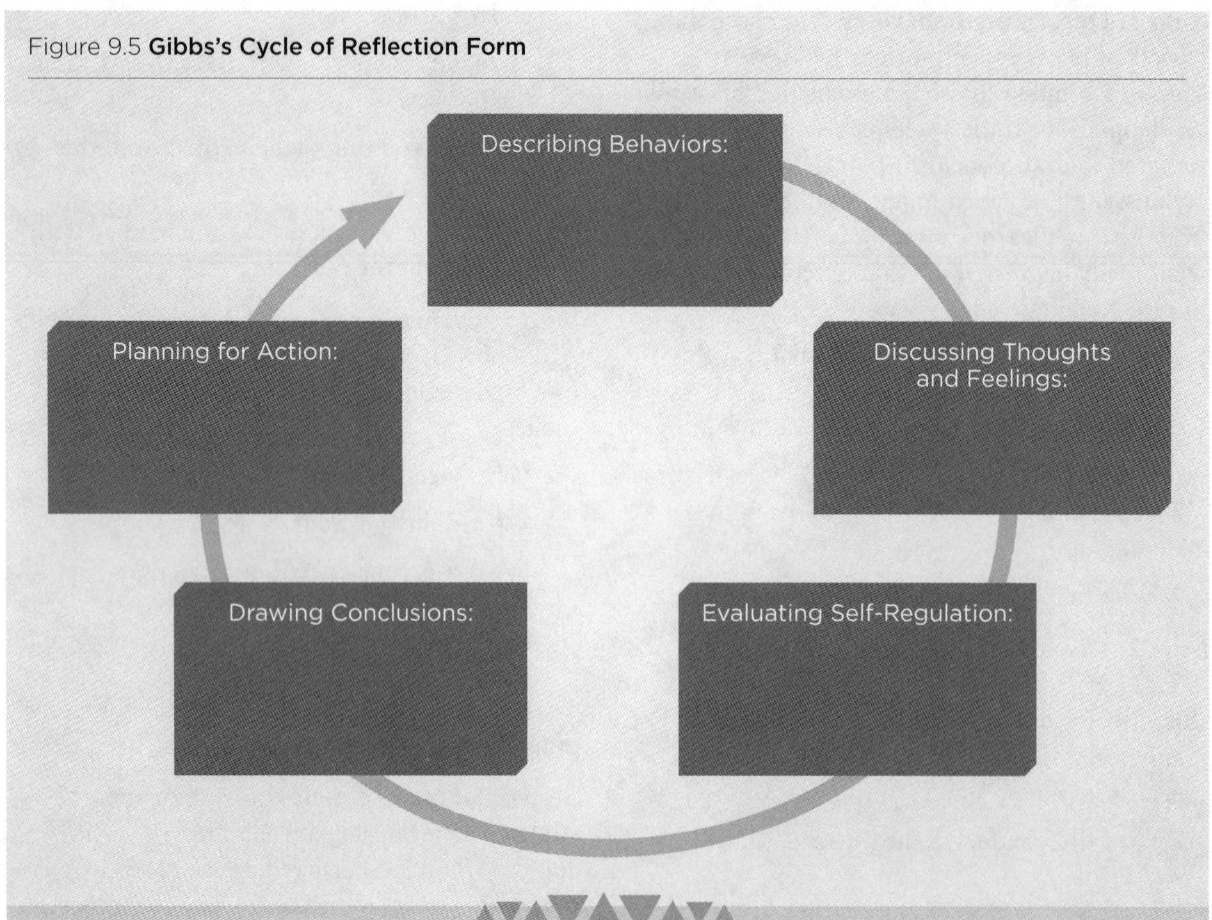

stage that the work is in, what they are doing to be successful and whether it is working, and how their thinking is developing over time. The product portfolio is a collection of final products that demonstrate mastery. For reflection purposes, students should make notations on each piece about its connection to the ABCs of self-regulation.

Conversations among students: Give students the opportunity to discuss their work in small groups to reflect on the learning process. They can compare notes, assist each other in maintaining a positive outlook on the class, or help each other when encountering difficulty. Keep these conversations between five and ten minutes to avoid students' diverging from the intent of reflection.

Coaching sessions: A coaching session is a one- to three-minute time period in which the student meets with the teacher to discuss the learning process—not outcomes of the learning. The teacher/coach asks leading questions such as: "How do you feel you are doing in learning this topic?" "What are your major stumbling blocks?" "What ways do you feel you learn best?" "How might you adjust the activities we do in class to fit the way you like to learn?" The questions are meant to guide the student in taking greater responsibility in the learning process and developing a greater sense of self-regulation.

Journal or diary: Students keep a daily journal or diary of what they learned, performed, or accomplished throughout the day. To organize their thinking, have them divide the page into three columns or rows and label the top row A (for Affect), B (for Behaviors), and C (for Cognition). In each row or column students can note what occurred throughout the day (see Figure 9.6).

Blog: Have students create blogs to post their ABCs using the format of a journal or diary. Blogs become powerful tools when students identify with the struggles or successes of their peers and can receive advice or suggestions from them. Take all necessary precautions when students post material on the Internet.

Peer review: A peer review is a student reflecting on another student's performance. Use a structure such as the "Peer Reflection Form" on page 131 to guide students in writing reflections that will inform another student about how he or she impacted others' feelings, what behaviors were productive, and how well he or she used thinking tools throughout the learning time.

Analogy reflection: Analogies relate one thing to something else and may help younger students reflect, especially on abstract concepts such as feelings. Use a simple three-column format to have children either sketch or write out simple statements about their ABCs of SRL (see Figure 9.7).

Study guides to prompt reflection: Study guides can provide support for students outside the classroom or during self-directed learning. They are a framework of questions or prompts that focus the student on salient points during review of materials. This can also be used for reflection prior to, during, and post-instruction. Study guide prompts can include:

- Before reading this chapter, write down what you already know about this topic. Keep your list close during the reading to check yourself for accuracy. When you are validated in what you know, highlight it in yellow. When you find that the reading is contrary to what you had thought, highlight it in pink. Write a correction based on the text. Focus on the pink highlights during your study time.
- During the reading, take notes of items that you found interesting, contradictory, oversimplified, beyond your understanding, and so forth. These items will be used during class time in discussions.
- After reading the chapter, ask questions of the author such as:
  - Where did you find your information?
  - Who or what were the sources?
  - Why did you write the text the way you did?
  - Could other points of view be considered?

- After reading the chapter, take a few minutes to summarize what you learned. Keep your summary to three to five sentences.

Exit/Entrance reflection tickets: Exit/Entrance tickets are simple notes that inform the student and teacher about items that "stuck" during instruction and/or are questions students have created post-instruction. The "ticket" is given to the teacher to enter the room or to exit the room. From this information the teacher can adjust instruction for the next day or take a quick sampling of where students are at in the learning process. For students, this can be a simple way to reflect on the lesson. See pages 132–136. Examples include:

- *3-2-1* is a listing of three new ideas gained during the lesson, two connections made with the new information, and one question that still remains.
- *Chirp:* In 140 characters including spaces, the student highlights or summarizes the learning. Students must come as close as possible to the 140 characters without going over.
- *Quick Sketch:* Using Quick Sketch is helpful for your visual learners. On a small piece of paper (4" x 5" or a 3" x 4" sticky note), have students sketch (not draw) a picture of the most important point they learned in the day's lesson. Emphasize this is a sketch, not a drawing, so students don't associate this with an art project or artistic work and spend all their reflective time perfecting the drawing. They should sketch with a few lines to capture the main idea and could use a few words to highlight their idea.
- *What's Your Question?* On a small piece of paper or through an email, a blog post, or an electronic bulletin board posting, each student writes at least one question he or she would like answered in the next class session. The question must pertain to the topic and not to unrelated subjects or "why do we need to learn this?" If students do ask "why do we need to learn this?" suggest they dig a bit deeper and ask a more pointed question such as, "In what ways do arrays help me understand my world?" or "What careers use algebra on a routine basis?"
- *Thumbs Up/Thumbs Down:* This simple form allows students to group thumbs up items (what they connected with, what made sense, or what they enjoyed about the lesson) and thumbs down items (what didn't make sense, what they did not connect with, or what was least enjoyable about the lesson).
- *I Felt, I Did, I Thought, I Learned:* This ticket helps students identify the dimensions of

Figure 9.6 **Journal or Diary Example**

A) Today I felt really good about coming to school, because in my FACS class we were going to begin our Muffin Madness competition. I really like Mrs. Swinick because she connects with me on a personal level and really gets me!

I was a little nervous about my fourth-hour class, because we were going to take a test on the vocabulary from the book we are reading in English. I knew that if I didn't do well on this test that it would affect my overall grade in this class. I really want to do well but don't feel the "love" from the teacher.

B) I know I worked really hard in most of my classes today, except for my last period. I think I was just tired from all the stuff we did all day. Plus, I was totally distracted by what I have to do when I get home. I'm going to have to squeeze in my study time along with babysitting my little brother (who is a pain!). Maybe I can find time to study once I (finally) get him to bed . . . that is if he doesn't put up too much of a stink . . . maybe I'll bribe him . . . LOL!

C) Well, I know that I learned I have to put more attention on practicing my math. I didn't do as well on the test as I thought I would, so I need to go back to the teacher and ask for some help on how to do those linear equations. Maybe if I knew how they were used in the "real world" I would understand how to do them. I'm going to plan to stop in and see Mr. Cash during our advisory period—maybe he'll give me a clue as to how this all works!

Figure 9.7 **Analogy Reflection Example**

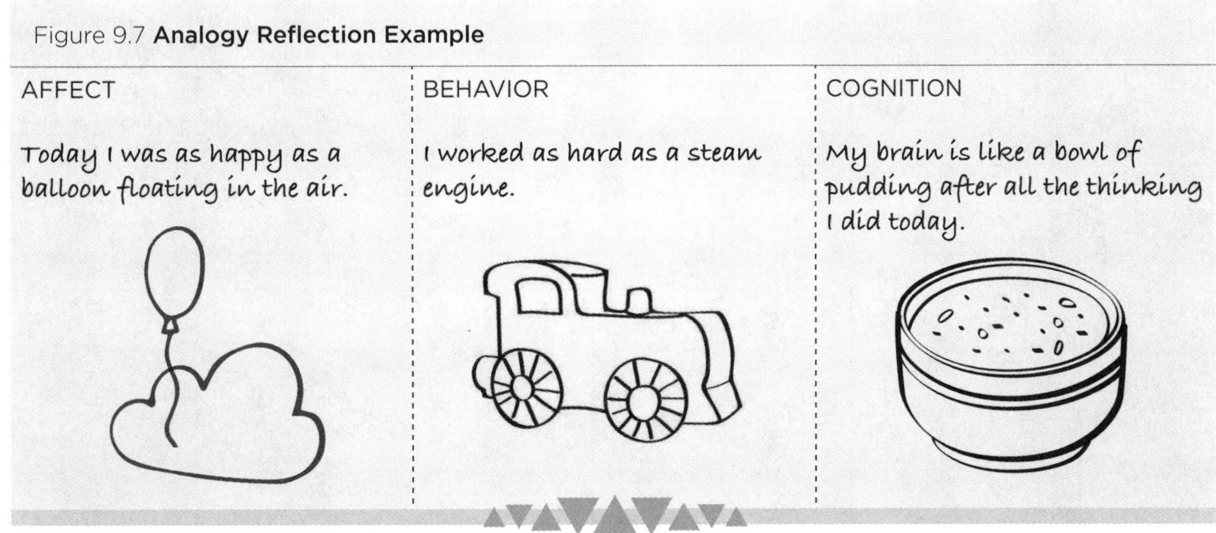

self-regulation during the learning process and leads them toward what they have learned.

Assessment as Reflective Practice

The Teaching and Learning Continuum in Figure 9.8 is a framework for building learning autonomy. Learning autonomy is having sufficient self-regulatory abilities to be self-directed in learning. The model gradually moves students from high dependency on teachers to learning independent of teacher control.

Stage 1: Didactic (Model and Observe)

At the lowest level of student self-regulation and autonomy is didactic instruction, which is directly delivered by the teacher through visual, auditory, or modeling actions. Didactic instruction is necessary for introducing information, igniting curiosity, and setting the stage for further learning. This type of instruction directly relates to Stage 1 in the SRL model. Even though student responsibility is limited, they are still active participants in building understanding of factual, procedural, and conceptual knowledge.

The teacher designs assessment at this stage to check for understanding in mainly paper and pencil formats. Most information gleaned from didactic assessment is based on recall, remembering, stating, or reciting—all at the lowest level of Bloom's Taxonomy. At the diagnostic (or pre-assessment), formative, and summative assessment levels the teacher is the main consumer of the information acquired. The essence of student self-regulation at this stage is attending to information (see Figure 9.9).

Reflection at this stage:

- is based on teacher prompts or initiation.
- is specific to the topic at hand.
- measures initial interest and focus toward learning.
- moves learners to the need for greater independence.
- includes formats such as
  - reviews of assessments to look for errors and accuracies.
  - entrance/exit tickets specific to a lesson or activity.
  - class discussion on what was learned and why it is important.
  - daily journal or diary writing to reflect on the day's occurrences.

Stage 2: Facilitated (Copy and Do)

Relating to Stage 2 of the SRL model is the facilitated level on the Teaching and Learning Continuum. The teacher starts to release control by arranging flexible group activities and offering more in the way of guiding questions and discussions. Students are now applying fundamentals of knowledge as well as self-regulatory practices.

Figure 9.8 **Teaching and Learning Continuum**[4]

TLC Level	Knowledge Level	Type of Assessment: Diagnostic	Formative	Summative
Consultative › Student designs assessment to develop, monitor, and evaluate own learning process	**Self-Regulatory*** › Create › Produce › Hypothesize › Build › Compose › Critique › Extend › Invent › Originate › Transform	› Student-directed investigation to find problems › Personal goal setting › Proposal development	› Case study › Hypothesis development › Personal goal-setting update › Website › Progress report › Expert feedback	› Student-designed rubric › Student-designed product › Assessment by audience/expert
Coached › Teacher and student collaborate to design assessment	**Conceptual** › Evaluate › Design › Support › Adapt › Discriminate › Analyze › Connect › Deconstruct › Differentiate › Examine › Infer › Integrate › Test for	› Interest survey › Contract › Self-preassessment	› Lab/experiment › Thesis statement › Self-assessment/ progress report › Discussion forum › Simulation › Wiki › Reciprocal teaching	› Student- and teacher-negotiated rubric › Teacher- and student-negotiated product › Self-assessment › Peer review › Portfolio › Research report › Contract completion
Facilitated › Teacher constructs assessment with options for individual learners or groups	**Procedural** › Construct › Perform › Solve › Reason › Understand › Analogize › Redesign › Predict › Map › Relate › Show › Examine › Inspect › Categorize › Classify › Clarify › Compare › Conclude › Contrast › Demonstrate › Distinguish › Explain › Illustrate › Interpret › Paraphrase › Predict › Represent › Reorganize › Summarize › Translate › Apply › Develop › Display › Execute › Implement › Model › Solve › Use	› KWL › Guided questioning › Group discussion › Mind map › Inventory of learning styles/modes/ preferences	› Discussions › Reflections › Demonstration › Homework › Research › Exit cards › Oral presentation › Games › Check-ins › E-bulletin boards/e-chats	› Subjective assessment (open-ended essay) › Poster › Research paper › Teacher-designed rubric › Debate › Group project › Assessment stations
Didactic › Teacher constructs assessment based on whole-group learning	**Factual** › Recall › Remember › Verify › Respond › Match › Choose › Define › Describe › Identify › Label › List › Locate/Find › Name › Recite › Say › Tell	› Teacher-constructed pretest	› Quizzes › Homework › Practice exams › Class participation › Performance assessments	› Objective assessment (multiple choice, true/false) › Standardized tests

Multiple Disciplines ↔ Single Discipline

Authentic ↔ Imitation

*Note: Self-regulatory replaces metacognitive as the fourth knowledge dimension in this chart.

4. Cash, 2011.

Students take on some responsibility for managing themselves as they act and respond.

Assessments during this stage are aimed at guiding students toward reaching goals and demonstrating their abilities in skill acquisition and conceptual generalizations. Students are applying basic understandings of the information. The teacher constructs the assessment so that students may make choices or have specific targets to reach. Both students and teachers are consumers of the information in the assessment products. Unlike the didactic level where assessments are singular in nature, at the facilitated stage, assessments should begin to cross over between subjects and disciplines. Students are building an awareness of the necessities of managing their feelings, actions, and thinking as they work in greater collaboration with others (see Figure 9.10).

Reflection at this stage:

- is based on teacher and student prompts or initiation.
- begins the crossover between subjects and disciplines.
- measures sustained or specific interests within the subject.
- moves learner toward independence through group discussion.
- includes formats such as:
  - reviews of assessments and products to look for accuracy of application.
  - entrance/exit tickets generalized to multiple lessons.
  - class discussion on how the information broadens understanding and the need for further investigation.
  - journal or diary writing to reflect on multiple lessons or activities.
  - collaborative rubrics focused on affect, behaviors, and cognition.

Stage 3: Coached (Practice and Refinement)

At the coached level the teacher and student collaborate on topics to study, goals to set, and ways to assess learning. The teacher acts as an observer of the student at work and offers specific descriptive feedback to ensure goal

Figure 9.9 **Assessment at Stage 1**

Diagnostic (Pre-Assessment)	Formative	Summative
Designed by the teacher or curriculum resources: Ensures students have proper background knowledge, prerequisite skills and strategies, and awareness of the conceptual ideas.	**Offered by the teacher based on general goal attainment:** Provides teachers and students an awareness of acquisition of basic information provided during instruction.	**Created by the teacher or curriculum resources for whole group:** Gives information about the retention of factual levels of information that is necessary for greater application; information for next topic.

Figure 9.10 **Assessment at Stage 2**

Diagnostic (Pre-Assessment)	Formative	Summative
Developed by the teacher with students in mind: Uncovers prior knowledge and experiences, and seeks out questions, levels of interest, and learning preferences.	**Performed by the teacher based on needs of groups of students:** Provides teachers and students with broader awareness of the topic and clarity of goal attainment.	**Designed by the teacher with options for individual or groups of students:** Offers information of the depth of understanding and simple application to other content areas and helps in preparing the student for further investigations; provides information for implications of work habits.

Figure 9.11 **Assessment at Stage 3**

Diagnostic (Pre-Assessment)	Formative	Summative
Collaboration between teacher and students: Develops, uncovers, or ignites interests in topics beyond the core; sets agreed-upon goals; measures motivation, skill development, and conceptual awareness.	**Initiated by teacher and sustained by student:** Provides students with specific feedback toward goal attainment; self-assessment on sustained motivation, skill development, and conceptual understanding.	**Created by the teacher with input from the student:** Measures goal attainment; offers opportunities for peer review, self-assessment on performance outcomes, and effort application; provides information for future study.

Figure 9.12 **Assessment at Stage 4**

Diagnostic (Pre-Assessment)	Formative	Summative
Determined by the student: Identification of situations, problems, or issues that have a personal value to the learner; articulation of the level of goal(s) to be set; definition of a process to be followed.	**Sought out by student:** Experts provide specific measurable feedback on goal attainment. Students do continuous self-assessment on motivation, skill implementation, and conceptual advancement.	**Designed by the student:** A jury of experts, peers, or an audience determines authenticity of the product; student self-assesses performance outcomes and effort application; student uses information to guide future practice.

attainment. The teacher is releasing control so the student can build greater self-regulatory abilities. In this way, students begin to manage their affect and motivation, maintain a focus by avoiding distractions, and utilize greater levels of metacognition and infra-cognition. Students do a much greater level of thinking, processing, and self-regulation based on the degree of freedom in the classroom (see Figure 9.11).

Reflection at this stage:

- is based on student initiation.
- crosses over between subjects and disciplines.
- measures specific attainment of pleasure in the learning.
- identifies the level of independence used throughout the activities.
- includes formats such as:
  - reviews of products to identify depth of understanding.
  - self-assessment of self-regulatory practices.
  - small-group discussion on the nature of learning.
  - student and teacher in a coaching session.
  - personal journal or diary writing that reflects on scholarship.
  - peer reviews focused on affect, behaviors, and cognition.

Stage 4: Consultative (Independence and Application)

At the most sophisticated level of the Teaching and Learning Continuum model is the consultative phase where the student takes charge of the learning process with the support and consultation of the teacher. Students are required to possess and enact the greatest amount of self-regulation. The teacher's role is to provide advice, support, and expert feedback. The student is responsible for designing, planning, monitoring, and assessing the final outcome.

In the consultative phase of the continuum, the student must continuously monitor the three dimensions of their self-regulation. The learners are responsible for adjusting the ABCs to pursue a goal and then skillfully reflect on implications of those adjustments. Note that not all students reach this level of autonomy throughout the course of a year or may not spend significant time at this level. Based on developmental and educational experiences, some students may attain this level early, while others may reach the consultative phase in later school years (see Figure 9.12).

Reflection at this stage:

- is student-initiated throughout the process.
- includes multiple disciplines and subject connections.
- measures goal setting, monitoring, attainment, and adjustments.
- identifies autonomy as the end product.
- includes formats such as:
  - personal reflection on the learning process.
  - self-assessment of self-regulatory application.
  - individual report on the nature of learning.
  - student and expert or teacher in consultation session.
  - personal journal or diary writing that reflects application and implications of scholarship.
  - audience/expert reviews focused on outcome and implications of product.

Encouraging Relaxation

In today's world, most students are constantly challenged by an overwhelming amount of information. Our students can't avoid the distractions that tempt them 24 hours a day and 7 days a week. Plus, our students have greater access to out-of-school activities—everything from coordinated extracurricular activities to communicating with friends, in person or virtually. All too often we hear of students who are burned out, stressed out, and just feeling down-and-out. Students with limited resources may have limited access to productive leisure activities and true relaxation when they are free of worries.

Balancing school and outside interests and finding leisure activities can be essential for developing students' self-regulation. Being able to incorporate leisure time and relaxation into the day is extremely important in finding happiness, well-being, and a positive outlook on life. Teaching students reflection and relaxation can have both an immediate and a long-lasting influence on their lives.

Ideas for Leisure Time Activities

Hobbies such as coin, card, or rock collecting; calligraphy; and electronics are examples. Help students identify their interests and have them look into hobbies. Show them how to find others with the same interests through online groups or after-school clubs.

Sports and physical recreation is a great way to foster an interest while getting physical exercise. Students can join an after-school program, seek out a community league, or join the YMCA/YWCA.

Arts and entertainment. Either watching or participating engages a part of the brain that more logical-sequential activities don't stimulate. The school drama group, art club, the local art museum, or a movie group all bring like-minded people together.

Recreation in nature such as hiking, biking, camping, or just taking walks through local parks can put the mind at ease and allow for new ideas to blossom. Also, look into the local arboretum, zoo, or park service for possible outings or opportunities for students to volunteer or get engaged.

Home-based activities. Examples are reading to and with someone, cooking or baking, fixing items around the house, gardening or tending to house plants, playing computer games that require face-to-face interactions with others, or watching classic movies with a group of friends.

Other ideas include:

- making time to spend with family and friends
- learning to play a musical instrument or to sing
- writing stories
- walking daily
- getting to know your neighborhood and neighbors

- setting up a small business to help neighbors, such as raking leaves, mowing lawns, or shoveling snow
- volunteering at the local museum, library, or community center
- learning to speak another language
- studying a topic such as hieroglyphs or codes used during war time

Relaxation Ideas

Encourage students to build relaxation activities into their daily schedules. Some examples are:

- Deep breathing: Inhale through your nose, hold it for three seconds, and then exhale through your mouth. You can add spreading your arms up like wings when inhaling and bringing them back down as you exhale. Take a deep breath at least 10 times per day.
- Performing yoga
- Listening to calming music
- Taking a leisurely walk in the park or around the neighborhood
- Playing a game of cards
- Reading a book, magazine, newspaper, or comic book for pleasure
- Meditating
- Talking with a friend or family member
- Playing with a pet
- Dancing
- Laughing every day!

Relaxation and building up leisure activities takes practice. Sometimes the student may need to try a couple of different activities and strategies to find what works best for them.

Chapter Summary

This chapter pulls together the ideas of reflection and relaxation as methods for increasing student self-regulation. The reflection theories of Kolb and Gibbs provide a foundation for the process and ways in which students can effectively use reflection in learning. Using the Teaching and Learning Continuum as a guide toward building greater levels of autonomy in learning through the instructional and assessment process suggests ways for teachers to release control so students develop greater self-regulatory responsibility. Finally, teaching students how to relax and engage in leisure activities can have a significant effect on their abilities to balance affect, behavior, and cognition to achieve self-regulation for learning.

Peer Reflection Form

Name: ______________________ Review of: ______________________

Subject: ______________________ Topic/Project: ______________________

	What You Did Well	Suggestions for Your Consideration	Questions for You
Affect Considerations › Is motivated › Attends to task › Cooperates › Takes responsibility for actions › Shares responsibility › Is a positive force			
Behavior Considerations › Stays on task › Puts forth effort › Uses time wisely › Is organized › Listens to others › Manages time › Is helpful › Actively engages in the learning › Completes work on time			
Cognition Considerations › Uses questions to understand › Is thoughtful › Thinks before speaking › Uses prior knowledge or experiences to connect › Applies what was learned › Seeks to know more › Contributes new or novel ideas			

Exit/Entrance Reflection Tickets

3-2-1

3 new ideas	
2 connections	
1 question	

Chirp

Quick Sketch: Example

The balance of power in the U.S. Government

continued ➡

Thumbs Up/Thumbs Down

I Felt, I Did, I Thought, I Learned

I felt:

I did:

I thought:

I learned:

continued ➡

If-Then

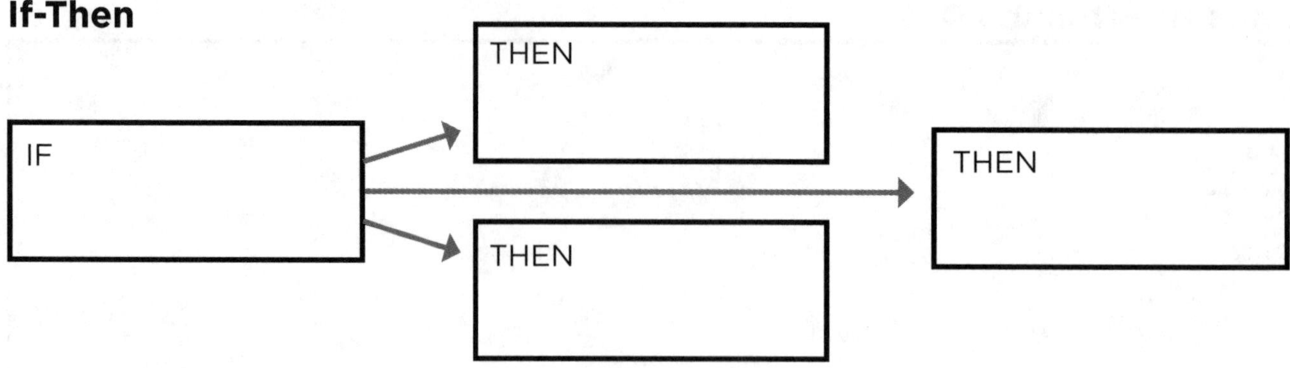

What Would Happen If . . .

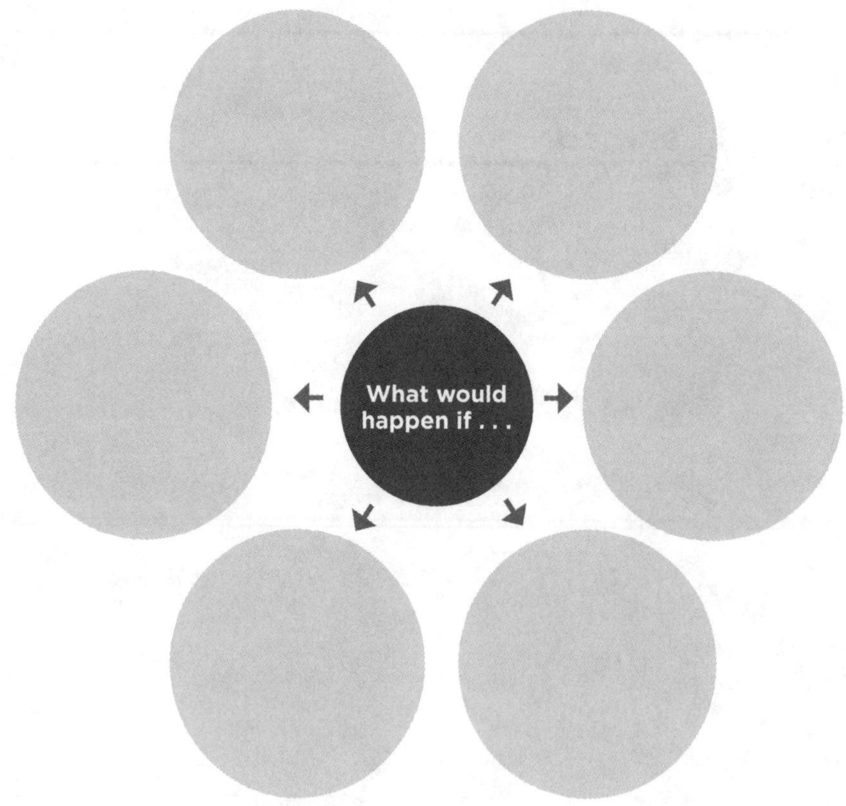

continued ➡

What, So What, Now What

What	
So What	
Now What	

5 Whys to Therefore

Statement:
Why
Why
Why
Why
Why
Therefore

continued ➡

Positive, Negative, Interesting

Statement:	Positive Outcome	Negative Outcome	Interesting Considerations

CHAPTER 10
Putting It All Together—A Classroom and School Plan

If we can bring our children understanding, comfort, and hopefulness when they need this kind of support, then they are more likely to grow into adults who can find these resources within themselves later on.

—Fred Rogers

For over four decades, self-regulation for learning (SRL) has been a popular topic of research in educational psychology. There are varied ways scientists have contextualized the theories and practices of SRL. Conversations continue to evolve about the most effective ways of developing self-regulation in students. Especially in these times of heightened accountability, changing standards, and advances in technology, its important dialogues include teachers, school leaders, and policy makers to ensure the theories are bridged to practice.

It is critical our students learn, practice, and apply appropriate self-regulation strategies to attain success in the increasingly complex world of the 21st century. To solve all the problems and achieve all the wonders of their futures, our students will need to maintain focus in spite of increasing distractions of technology and learn to be both collaborative and independent. We must embed the direct instruction, practice, and application of managing affects, behavior, and cognition.

Our students come to the classroom with social, emotional, behavioral, and cognitive variations. Just as differentiation has become a common term in the language of teaching and learning, it must also become a common term in the development of self-regulation for learning. Students will have differing SRL needs in the various stages and phases of learning.

This book has explained how the ABC (affect, behavior, cognition) dimensions and the four stages SRL interact with the four phases of engaging in learning (EiL) to provide classroom teachers, program managers, and district authorities a framework for increasing student engagement, achievement, and success. Some people believe that students who are successful in school possess greater degrees of intelligence and ability than those who are not successful. However, the significant amount of research discussed in previous chapters shows that the qualities of self-regulation matter more than intelligence and ability in achieving success. Regardless of intellectual ability or aptitude levels, without persistence, self-control, curiosity, self-confidence, determination, and grit, success remains elusive.

In this chapter I highlight strategic methods for implementing self-regulation—from the classroom to a school-wide plan. You will move from knowing and understanding the different types of learners in every classroom, to setting a classroom or school goal of implementation, to direct instruction in the strategies of developing self-regulation. The key to the development of self-regulated learners is a community-wide approach. Working with all stakeholders in the school community is essential to ensure our students are prepared to take on the challenges before them.

A Framework for Classroom Practice

Significant research shows that students who learned self-regulatory techniques along with literacy strategies outperformed those students who only learned literacy strategies.[1] This was especially true for students who struggled or had low initial learning motivation. Such evidence shows us we must incorporate self-regulatory strategies along with content strategies to ensure our students not only have the tools of the content but also have the tools to become autonomous learners. Using specific and differentiated classroom applications can be an effective method for moving learners toward autonomy and proficiency.

Figure 10.1 shows the four focus areas to consider as you plan for teaching students the four stages of self-regulation. The four areas (Awareness, Management, Instruction, and Community) comprise a powerful learning environment in which developing self-regulation includes the personal, academic, and social experience.

Each of the four focus areas has an influence on how learners acquire the regulatory strategies for the fusing of skill and will. Figure 10.2 shows a summary of the classroom applications of SRL to the four focus areas.

1. Paris and Paris, 2001.

Figure 10.1 **Classroom Application Model of SRL**

	Awareness	Management	Instruction	Community
Model & Observe	Teacher provides students assessments on learning types or preferences, interests, and strengths/limitations.	Teacher provides the goal and tells students how to manage the tasks.	Teacher provides students with explicit instruction of self-regulation strategies.	Teacher defines the expectations and norms of the classroom community.
Copy & Do	Teacher helps students investigate various interests and areas of strength/limitations.	Teacher focuses students on the goals and assists the student in managing the tasks.	Teacher defines the self-regulation strategies to practice and guides students toward acquisition.	Students can articulate the expectations and norms of the classroom community and directly follow them.
Practice & Refinement	Students focus or adjust their learning preferences when approaching a task, do a self-check on topics of interest, and consider their strengths/limitations when working on a task.	Students and teacher agree upon goals. Students self-assess how well they are managing tasks to reach a goal.	Students use peer assistance to implement self-regulation strategies. Peers check each other for proficiency.	Students monitor self and peers in meeting the expectations and norms of the classroom community.
Independence & Application	Students reflect on how well they focused their learning type, overcame limitations, and utilized strengths to meet goals.	Students set goals and define the management techniques necessary to accomplish goals.	Students select and independently apply strategies to achieve learning goals.	Students collaboratively refine expectations and norms or individuals set personal expectations and norms.

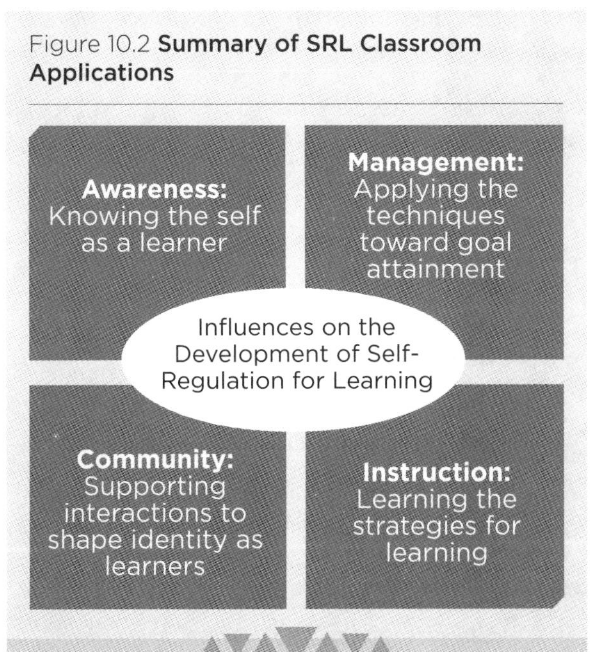

Figure 10.2 **Summary of SRL Classroom Applications**

Awareness

Students must be aware of and possess knowledge about learning types and preferences, interests, and academic strengths and limitations. This awareness helps the learner know where, when, and how to apply degrees of effort to learning tasks. Analyzing their personal learning type (preferring to learn through reading, listening to, or interacting with material) and comparing themselves to others in the classroom community enables students to appreciate that all people learn in different ways. It is important for students to periodically reflect on how they are learning, what positive/negative habits they are forming, what is promoting/inhibiting their progress, and what techniques are moving them toward greater self-efficacy.

AWARENESS STRATEGIES FOR THE MODEL AND OBSERVE STAGE

Teachers should share information about the different types of learning styles and allow students to explore the different types to learn more about how they perceive the world and understand new information. There are many options and lots of materials readily available online. Whichever you use, give students examples and models to help them start observing how they learn.

- *Gardner's multiple intelligences theory* includes the following learning styles: visual-spatial, logical-mathematical, bodily-kinesthetic, musical-rhythmical, verbal-linguistic, interpersonal, intrapersonal, as well as other potential candidates: naturalist, spiritual-existential, and moral.[2] Teachers can distribute an inventory of Gardner's learning styles. Even elementary students can gain meaningful information from this activity.
- *Kolb's four learning modes* include accommodators, divergent thinkers, convergent thinkers, and assimilators. These are discussed in Chapter 9. Teachers can define and model the four modes so that students can identify which best describes them.
- *Myers and Briggs* personality types include extraversion, introversion, sensing, intuition, thinking, feeling, judging, and perceiving. Teachers who choose to use this categorization of personality types can use general overviews of the types available on the Internet rather than the technical inventory, which must be administered by a clinician.
- *Sternberg's successful intelligence theory* delineates three ability dimensions: analytical, practical, and creative. We all have each of these but vary our preferences among them.
- *Four types of thinkers* categorizes thinkers into four groups: receivers, intuitive thinkers, sequential thinkers, and connected thinkers.
- *Learning modalities* include visual, auditory, and kinesthetic.
- *Gregorc's model* uses four categories: random learning, sequential learning, concrete processing, and abstract processing.[3] For more on Gregorc's model in the classroom, see Figure 10.3.
- *Four kinds of learners* categorizes learners into sequential, emotional, problem-solving, and creative learners. Although everyone has all four areas of learning, one or two categories dominate most learning preferences. This model is described in the next section of the chapter (see page 143).

2. Gardner, 1993, 1999.
3. Gregorc, 1998.

In addition to taking assessments or surveys to identify learning preferences, give an example of how you know what your own learning preference is.

Use pre-assessments to identify student strengths and limitations. For example, at the beginning of a math unit on rational numbers, provide students with a series of numbers, some rational and some irrational. From this quick checklist the teacher can identify who does and does not have an understanding of the concept of rational numbers. The teacher then designs lessons to expand on the knowledge of those who have an understanding of rational numbers and designs lessons to support those who need a greater understanding.

Awareness Strategies for the Copy and Do Stage

- Students and teacher analyze learning preference surveys.
- Students and teacher analyze interest surveys.
- Students and teacher analyze pre-assessments.
- Teacher helps students interpret data from surveys and assessments.

Figure 10.3 **Strategies Based on Gregorc's Model of Learning Preferences**

Processing		Learning: **Sequential**	**Random**
	Concrete	***Concrete-Sequential Preference Learners*** - Need real-world examples - Like ordered, linear ways of gathering information - Detect through senses (sight, touch, sound, taste, smell) - Recall details, facts, formulas, and rules easily - Enjoy hands-on experiences - Require step-by-step instructions - Tend to work alone - Require timelines/deadlines/outlines	***Concrete-Random Preference Learners*** - Love to experiment - Need real-world examples - Use trial-and-error in learning - Make intuitive leaps - Need to find alternative ways to do things - Prefer to do things their own way - Rely upon their abilities to think divergently - Enjoy multiple perspectives - Like to solve problems - Give themselves deadlines - Accept change - Try to work with others who value divergent thinking
	Abstract	***Abstract-Sequential Preference Learners*** - Love the world of theory and abstract thought - Think conceptually and analytically - Are philosophical - Enjoy research - Easily zoom in on what's important - Are logical, rational, and reflective thinkers - Enjoy reading - Thoroughly investigate - Generally prefer to work alone - Like exercises in logic - Continually feed their mind - Prefer highly structured situations	***Abstract-Random Preference Learners*** - Thrive in unstructured settings - Reflect on information to organize - Absorb the world through feelings and emotions - Associate ideas in unique ways - Remember best when information is personalized - Do not like to be restricted or in structured environments - Have natural abilities to work with others - Recognize how emotions can effect production - Learn through association - Need the big picture - Must be given time to work - Use visual clues to assist in gathering information

Based on work by A. Gregorc, 1998.

- Teacher assists students in documenting the way they
  - like to learn.
  - enjoy gathering information.
  - like to focus on their interests in study.
  - can use their strengths to support limitations.

Awareness Strategies for the Practice and Refinement Stage

- Teachers encourage students to
  - use their learning preferences in approaching a task.
  - focus their interest in the topic or find areas of interest in the topic.
  - check for strengths and limitations.
- Teachers guide students to
  - adjust their learning preference to accomplish the task.
  - find interests within and around the topic.
  - utilize strengths to complete tasks.

Awareness Strategies for the Independence and Application Stage

- Students reflect on how well they
  - utilized, monitored, adjusted, and performed within their learning type or preference.
  - avoided distraction by keeping focused on the goal.
  - were able to overcome obstacles, limitations, or hurdles in the way they approached the learning goal.

Management

When a student possesses self-management of affect, behavior, and cognition, they are more likely to adapt to different situations, persist at complex activities, and flexibly approach difficult problems as well as be more learning goal oriented. Students who self-manage set appropriately challenging goals, allocate time and resources effectively, and monitor progress to be able to adjust when necessary. They also are more proficient at reviewing their learning and use that reflection to approach new learning without fear.

Management Strategies for the Model and Observe Stage

- Teachers provide the learning and self-regulation goal for the students.
- Teachers model and instruct students with specific techniques for
  - managing time.
  - organizing materials.
  - asking for help.
  - staying focused on the task.
  - taking breaks.
  - reflecting.

Management Strategies for the Copy and Do Stage

- The teacher helps students focus on the goals to be achieved.
- The teacher monitors the students' implementation of the management tools.
- Students are asked to consciously/overtly explain the tools and techniques they are using and analyze how well they are working.

Management Strategies for the Practice and Refinement Stage

- Together with the teacher, students declare their learning goals.
- The teacher assists students in monitoring the use of the tools.
- The teacher reminds students to self-assess their approach to the goals.

Management Strategies for the Independence and Application Stage

- Students set their own learning goals.
- Students define which strategies they will use and when.
- Students automatically reflect on their level of success in achieving the goals.

Instruction

Students need diverse ways of acquiring the strategies and techniques for self-regulation. There are no definitive instructional methods. Some students will learn best through explicit direct instruction, directed reflection, and close monitoring by the teacher. Other students may find it most beneficial to observe others enacting the strategies and involve themselves in activities where the strategies are practiced and analyzed for effect. All students benefit from the self-assessment process. Whether the assessments be graphing achievement, discussions with teacher or peers, or documenting their personal growth, self-assessment is a critical tool for developing SRL.

Instructional Strategies for the Model and Observe Stage

- The teacher explicitly instructs on self-regulatory tools.
- The teacher models the tools for the students.
- The teacher ensures students know the strategies and have access to reminders.

Instructional Strategies for the Copy and Do Stage

- The teacher has the students directly implement the tools of self-regulation.
- The teacher closely monitors the students' use of the tools.
- The teacher asks the students to define how the strategies are applied and when they are most beneficial.

Instructional Strategies for the Practice and Refinement Stage

- In cooperation with the teacher's recommendations, students apply strategies to meet the situation's requirements.
- The students monitor the application and outcome of the practice.
- The students adjust the strategies when necessary.

Instructional Strategies for the Independence and Application Stage

- Without prompts, students freely apply strategies to address situations.
- Students seek out peer assistance in implementing effective strategies.
- The students reflect on progress toward autonomy.

Community

Learning to self-regulate must be woven into the social fabric of the classroom experience. All people desire and strive for an individual identity. In achieving our identity we take cues from our interactions, our environment, and the reactions of others to conceptualize our identity. The first step in forming identity as a learner is to gain perspective on personal beliefs about the worth and value of education. Those who don't find the worth or value in the learning are more likely to avoid rather than approach goals. Individual students must appraise, monitor, and adjust their affect, behaviors, and cognition to achieve worthy and valuable goals and remain consistent with how they desire to be identified by others. Working within the designated expectations and learning norms, the student must also consider how they interact with others in the classroom community. Groups of students should analyze the effectiveness of collaborative efforts and efficiencies of process. Finally, the classroom community should reflect on how well expectations, norms, and the environment have been enhanced for all.

Community Strategies for the Model and Observe Stage

- The teacher sets and defines classroom expectations and norms that are framed around the acquisition of self-regulation and the development of a learning community.
- The teacher models or provides examples of application of the expectations and norms.
- The teacher posts and continually refers to expectations and norms.

Community Strategies for the Copy and Do Stage

- The teacher requires students to recite or cite classroom expectations.
- The teacher arranges and groups students in ways to encourage community development.
- The teacher provides options, such as learning centers or stations, for students to apply expectations/norms and community practices.

Community Strategies for the Practice and Refinement Stage

- Students self-monitor their application and adherence to classroom expectations/norms and community development.
- Students work together to ensure all members of the community abide by the expectations and norms.
- Students offer each other support in maintaining expectations and norms.

Community Strategies for the Independence and Application Stage

- Students no longer need reminders for applying and monitoring classroom expectations.
- Students may set individual expectations or norms to improve their performance.
- Students work together with little guidance or maintenance from the teacher.
- As a class, the students reflect on the classroom environment and its importance to learning.

Keep in mind that the intervention strategies to acquire self-regulation for learning are not meant to be prescriptive—what works for one student may not work for another student. Nor should the strategies be highly scripted in their delivery. Teachers must model, apply, reinforce, and assess fluidly and within the context of the environment. The strategies listed throughout this book are an array of ideas and suggestions that should be adapted, adjusted, or aligned to the child, the setting, and the context. See Figure 10.4.

Figure 10.4 **Six Keys to Self-Regulation Development**

1. Students must be **offered an array of strategies** from which to choose.
2. **Strategies must be modeled in context** by the teacher and others.
3. Students must **learn how to apply effort** when using strategies.
4. Students must **rely on peers when using strategies**, from working collaboratively to seeking assistance.
5. Students must **transfer the use of strategies from one action/context to another.**
6. Students must **work within authentic experiences to apply the strategies.**

Four Kinds of Learners

Helping students understand how they learn best can be an effective way for them to deal with stressful situations. When students encounter difficult situations they may be relying upon strategies that are not effective, thus causing them to be ineffective or frustrated. Take for example a student who is very organized and prefers to learn things in a sequential process. When this student works on an open-ended activity with the possibility of multiple outcomes, the student may not know where or how to begin. In this case, adopting a more flexible attitude or style during the activity can be beneficial.

History

Learning styles, popularized in the 1980s, became a way for teachers to differentiate learning in the classroom. The concept of learning styles comes from a long history in psychology from Carl Jung (1923) to Myers-Briggs's work on the Type Indicator (1962/1998) to common literature by educational experts Harvey Silver and Richard Strong (2004).

Controversy

Recently, there has been a flurry of controversy about whether acknowledging and using learning styles in the classroom can increase student achievement. Many practitioners will attest to the usefulness of varying tasks based on how students like to learn. In fact, research conducted by Robert Sternberg showed how asking students to learn information in a variety of ways led to significant increases in academic achievement.[4]

Four Categories

Using Silver and Strong's work, I have found it helpful to categorize learners into four general categories to help them strengthen their emotional regulation (see Figure 10.5). Not based in any specific research, this typology is based on my experiences with people and what is known about how we learn. Every person is a composite of all four types, though many favor one or two types when learning or interacting with the world. Some students will be able to shift from one type to another when necessary to complete a task. When students struggle in your classroom, consider the following possible reasons:

- They don't understand the information due to the method in which it was delivered.
- They find it hard to shift from one type of learning to another when the experience requires it.
- They clash with the teacher's preferred method of instruction.
- They can't recognize what type of learner they are or need to be.
- When in groups, they are mismatched with other types.

Type I: Paper Clip

A *paper clip* learner is one who likes order, sequence, and timelines. These learners prefer to know what is coming and precisely what's expected of them. They feel more comfortable in neat surroundings that are organized and efficient. Paper clips enjoy keeping time, creating and checking off a to-do list, and maintaining order. They enjoy working through facts and details. They consider themselves get-it-done-type mastery learners.

These learners may struggle or be uncomfortable with random conversations, inaccurate

4. Sternberg and Grigorenko, 2007.

Figure 10.5 **Four Kinds of Learners**

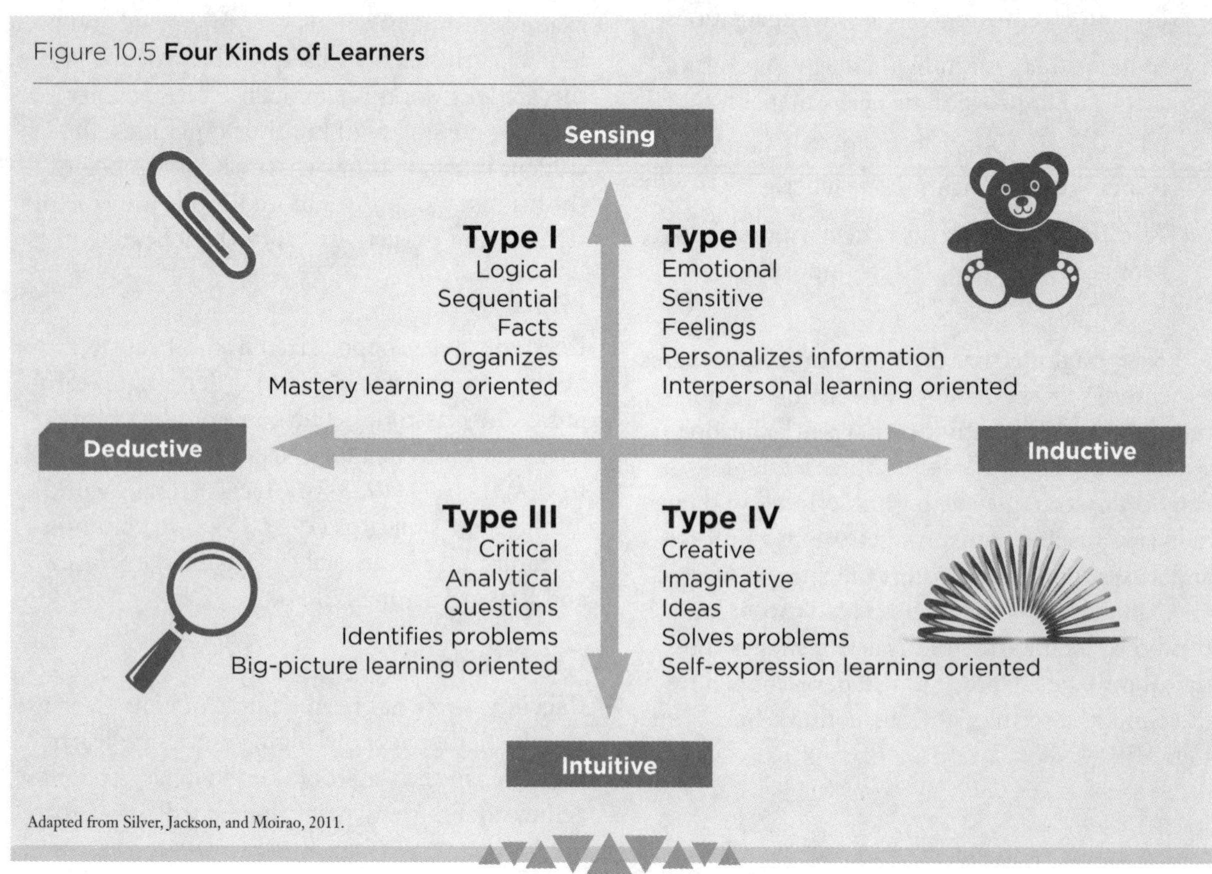

Adapted from Silver, Jackson, and Moirao, 2011.

information, sudden schedule changes, and too much flexibility. To stretch this type of learner, consider including open-ended activities or "messy" problems where there is not one right answer or procedure. Encourage paper clip learners to think creatively through collaborative group work. Let them know it is safe to take intellectual risks and be wrong from time to time.

Paper clip personalities are valuable in situations where timelines and rules take priority, order is required, and problems can be solved sequentially. Typically, paper clips do well in the lower grades and comprise about a third of the student population.

Type II: Teddy Bear

The *teddy bear* is an emotional learner. These learners recognize and pay attention to their own and others' feelings and behaviors. They like to make others feel comfortable, are interested in the other person's affect, and have a deep need for an affirmative environment. Teddy bears are considered contextual or personalized learners—they learn in context, through the wholeness of an experience or from their prior experiences. Teddy bears prefer to work in groups, set the tone and mood of the group, encourage others, and participate in service-learning projects. These are your "positive-type" learners—always seeing the best in others.

This type of learner may find it difficult to debate, watch others struggle, see the factual side of highly charged events (such as the Holocaust or acts of aggression), or be critical. To stretch the teddy bear to feel more comfortable in learning, teach the art of making decisions through reasoning and consensus building. Teddy bear learners should practice working independently on situations that may not be "real" or authentic and build their ability to ask critical or convergent type questions.

Teddy bears are effective when cooperation, inclusion of others, and sensitivity toward others are required. Learning how to be helpful, courteous, and kind will come in handy when situations become stressful—when people are angry, relationships need repair, and teams need to be productive. Teddy bears comprise about a third of the student population. Many teddy bear students may be challenged when they work with facts, with little real-world connections, and with no partners.

Type III: Magnifying Glass

The *magnifying glass* signifies detective work. These learners like to see the big picture and then look closely at issues within the picture to find problems. Magnifying glasses are critical and sometimes emotionless in their pursuits. They can be argumentative—they say, "Yes, but . . ." Like paper clips, magnifying glasses prefer a logical order to information. These learners love to debate, question, find problems, critically analyze tough issues, and form individual opinions. "Straightforward" thinkers, they may find it difficult to work with teddy bears.

They may find it difficult to use empathy in the decision-making process and to listen with their hearts when trying to understand differing points of view. Therefore, they need to learn consensus-building strategies and how to take into account the affective side of learning and interactions. Helping magnifying glasses learn to work in collaborative teams through open-ended situations where creativity is required can help them stretch and be more flexible.

Type IV: Slinky

The *Slinky* is a creative, abstract student. These learners know where they want to go, but they may take multiple pathways to get there. "Coloring outside the lines," they generate new ideas and ways to do things, do projects their own way, think imaginatively, and create fantasies. These are true "out of the box" thinkers and doers. These students are self-expressive in that they share their learning overtly and through personalization. They need space to move and create, like open-ended activities, and are quick to find solutions.

Because they have difficulty with too much structure and get restless when not flexing their creative muscle, the Slinky is easily annoyed by the paper clip. To stretch the Slinky, use checklists and graphic sequences (such as timelines or calendars). Have Slinkys focus on meeting deadlines by using contracts; have them refer to the contracts throughout the work process. Also, encourage them to use wait-time and think-time to ponder ideas, rather than coming to quick solutions.

Left and Right (of Figure 10.5)

Another way to think about the four types is based on how the brain is organized. The left hemisphere of the brain is the logical-sequential or deductive thinking side (the paper clip and magnifying glass types), whereas, the right hemisphere is considered the abstract-contextual or inductive thinking side (the teddy bears and Slinkys). Deductive thinkers tend to use the factual information at hand to come to a conclusion. Inductive thinkers consider all kinds of information including feelings and behaviors to reason through situations. When these two sides work in harmony, we are more likely to accomplish complex tasks efficiently and with greater success.

Top and Bottom (of Figure 10.5)

The frames across the top of the diagram where the paper clip and teddy bear reside are those students who use more of their senses and direct experience to solve problems and think through situations. The magnifying glass and Slinky in the bottom frames may rely upon their gut feelings, subconscious, or "sixth sense" to process data and solve problems. Using both our senses and intuition can be highly valuable in solving problems with which we have no prior experiences to draw upon.

It is always good practice to assist students in identifying their areas of strength and limitations—this includes knowing the way(s) they prefer to learn. Ask your students to identify the one or two types of learning they prefer, as well as the one or two types in which they struggle. Then, encourage them to strengthen their limitations and understand those who are strong in those areas. I always found it helpful to assign students to partner with an oppositional type of learner, so they could support each other when it came time to do tasks that required specific types of strengths.

In designing classroom environments conducive to all types of learners, keep in mind:

***Paper clips* need:**

- posted schedules
- notification when schedules change
- timelines and due dates
- linear instruction that follows an outline
- an organized classroom environment

***Teddy bears* need:**

- connectivity with others
- contextualized experiences or service-learning projects
- study topics with emotional connections
- flexible grouping
- inclusion of the arts in the classroom

***Magnifying glasses* need:**

- time to investigate complex issues
- opportunities to debate and discuss ideas
- chances to problem-find and problem-solve
- experiences that require making decisions
- logical order to units of study

***Slinkys* need:**

- open-ended questions and activities
- chances to think, act, and be outside the box
- time to express themselves
- ample opportunities to move
- space, opportunities, and materials to be creative

Assessing the Development of SRL

As we build the framework of developing self-regulation for learning in our classroom, it is important for us to keep the focus on releasing the controls to help students take on the responsibilities for learning. An important aspect of developing lifelong learning skills and self-regulation for learning is for the student to take more responsibility for identifying and managing their own affect, behavior, and cognition to become strategic learners. Having students provide their own assessment and feedback can help strengthen their abilities to become more self-regulated. Teachers can assist students in their own assessments by following the phases of engaging in learning (see Chapter 3) to identify their levels of confidence, make a plan for learning, monitor their learning, and then reflect upon what they have learned.

The Forms

Based on the phases of engagement in learning, the Student Assessment Questionnaire for SRL informs students where they are in the learning phases and offers teachers indications for interventions in each of the four phases. The questionnaire is divided into four "frames" to align to each of the four phases.

The "Student Assessment Questionnaire for SRL—Primary" handout is for grades kindergarten through second. The questionnaire for elementary and secondary is most appropriate for grades three and up. However, the primary form could be modified for third-grade students and the elementary through secondary form could be modified for second-grade students. The primary form has fewer questions than the elementary and secondary form. All the forms are framed around the concept of affect, behavior, and cognition (ABC) in each phase of engaging in learning.

Using the Forms

Use the questionnaire four times: prior to introducing a task or activity (Phase 1); before the start of a task/activity (Phase 2); during the task/activity (Phase 3); and after completion of the task/activity (Phase 4). It works best for students to use the questionnaire when approaching a large task or activity rather than when working on daily lessons. To use the questionnaire at the beginning, during, and end of a week, simply modify the language in each of the phases to fit the situation. For primary students, use it with the entire class or one-on-one with students. Elementary through secondary students can take the assessment on their own.

When reviewing students' responses to each of the frames, select ideas and strategies in prior chapters to provide interventions or techniques that support students or increase their levels of regulatory actions. Some strategies will be more effective than others to address particular student needs for support. On the stages of self-regulation for learning, if children rate themselves low (strongly disagree toward uncertain/unsure), then more modeling and copying of strategies may be appropriate. If children rate themselves higher (toward strongly agree), then they need practice and independence. Always look at children's self-assessment through your lens as the educational leader in the classroom—they may either underestimate or overestimate their self-regulatory development.

Phase 1: Estimating Confidence Level

Students should take this questionnaire frame to check their ABCs about the learning environment. Refer to Chapter 4 for ideas on improving students' emotional state, igniting their interests in learning, building their self-beliefs, and developing self-efficacy. The responses in this frame can also offer the teacher indications of the power of the learning environment—how collaborative and encouraging the classroom community coexists.

Phase 2: Preparing and Planning

Prior to an activity, students should complete this frame of the Student Assessment Questionnaire. Information gathered from the questionnaire can provide the student and teacher information about implementing prerequisite training and supports. Chapter 5 provides numerous strategies and ideas for "front loading" the tools for learning and engaging in learning tasks.

Phase 3: Monitoring and Adjusting

During the task or activity, students use this frame to check themselves on the goals they have set. Chapter 6 identified different levels of goal sets. For daily or weekly tasks/activities, students should focus on learning/performance goals (SMARTS/S goals), to be able to adjust feelings, actions, or thinking. Chapter 7 offers ideas for helping students avoid distractions, manage their time and materials, deal with stress, and maintain focus. Teachers can use this frame to provide students descriptive feedback on performance and goal attainment. See Chapter 8 for help in using feedback, teaching students to ask for help, and building habits of study.

Phase 4: Reflecting and Assessing

Using ideas from the first part of this chapter, students can reflect on their performance and plan their approach to the next task/activity. This frame can be used as an individual reflective tool or as a community building tool to identify how students can assist and support others during the learning process. The Student Assessment Questionnaire for SRL is intended to be a non-evaluative tool to assist students in developing greater responsibility for learning. Use it in a cyclical manner; after one cycle through all four frames, the students use it when approaching another task—referring to previously completed forms to monitor their self-regulatory development.

Parent/Guardian Support of SRL

In most cases, parents may not be aware of the tools necessary in developing self-regulation for learning. To assist parents in guiding their child toward greater self-regulation, teachers can offer them support that extends the classroom practices into the home. Be sure to share with parents the strategies you are using in the classroom, so they can practice them at home with their child. Keep the parents knowledgeable about the topic of self-regulation by providing them with tips and ideas (see "Tips for Parents on Supporting Their Child's Development of Self-Regulation for Learning"). The ideas can be shared in newsletters, emails, posted on classroom or district websites, or shared during parent/teacher/student information nights or conferences.

Depending on the child's stage of development and how well he or she balances ABCs, some strategies will work better than others. Providing parents with specific strategies that you have found useful or that are working well for the child is better than providing numerous tips or tricks. This could be overwhelming for some parents and may not be useful in their home situation.

Chapter Summary

Early methods of didactic instruction positioned the student as a passive participant in the learning process. As advances in the science of teaching continue to develop, we know that the student must be an active participant who interacts with relevant and meaningful content. Students need to be active learners in the curriculum that is aimed at teaching the whole child by integrating both specific and multidisciplinary strategies with the techniques of self-regulation for learning. Finally, the development of self-regulation for learning is a community effort. Teachers, schools, parents, and students all have responsibilities in the process of lifelong learning as Figure 10.6 shows.

Figure 10.6 **Responsibilities of Student, Teacher, School, and Parent**

Student	Teacher	School	Parent
Commit effort in learning.	Establish a culture in the classroom that values effort.	Make learning a valuable asset in the school community.	Praise your child's effort over achievement.
Set and strive for appropriate goals.	Support students in setting and attaining goals.	Post school-wide goals and the process to achieve the goals.	Show your child how you set goals and work to achieve them.
Learn to persist even when things get tough.	Provide safe opportunities for students to struggle with challenges.	Recognize students when they show persistence and perseverance.	Discuss how you persist at difficult tasks and value your child's persistence.
Know your strengths and limitations.	Provide opportunities for your students to know their strengths and limitations.	Display different ways of being successful.	Tell your child what you are good at and share your limitations.
Learn how to work collaboratively and independently.	Offer choices for students to work together and independently.	Staff should demonstrate for students how they work together to achieve school goals.	Show your child how you work with others and how you work alone.
Learn to study.	Give students training on the habits of study.	Set school-wide expectations for home study (rather than homework).	Assist your child in developing study habits.
Seek out appropriate challenges.	Provide a challenging and robust learning environment that is engaging and develops student interests.	Insist upon quality curriculum that encourages depth and complexity.	Show your child how you enjoy challenges and are a continual learner.
Learn to find and solve problems.	Offer opportunities for students to investigate and solve problems worth solving.	Encourage a student-centered school environment that focuses on service learning.	Encourage your child to participate in community events and even volunteer for local agencies to help others.

Student Assessment Questionnaire for SRL—Primary

Phase 1: Estimating Confidence Level

How well do I think I will do?

In this classroom:	☺	😐	☹
I feel good about learning.			
I know what the rules are.			
I like to think about different ideas.			
I have friends who help me.			
I like to work with others.			
I like being here.			

Phase 2: Preparing and Planning

What will I do to do well?

Before we start:	☺	😐	☹
I am happy to do this activity.			
I know what to do.			
I can do it.			
I know who can help me.			
I can work with others.			
I know who to ask for help.			

continued ➡

Phase 3: Monitoring and Adjusting

How well am I doing at doing well?

While we are working:	☺	😐	☹
I feel good about what I am doing.			
I know what to do next.			
I am doing a good job.			
I am asking for help when I need it.			
I am working well with others.			
I enjoy what we are doing.			

Phase 4: Reflecting and Assessing

How well did I do at doing well?

Now that we have finished:	☺	😐	☹
I feel good about what we did.			
I followed the rules.			
I did a good job.			
I used my friends to help me.			
I liked working with others.			
I liked doing the activity.			

Student Assessment Questionnaire for SRL—Elementary & Secondary

Phase 1: Estimating Confidence Level

How well do I think I will do?

In this classroom:	1 Strongly Disagree	2	3 Uncertain or Unsure	4	5 Strongly Agree
I feel confident I can learn.					
I know what is expected of me.					
I am free to think differently than others.					
I am encouraged by others.					
I can work with others.					
I am challenged to come up with new ideas.					
I have others who like me.					
I know what to do when assigned a task.					
I am given opportunities to be creative.					
I enjoy learning.					

Phase 2: Preparing and Planning

What will I do to do well?

For this activity:	1 Strongly Disagree	2	3 Uncertain or Unsure	4	5 Strongly Agree
I feel confident I can do it.					
I know what is expected.					
I know what tools to use to accomplish the task.					
I know who will encourage me to do well.					
I know who to work with so I can be productive.					
I know what to do when I have questions.					
I know what to do to stay positive.					
I know where to find materials, resources, or supports.					
I know ways I can expand on or include new ideas.					
I know what will make learning enjoyable.					

continued ➡

Student Assessment Questionnaire for SRL—Elementary & Secondary (continued)

Phase 3: Monitoring and Adjusting

How well am I doing at doing well?

During this activity:	1 Strongly Disagree	2	3 Uncertain or Unsure	4	5 Strongly Agree
I am feeling good about what I am doing.					
I am doing what is expected.					
I am using tools well to accomplish the task.					
I am being encouraged by others.					
I am working with others who are helping me be productive.					
When I have questions, I am asking them.					
When I have questions, I am getting them answered.					
I am staying positive.					
I am using the materials, resources, and supports when necessary.					
I am expanding on or including new ideas when appropriate.					
I am enjoying what I am doing.					

Phase 4: Reflecting and Assessing

How well did I do at doing well?

Reflecting on the activity:	1 Strongly Disagree	2	3 Uncertain or Unsure	4	5 Strongly Agree
I feel good about what I did.					
I knew what to do and did it.					
I used tools well to accomplish the task.					
I felt encouraged by others.					
I worked with others who kept me on task and helped me be successful.					
I asked questions when necessary.					
When I had questions, the answers were helpful.					
I stayed positive during most of the activity.					
I used the materials, resources, and supports correctly.					
I expanded on or included new ideas when given the opportunity.					
I enjoyed what I did.					

Tips for Parents: Supporting Your Child's Development of Self-Regulation for Learning

Self-regulation for learning (SRL) is the ability to balance affect (feelings), behavior, and cognition (ABCs) to be successful. SRL develops in four stages:

1. Children observe others modeling appropriate ABCs in achieving success.
2. Children must copy and perform the strategies with support and guidance.
3. Children must practice the strategies in different contexts and places to be able to refine them to fit the situation and achieve success.
4. Children must take time to reflect on how well strategies work, what may need to change, and then be allowed to apply them on their own.

You can support your child's development of the ABCs by:

Modeling strategies for your child

- Talk to your child about how you handle feeling bad, being excited, and feeling stressed out.
- Show your child positive ways to deal with difficult situations.
- Think out loud so your child can hear how you plan, organize, and think through situations.

Copying and doing

- Help your child talk through his or her feelings and think of ways to remain positive, reduce stress, and deal with difficult people.
- Have your child think out loud with you as he or she plans, organizes, and deals with difficult situations.

Practicing strategies

- Daily, ask how your child managed his or her feelings, motivation, and drive during school.
- Watch your child and offer advice when he or she is working through a difficult situation.
- Throughout the day, ask your child to give you examples of how he or she is thinking at that moment.

Independence and application

- Check in with your child on a routine basis to have him or her identify feelings and levels of motivation.
- Have your child tell you how he or she works through complex issues or situations both inside and outside of school.
- Have your child explain to you the way he or she thinks about what he or she is doing and his or her future.

More ideas

- Be open and honest about emotions: everyone has them and everyone deals with them differently. What matters is that we are able to recognize the impact our emotions have on how we deal with situations, on how we react to the environment, and on others around us.
- Talk to your child about how people deal positively and negatively with their emotions.
- Talk with your child about how people behave positively and negatively.
- Show your child that positive emotions and behaviors have a greater effect on being successful than negative emotional reactions and behaviors.

continued ➡

Tips for Parents (continued)

- Use affirmative language rather than negative language with your child:
  - "I like it when you follow my directions" rather than, "Why are you not doing what I told you to do?"
  - "I appreciate when you talk to me in a calm manner" rather than, "Don't talk to me like that."
- Help your child identify what he or she is naturally good at and what causes him or her difficulty.
- Tell your child "No one is good at everything, but everyone is good at something."
- Help your child recognize in difficult situations that you can:
  - Learn to adapt to the situation.
  - Ask for a change in the situation.
  - Avoid getting into the situation in the future.
- Give your child constructive feedback focused on how to improve his or her performance—be specific and focused in your feedback to your child.
- Praise your child's effort not your child's ability.
  - Work through challenges worth solving with your child. The challenges must be enjoyable and intriguing.
- Remind your child that:
  - All skills and processes are learnable.
  - Patience, persistence, and perseverance are essential to success.
  - Feedback is meant to build confidence and resilience.
- Teach your child how to:
  - Believe in himself or herself.
  - Seek out help from others.
  - Organize materials to get the job done.
  - Ask questions, or ask for help.
  - Request, require, and advocate for more support, information, and resources.
- Help your child see how the skill/content is important to future learning.
- Balance your praise and support.
- Encourage your child to practice until he or she feels confident in what he or she can do.
- Provide time for your child to reflect on learning.
- Assist your child in making connections between school and his or her life, fields of study, and careers.
- Live the growth mindset:
  - Show your child your love for challenges.
  - Use your mistakes as a learning tool.
  - Discuss the effort you put in daily.
  - Display your continued learning.
- Seek professional help (social worker, psychologist, therapist, doctor) when you don't know how to support your child.

References and Resources

Ames, Carole. "Classrooms: Goals, Structures, and Student Motivation." *Journal of Educational Psychology, 84(3)* (1992): 261–271.

Babbitt, N. *Tuck Everlasting*. New York: Farrar, Strauss and Giroux, 1975.

Bandura, A. *Self-Efficacy: The Exercise of Control*. New York: Freeman, 1997.

Bandura, A. *Social Foundations of Thought and Action: A Social Cognitive Theory*. Englewood Cliffs, NJ: Prentice Hall, 1986.

Barab, S. A., and J. A. Plucker. "Smart People or Smart Context? Cognition, Ability and Talent Development in an Age of Situated Approaches to Knowing and Learning." *Educational Psychologist, 37(3)* (2002): 165–182.

Baumeister, R. F., and K. D. Vohs (eds.). *Handbook of Self-Regulation: Research, Theory, and Applications*. New York: Guilford Press, 2004.

Beyer, B. K. *Practical Strategies for the Teaching of Thinking*. Newton, MA: Allyn and Bacon, 1987.

Boekaerts, M., and E. Cascallar. "How Far Have We Moved Toward the Integration of Theory and Practice in Self-Regulation?" *Educational Psychology Review, 18(3)* (2006): 199–210.

Boekaerts, M., and L. Corno. "Self Regulation in the Classroom: A Perspective on Assessment and Intervention." *Applied Psychology, 54(2)* (2005): 199–231.

Brookfield, S. D. *The Skillful Teacher: On Technique, Trust, and Responsiveness in the Classroom*. Hoboken, NJ: John Wiley & Sons, 2009.

Brown, P. C., H. L. Roediger, and M. A. McDaniel. *Make It Stick: The Science of Successful Learning*. Cambridge, MA: Belknap Press, 2014.

Carey, B. *How We Learn: The Surprising Truth About When, Where, and Why It Happens*. New York: Random House, 2014.

Carr, N. *The Shallows: What the Internet Is Doing to Our Brains*. New York: Norton, 2011.

Carver, C. S., and M. F. Scheie. *On the Self-Regulation of Behavior*. New York: Cambridge University Press, 1998.

Cash, R. M. *Advancing Differentiation: Thinking and Learning for the 21st Century*. Minneapolis: Free Spirit Publishing, 2011.

Collins, N. "Practice Doesn't Always Make Perfect." *Scientific American Mind, 25(6)* (2014): 12–12.

Colvin, G. *Talent Is Overrated: What Really Separates World-Class Performers from Everybody Else*. New York: Portfolio, 2008.

Cooper, H., J. Civey, and E. A. Patall. "Does Homework Improve Academic Achievement? A Synthesis of Research, 1987–2003." *Review of Educational Research*, 76 (2006): 1–62.

Corsini, R. J., and D. Wedding. *Current Psychotherapie*. Belmont, CA: Brooks/Cole, 2011.

Covey, S. *The Seven Habits of Highly Effective People*. New York: Simon & Schuster, 1989.

Cox, A. J. *No Mind Left Behind: Understanding and Fostering Executive Control—The Eight Essential Brain Skills Every Child Needs to Thrive*. New York: Perigee, 2007.

Danckert, J. "Descent of the Doldrums." *Scientific American Mind, 24(3)* (2013): 54–59.

Dembrowsky, C. *Personal and Social Responsibility*. La Luz, NM: Institute for Affective Skill Development, 1988.

Dewey, J. *Art and Education*. Merion, PA: Barnes Foundation Press, 1926.

Dewey, J. "Individuality and Experience." In *Later Works of John Dewey* (Vol. 2). Carbondale, IL: Southern Illinois University Press, 1984.

Dignath, C., and G. Büttner. "Components of Fostering Self-Regulated Learning Among Students. A Meta-Analysis on Intervention Studies at Primary and Secondary School Level." *Metacognition and Learning, 3(3)* (2008): 231–264.

Dillon, D. G., and K. S. LaBar. "Startle Modulation During Conscious Emotion Regulation Is Arousal-Dependent." *Behavioral Neuroscience, 119(4)* (2005): 1118.

Dweck, C. *Mindset: The New Psychology of Success*. New York: Random House, 2006.

Eccles, J. S., and A. Wigfield. "Motivational Beliefs, Values, and Goals. *Annual Review of Psychology, 53(1)* (2002): 109–132.

Elliot, A. J. "Approach and Avoidance Motivation and Achievement Goals." *Educational Psychologist, 34(3)* (1999): 169–189.

Elliot, A. J., and C. S. Dweck (eds.). *Handbook of Competence and Motivation*. New York: Guilford Press, 2005.

Elliot, A. J., and H. A. McGregor. "A 2 x 2 Achievement Goal Framework." *Journal of Personality and Social Psychology, 80* (2001): 501–519.

Emmet, D. M. *The Nature of Metaphysical Thinking*. London, England: MacMillan, 1945.

English, H. B., and A. C. English. *A Comprehensive Dictionary of Psychological and Psychoanalytical Terms: A Guide to Usage*. New York: Longmans, Green, and Co., 1958.

Flavell, J. H. "Metacognition and Cognitive Monitoring: A New Area of Cognitive–Developmental Inquiry." *American Psychologist, 34(10)* (1979): 906.

Freud, S. *An Outline of Psychoanalysis*. New York: W. W. Norton, 1940.

Fuchs, L. S., and D. Fuchs. "Curriculum-Based Assessment of Progress Toward Long-Term and Short-Term Goals." *The Journal of Special Education, 20(1)* (1986): 69–82.

Galbraith, J., and J. Delisle. *When Gifted Kids Don't Have All the Answers*. Minneapolis: Free Spirit Publishing, 2015.

Gardner, H. E. *Intelligence Reframed: Multiple Intelligences for the 21st Century*. New York: Basic Books, 1999.

Gardner, H. E. *Multiple Intelligences: The Theory in Practice: A Reader*. New York: Basic Books, 1993.

Gibbs, G. *Learning by Doing: A Guide to Teaching and Learning Methods*. Oxford, England: Oxford Polytechnic, 1988.

Gobet, F. "Deliberate Practice and Its Role in Expertise Development." In *Encyclopedia of the Science of Learning*, edited by N. M. Seel. New York: Springer, 2012.

Gregorc, A. F. *Mind Styles Model: Theory, Principles, and Applications*. Columbia, CT: Gregorc Associates, 1998.

Gross, J. J., and R. A. Thompson. "Emotion Regulation: Conceptual Foundations." *Handbook of Emotion Regulation, 3(24)* (2007).

Halvorson, H. G., and E. T. Higgins. *Focus: Use Different Ways of Seeing the World for Success and Influence*. New York: Hudson Street Press, 2013.

Hattie, J. A. C. *Visible Learning: A Synthesis of Over 800 Meta-Analyses Relating to Achievement*. Abingdon, England: Routledge, 2009.

Heacox, D. *Differentiating Instruction in the Regular Classroom: How to Reach and Teach All Learners*. Minneapolis: Free Spirit Publishing, 2012.

Heacox, D. *Making Differentiation a Habit: How to Ensure Success in Academically Diverse Classrooms*. Minneapolis: Free Spirit Publishing, 2009.

Heacox, D., and R. Cash. *Differentiation for Gifted Learners: Going Beyond the Basics*. Minneapolis: Free Spirit Publishing, 2014.

Hearn, J. "From Hegemonic Masculinity to the Hegemony of Men." *Feminist Theory, 5(1)* (2004): 49–72.

Hidi, S., and M. Ainley. "Interest and Self-Regulation: Relationships Between Two Variables That Influence Learning." In *Motivation and Self-Regulated Learning: Theory, Research, and Application*, edited by D. Schunk and B. J. Zimmerman. New York: Routledge, 2008.

Higgins, E. T. "Making a Good Decision: Value from Fit." *American Psychologist, 55* (2000): 1217–1230.

Higgins, E. T. "Promotion and Prevention Experiences: Relating Emotions to Nonemotional Motivational States." In *Handbook of Affect and Social Cognition*, edited by Joseph P. Forgas. Mahwah, NJ: Lawrence Erlbaum Associates Publishers, 2001.

Jensen, E. *Teaching with Poverty in Mind: What Being Poor Does to Kids' Brains and What Schools Can Do About It*. Alexandria, VA: ASCD, 2009.

Jung, C. G. *Psychological Types: Or the Psychology of Individuation*. Oxford, England: Harcourt, Brace, 1923.

Kimura, D. "Sex Differences in the Brain." *Scientific American*, *287* (2003): 32–37.

Kolb, D. A. *Experiential Learning: Experience as the Source of Learning and Development* (Vol. 1). Englewood Cliffs, NJ: Prentice-Hall, 1984.

Kolb, D. A., and R. E. Fry. "Toward an Applied Theory of Experiential Learning." In *Theories of Group Processes*, by Cary L. Cooper. New York: Wiley, 1975.

Kurman, J., and C. Hui. "Promotion, Prevention or Both: Regulatory Focus and Culture Revisited." *Online Readings in Psychology and Culture*. Retrieved from scholarworks.gvsu.edu/orpc/vol5/iss3 (2011).

Lamont, M., J. Kaufman, and M. Moody. "The Best of the Brightest: Definitions of the Ideal Self Among Prize-Winning Students." *Sociological Forum*, *15(2)* (2000): 187–224.

Lipsett, A. "Supporting Emotional Regulation in Elementary School: Brain-Based Strategies and Classroom Interventions to Promote Self-Regulation." *LEARNing Landscapes*, *5(1)* (2011).

Livingston, J. A. "Metacognition: An Overview." Retrieved from gse.buffalo.edu/fas/shuell/CEP564/Metacog.htm (1997).

Locke, E. A., and G. P. Latham. *A Theory of Goal Setting and Task Performance*. Englewood Cliffs, NJ: Prentice-Hall, 1990.

McLeod, S. A. "Kolb - Learning Styles." Retrieved from www.simplypsychology.org/learning-kolb.html (2010).

McMahon, M., and J. Luca. "Assessing Students' Self-Regulatory Skills." In *Proceedings of the Annual Conference of the Australasian Society for Computers in Learning in Tertiary Education*, 2001.

Mischel, W., Y. Shoda, and P. K. Peake. "The Nature of Adolescent Competencies Predicted by Preschool Delay of Gratification." *Journal of Personality and Social Psychology*, *54(4)* (1988): 687–696.

Montalvo, F. T., and M. C. G. Torres. "Self-Regulated Learning: Current and Future Directions." *Electronic Journal of Research in Educational Psychology*, *2(1)* (2004): 1–34.

Murphy, S. "Surfing Our Way to Stupid." *New Scientist*, *207(2775)* (2010): 28.

Newberg, A., and M. R. Waldman. *Words Can Change Your Brain: 12 Conversation Strategies to Build Trust, Resolve Conflict, and Increase Intimacy*. New York: Penguin, 2012.

Pajares, F., and D. Schunk. "The Development of Academic Self-Efficacy." In *Development of Achievement Motivation*, edited by A. Wigfield and J. Eccles. San Diego: Academic Press, 2002.

Paris, S. G., and A. H. Paris. "Classroom Applications of Research on Self-Regulated Learning. *Educational Psychologist*, *36(2)* (2001): 89–101.

Paul, R., and L. Elder. *Critical Thinking: Tools for Taking Charge of Your Professional and Personal Life*. Upper Saddle River, NJ: Pearson FT Press, 2014.

Peterson, J. S. *The Essential Guide to Talking with Gifted Teens*. Minneapolis: Free Spirit Publishing, 2008.

Piaget, J. *The Construction of Reality in the Child* (Vol. 82). London, England: Routledge, 2013 (originally published in 1937).

Pink, D. H. *Drive: The Surprising Truth About What Motivates Us*. New York: Penguin, 2009.

Pryor, J. H., et al. *The American Freshman: Forty Year Trends*. Los Angeles: Higher Education Research Institute, 2007.

Roberts, P. "Instant Gratification." *The American Scholar* (Autumn 2014).

Rogers, C. *Client-Centered Therapy: Its Current Practice, Implications and Theory*. London, England: Constable, 1951.

Rogoff, B., et al. "Firsthand Learning Through Intent Participation." *Annual Review of Psychology, 54(1)* (2003): 175–203.

Rothman, A. J., et al. "Self-Regulation and Behavior Change: Disentangling Behavioral Initiation and Behavioral Maintenance." In *Handbook of Self-Regulation. Research, Theory, and Applications*, edited by R. F. Baumeister and K. D. Vohs, 2004.

Schunk, D. H. "Peer Models and Children's Behavioral Change." *Review of Educational Research, 57(2)* (1987): 149–174.

Schunk, D., and B. J. Zimmerman (eds.). *Motivation and Self-Regulated Learning: Theory, Research, and Application*. New York: Routledge, 2012.

Schwartz, D. "Calmly We Walk Through This April's Day." *Selected Poems (1938–1958): Summer Knowledge.* New York: New Directions Publishing, 1967.

Silver, H., J. Jackson, and D. Moirao. *Task Rotation: Strategies for Differentiating Activities and Assessments by Learning Style.* Alexandria, VA: ASCD, 2011.

Silver, H. F., and R. W. Strong. *Learning Style Inventory for Students*. Ho-Ho-Kus, NJ: Thoughtful Education Press, 2004.

Skinner, B. F. "The Steep and Thorny Way to a Science of Behavior." *American Psychologist, 30(1)* (1975): 42.

Sternberg, R. *Successful Intelligence: How Practical and Creative Intelligence Determine Success in Life.* New York: Plume, 1997.

Sternberg, R. J. *Wisdom, Intelligence, and Creativity Synthesized*. New York: Cambridge University Press, 2003.

Sternberg, R. J., and E. L. Grigorenko. *Teaching for Successful Intelligence: To Increase Student Learning and Achievement.* Thousand Oaks, CA: Corwin Press, 2007.

Sungur, S., and C. Tekkaya. "Effects of Problem-Based Learning and Traditional Instruction on Self-Regulated Learning." *The Journal of Educational Research, 99(5)* (2006): 307–320.

Svinicki, M. D. "Student Goal Orientation, Motivation, and Learning" (2008). Retrieved from www.education.com/reference/article/Ref_Student_Goal in 2015.

Sylwester, R. "The Downshifting Dilemma: A Commentary and Proposal." *International Journal of Interdisciplinary Education, 1(1)* (2013): 1–5.

Sylwester, R. (ed.). *Student Brains, School Issues: A Collection of Articles*. Newbury Park, CA: Corwin Press, 1998.

Torrance, E. P. *The Search for Satori and Creativity.* New York: Creative Education Foundation, 1979.

Tough, P. *How Children Succeed.* New York: Houghton Mifflin Harcourt, 2012.

"Understanding Procrastination." Retrieved from www.sas.calpoly.edu/docs/asc/ssl/procrastination.pdf.

Vygotsky, L. S. "Thinking and Speech." In *The Collected Works of L. S. Vygotsky, Vol. 1: Problems of General Psychology*, edited by R. W. Rieber and A. S. Carton, translated by N. Minick, New York: Plenum Press, 1987.

Vygotsky, L. S., and M. Cole. *Mind in Society: The Development of Higher Psychological Processes*. Cambridge, MA: Harvard University Press, 1978.

Walsh, L., et al. "The Role of Technology in Engaging Disengaged Youth: Final Report." *Australian Flexible Learning Framework* (2011). Retrieved from https://www.fya.org.au/app/theme/default/design/assets/publications/Final-Report-AFLF-280411.pdf.

Walters, K. S. (ed.). *Re-Thinking Reason: New Perspectives in Critical Thinking*. Albany, NY: SUNY Press, 1994.

Weinstein, N. D. "Testing Four Competing Theories of Health-Protective Behavior." *Health Psychology, 12(4)* (1993): 324.

Wiggins, G. "Feedback for Learning." *Educational Leadership 70(1)* (2012): 10–16.

Wilson, N. S., and H. Bai. "The Relationships and Impact of Teachers' Metacognitive Knowledge and Pedagogical Understandings of Metacognition." *Metacognition and Learning, 5(3)* (2010): 269–288.

Wood, R. E., and E. A. Locke. "The Relation of Self-Efficacy and Grade Goals to Academic Performance." *Educational and Psychological Measurement, 47(4)* (1987): 1013–1024.

Zimmerman, B. J. "Attainment of Self-Regulation: A Social Cognitive Perspective." In *Self-Regulation: Theory, Research, and Applications*, edited by M. Boekaerts, P. Pintrich, and M. Zeidner (pp. 13–39). Orlando, FL: Academic Press, 2000.

Zimmerman, B. J. "A Social Cognitive View of Self-Regulated Academic Learning." *Journal of Educational Psychology, 81(3)* (1989): 329–339.

Zimmerman, B. J., and A. Kitsantas. "The Hidden Dimension of Personal Competence: Self-Regulated Learning and Practice." In *Handbook of Competence and Motivation*, edited by A. J. Elliot and C. S. Dweck. New York: Guilford Publications, 2005.

Zimmerman, B. J., and D. H. Schunk. "Reflections on Theories of Self-Regulated Learning and Academic Achievement." In *Self-Regulated Learning and Academic Achievement: Theoretical Perspectives*, edited by B. J. Zimmerman and D. H. Schunk (pp. 289–300). Mahwah, NJ: Erlbaum, 2001.

Zimmerman, B. J., S. Bonner, and R. Kovach. *Developing Self-Regulated Learners: Beyond Achievement to Self-Efficacy.* Washington, DC: American Psychological Association, 1996.

Index

Page numbers in *italics* refer to figures; those in **bold** refer to reproducible forms.

C

D

E

About the Author

Richard M. Cash, Ed.D., received his post-baccalaureate degree in elementary education from the University of Minnesota, master's degree in curriculum and instruction from the University of St. Thomas (St. Paul, Minnesota), and doctoral degree in educational leadership also from the University of St. Thomas.

After receiving his master's, Richard became a curriculum specialist and developed training modules, curriculum formats, and differentiated learning archetypes that assisted teachers in creating higher-level experiences to meet the needs of all children. After completing his doctorate, Richard served as the administrator of gifted programs in Rochester, Minnesota, and as director of gifted programs for the Bloomington Public Schools in Minnesota. In Bloomington, he realigned the gifted programs to service more students during a budget deficit and incorporated differentiated instruction into the total school curriculum.

Richard has given hundreds of workshops, presentations, and staff development sessions throughout the United States and internationally. The research-based strategies and techniques he offers are proven to increase student achievement. His greatest passion is helping teachers recognize the various talents all children possess and create engaging learning experiences to encourage those talents to flourish.

Richard is a member of several professional organizations including the National Association for Gifted Children, the Council for Exceptional Children, and ASCD. He has authored numerous articles on quality instructional practices and is considered by many to be an exceptionally engaging, motivating, and enlightening presenter.

Richard's other books include *Advancing Differentiation: Thinking and Learning for the 21st Century* and *Differentiation for Gifted Learners: Going Beyond the Basics* with coauthor Diane Heacox, Ed.D.

Richard offers on-site (in person or via Skype) professional development on differentiated instruction, thinking skills, brain-compatible learning, creativity, and gifted education, among other topics. He provides one-on-one consulting as well as group workshops. To learn more, visit www.nrich.consulting.

Other Great Resources from Free Spirit

Advancing Differentiation
Thinking and Learning for the 21st Century (Revised & Updated Edition)
by Richard M. Cash, Ed.D.
For teachers and administrators, grades K–12.
240 pp.; paperback; 8½" x 11"; includes digital content.
Free PLC/Book Study Guide
freespirit.com/PLC

Differentiation for Gifted Learners
Going Beyond the Basics
by Diane Heacox, Ed.D. and Richard M. Cash, Ed.D.
K–12 teachers, gifted education teachers, program directors, administrators, instructional coaches, curriculum developers.
224 pp.; paperback; 8½" x 11"; includes digital content.
Free PLC/Book Study Guide
freespirit.com/PLC

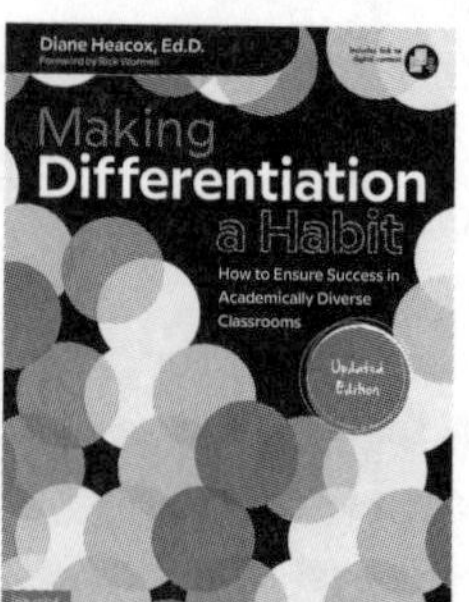

Making Differentiation a Habit
How to Ensure Success in Academically Diverse Classrooms (Updated Edition)
by Diane Heacox, Ed.D.
For teachers and administrators, grades K–12.
192 pp.; paperback; 8½" x 11"; includes digital content.
Free PLC/Book Study Guide
freespirit.com/PLC

Differentiating Instruction in the Regular Classroom
How to Reach and Teach All Learners (Updated Anniversary Edition)
by Diane Heacox, Ed.D.
Teachers and administrators, K–12.
176 pp.; paperback; 8½" x 11"; includes digital content.

Making Curriculum Pop
Developing Literacies in All Content Areas
by Pam Goble, Ed.D., and Ryan R. Goble, M.A.
Teachers, administrators, curriculum directors, grades 6–12.
224 pp.; paperback; 8½" x 11"; includes digital content.
Free PLC/Book Study Guide
freespirit.com/PLC

The Power of Self-Advocacy for Gifted Learners
Teaching the 4 Essential Steps to Success
by Deb Douglas
For teachers of gifted students in grades 5–12, counselors, gifted program coordinators, administrators, parents, youth leaders.
208 pp.; paperback; 8½" x 11"; includes digital content.
Free PLC/Book Study Guide
freespirit.com/PLC

Teaching Gifted Children in Today's Preschool and Primary Classrooms
Identifying, Nurturing, and Challenging Children Ages 4–9
by Joan Franklin Smutny, M.A., Sally Yahnke Walker, Ph.D., and Ellen I. Honeck, Ph.D.
Teachers, grades preK–3.
248 pp.; paperback; 8½" x 11"; includes digital content.
Free PLC/Book Study Guide
freespirit.com/PLC

Teaching Gifted Kids in Today's Classroom
Strategies and Techniques Every Teacher Can Use (Updated Fourth Edition)
by Susan Winebrenner, M.S., with Dina Brulles, Ph.D.
Educators of grades K–12.
256 pp.; paperback; 8½" x 11"; includes digital content.

Interested in purchasing multiple quantities and receiving volume discounts?
Contact edsales@freespirit.com or call 1.800.735.7323 and ask for Education Sales.

Many Free Spirit authors are available for speaking engagements, workshops, and keynotes.
Contact speakers@freespirit.com or call 1.800.735.7323.

For pricing information, to place an order, or to request a free catalog, contact:

Free Spirit Publishing Inc. • 6325 Sandburg Road, Suite 100 • Minneapolis, MN 55427-3674
toll-free 800.735.7323 • local 612.338.2068 • fax 612.337.5050
help4kids@freespirit.com • www.freespirit.com